BRITISH BURMA

AND ITS PEOPLE

BRITISH BURMA

AND ITS PEOPLE:

BEING SKETCHES OF

NATIVE MANNERS, CUSTOMS, AND RELIGION.

BY CAPT. C. J. F. S. FORBES,

F.R.G.S., M.R.A.S., &C.

GYAN

Published by

Gyan Publishing House
5, Ansari Road
Daryaganj, New Delhi-110002
Phone: 011-47034999, 9811692060
E-mail: books@gyanbooks.com

Distribution Network
gyanbooks.com
India, USA, Canada, UK, Australia

ISBN: 978-93-6208-249-7 (PB)
First Published, 1878

2nd Impression 2024

Printed at: Gyan Press, Delhi.

BRITISH BURMA AND ITS PEOPLE
Author: C. J. F. S. FORBES

TO

SIR ARTHUR PURVIS PHAYRE, K.C.S.I., C.B.

THE STATESMAN AND ADMINISTRATOR TO WHOM

BRITISH BURMA OWES SO MUCH

THIS LITTLE WORK IS DEDICATED

AS A MARK OF THE RESPECT AND ESTEEM OF THE AUTHOR

THARRAWADDY, B. BURMA
Oct. 1, 1878

PREFACE.

The following pages owe their origin to a remark in the Report on the Census of British Burma in 1872, page 27:

'There are similarities of language, physical type, and traditions, which establish an ethnical affinity between all the races situated among the immense sweep of mountain country, which hems in Burma on three sides. But the evidences of this relationship have never yet been compendiously collated; and the industry, displayed in this direction by individual officers, whose duty has brought them into contact with one or other of the several tribes, has not yet borne fruit in the form of a general inquiry. A systematic examination of the dialects, or even a scientific comparison of the vocabularies which have already been compiled, would probably throw much light upon their mutual relationship; but, as it is, a great deal of the speculation on the subject is necessarily guesswork.'

The first intention of the writer was to endeavour in some degree to supply the want above alluded to, but in a form suitable only to the pages of a scientific journal, such as that of the Asiatic Society; but, since his return to Europe, he has been so much struck with the fact that while Burma, and the Chinese trade route through Burma, are often mentioned, the English public, even the educated and reading class, have as a rule the faintest possible idea of the country, or of the people.

It is considered generally to be a part of India, inhabited by a people only slightly differing from, and in fact being one of, the many races of Hindustán. It may seem presumptuous to endeavour to convey information upon some subjects, such as Buddhism and its origin, which have been so learnedly and completely treated of by able Orientalists, both English and Continental; but there are two reasons, which seem to render it necessary for our purpose in this little work: first, it would be impossible to give a complete idea of Burma and the Burmese without including a clear account of their religion, as this explains much of their character and customs; secondly, Buddhism has not been considered, in special connection with Burma, in books now generally accessible to the public, although in the opinion of the Burmese this widespread religion in its purest form is now to be found in that country, and not in China, Tibet, or even in the sacred Isle of Ceylon.

As an instance of the want of accurate knowledge respecting Burma, we may mention that not many years ago, the 'Illustrated London News' named Martaban, a pretty village of about 200 houses, as one of the three great seaports of Burma, doubtless mistaking it for the neighbouring city of Maulmain. Again, the same generally well-informed paper, in the number for October 21, 1876, in a description of some sketches in Burma, contains the following: 'Pagodas erected on square terraces, rising one above the other, beneath which *are vaults inhabited by the priests.* Near the ancient city of Paghan, which flourished 1,000 years ago, the bank of the river for a length of eight miles is lined with remains of this quaint architecture and sculpture. It is not known by what nation of old times they were constructed, for

Burman history is apocryphal.' This is a most incorrect description of the Burmese pagodas; and, moreover, the priests, or rather monks, *never* live in or under the pagodas, but in regular monasteries; and the builders of the temples of Paghan are well known.

A province such as British Burma, which, during the twenty years between 1855 (that is, two years after its annexation) and 1875–76, has increased in annual revenue from 532,100*l.* to 1,527,296*l.*; in its commerce from 4,856,400*l.* to 14,665,286*l.*; and in its population from 1,274,640 to 2,896,368 souls: a province, which is now looked on by the commercial world as the trade high-road into the vast regions of Western China, we think deserves to be a little better known to all classes.

Of the works which have been published on Burma since our occupation, there are four of the highest value. First comes Colonel Yule's magnificent folio, 'An Embassy to the Court of Ava;' but this only records the manners and customs of the people, as they struck the traveller in Upper Burma during a stay of a month or so, and, interesting and most valuable as it is, contains little allusion to our own provinces.

Dr. F. Mason's 'Burmah; its People and Natural Productions,' is a scientific rather than a popular descriptive work, and is more a book of reference than of general reading.

Bishop Bigandet's 'The Life or Legend of Gaudama, with Annotations,' contains a clear and almost exhaustive summary of Burman Buddhism, but, naturally, treats of no other subject.

Lastly, Sir A. Phayre's valuable 'Histories of the Burman Race,' 'of Arracan,' and 'of Pegu,' give all that is known of these nations, in an historical point of view, from their own and from foreign records; but these are hidden away in the pages of a scientific journal, and are, moreover, too diffuse for the ordinary reader.

I trust, therefore, that it will be allowed, that there is room for such a book as I have attempted. It is offered as the result of an experience derived from thirteen years of close intercourse with the people of Burma, both officially and privately. How far it will supply the want above alluded to, must be left to the indulgent verdict of my readers.

CONTENTS.

BRITISH BURMA.

CHAPTER I.

PHYSICAL GEOGRAPHY.

BURMA, including under this designation both the British province and the independent Kingdom of Burma, extends along the eastern shore of the Bay of Bengal from the Chittagong division of Lower Bengal to the Isthmus of Kraw. It is bounded on the east by the Empire of Siam and the Kingdom of Cambodia to about 21° 30′ N. lat., and thence to its northernmost extremity by the Chinese province of Yu-nan. Its northern boundary can hardly be defined; it apparently runs up into an angle among the Snowy Ranges of Eastern Tibet, in about 28° N. lat. Thence it stretches westerly, bordering on Upper Assam, Munipúr, the Lushai Hills, and the Chittagong division of Bengal to the Naaf River.

Omitting the long narrow strip of mountainous

country and sea-coast which forms the Tenasserim Province below Maulmain, British Burma may, roughly speaking, be said to consist of three broad mountain ranges, having outside them on the west the seaboard province of Arracan, enbracing between them the two great valleys of the Irrawaddy and the Sittoung, which form south of Rangoon one vast plain, the centre range of the three mountain chains being shorter than are the other two.

The whole of the seaboard is exclusively British territory; and the mighty Empire of Burma, that once stretched from Dacca to the Gulf of Siam, and was, even at the commencement of the present century, regarded by the European Powers in the East with the feelings of wonder and fear due to the vague and the unknown, has shrunk into an inland State, without a single avenue or outlet for her trade except at the will of a foreign Power. Even within the boundaries above given, her authority on the more northern, eastern, and western frontiers is but nominal.

The division between the independent Kingdom of Burma and the British territory is formed on the west by the great chain of mountains that runs down from Sylhet and Cachar, in Lower Bengal, to Cape Negrais; this portion is known as the Arracan Yoma (or 'Ridge'). A stone pillar on the Kyeedoung Peak of this range in 19° 29′ 3″ N. lat., and thence an arbitrary line, marked at certain distances by pillars and cairns, continues to define the northern boundary in a straight line to the range of mountains east of the Sittoung River. There the independent State of Karennee intervenes, completing the boundary between Upper Burma and the British province, which marches on the west with the Siamese Empire.

British Burma is both naturally and geographically separated into five divisions—namely, Arracan, the Irrawaddy Valley, the Sittoung (or Sittang) Valley, the Salween Valley, and Tenasserim. Of these, the first three are formed by the Arracan, Pegu, and Poungloung ranges, which traverse the country in a north and south direction, and form the watershed of the Irrawaddy and Sittoung Rivers. The valleys of these two streams unite in their southern portions into an enormous littoral plain stretching from the southern end of the Arracan mountains (near Cape Negrais) along the whole coast to Martaban, at the mouth of the Salween.

The province contains politically three 'Divisions,' Arracan, Pegu, and Tenasserim. The total area is 93,664 square miles, being about 4,000 square miles larger than Great Britain.

Of the whole, about 36,204 square miles are

cultivable, but in 1875 only 3,450 were actually under cultivation.

The Arracan division consists chiefly of more or less mountainous tracts; and lying between the hills and the sea is a narrow strip of country which is intersected by a perfect labyrinth of tidal creeks of all sizes, that afford safe navigation for the country boats the whole length of the coast, during the flood tides, without their ever risking the open sea. The chief town is Akyab, which is known at home as one of the rice ports of Burma, rice being the chief article both of produce and export from this tract.

The two valleys of the Irrawaddy and the Sittoung are similar in character, though the latter is the narrower. Both commence above the British boundary line, the noble and fertile Irrawaddy Valley opening out widely as it trends southward until, at the extremity of the Pegu range (on the last spur of which is situated the great golden pagoda of Rangoon), it joins the Sittoung Valley, the two forming the great coast plain. Both these valleys are more or less cultivated, rice being the chief staple; but it is in the great plain that stretches from the south-eastern slopes of the Arracan range to the promontory of Martaban that the larger portion of the enormous rice crop is raised. From the Pegu division alone the annual export exceeds 570,000 tons, valued at over two-and-a-half millions sterling.

The extraordinary development of the rice trade of Burma is a singular and interesting question. Not to go as far back as we might, and taking only the twelve years from 1862 to 1874, we find that the export of rice from British Burma was in the former of these years 284,228 tons; in the latter, 811,106 tons; and there seems to be every sign that as fast as Burma, with its limited population, can increase the outturn, it will be absorbed by commerce. The question naturally presents itself, whence arises this enormous increase in the world's consumption of rice, as there was twelve years ago no other source of supply now closed, the place of which has been occupied by Burma?

The great Irrawaddy River (of which the sources, though unknown, are placed in the Snowy Range of Eastern Tibet), after draining the great plain of Upper Burma, enters, as it approaches the British frontier, a narrow valley lying between the spurs of the Arracan and Pegu ranges, and extending below the city of Prome. Thence the mighty stream rolls on through the widening vale, until, about ninety miles from the sea, it bifurcates; one branch flows to the westward and forms the Bassein River, while the main channel in the lower part of the delta subdivides and finally enters the sea by ten mouths. It is navigable for river steamers for 840 miles from the sea; but it is during the rainy season (or monsoon) that it is seen in its full grandeur. The stream then rises forty feet above its summer level, and, flooding over the banks, presents in some places, as far as the eye can reach, a boundless expanse of turbid waters, the main channel of which rushes along with a velocity of five miles an hour.

The Sittoung River, which drains the valley to the east of the Pegu range, is very far inferior to the Irrawaddy both in the length of its course and in its size; but it possesses similar characteristics. Its chief peculiarity is the great tidal wave or 'bore,' that renders its navigation in the lower part very dangerous. At about forty miles from its mouth it takes an exaggerated bend, like a gigantic ᔕ, from which 'it widens so rapidly into the Gulf of Martaban that it is difficult to decide where the river ends and the gulf begins. Owing to the meeting in this gulf of the great tidal wave of the Indian Ocean from the south-west, and the currents along the Tenasserim coast from the south-east,' when the spring tides make an enormous wave, the 'bore,' with a curling crest of foam from nine to twelve feet high, rushes up the funnel-like channel, dashes and breaks first on one bank, then gathers itself together again, rushes on at a speed of at least twenty miles an hour, and dashes and breaks against the opposite side; and woe betide boat or vessel that it meets in its path! Three waves succeed each other in this manner; the boats that have been lying sheltered in some side creek then push out, and are safely and swiftly borne along upon the rushing stream. But still accidents constantly occur, and some years ago a whole wing of a native Sepoy regiment was lost in this dangerous locality.

The Tenasserim division of British Burma is very nearly equal in area to both the other divisions together; it alone contains 46,730 out of the total of 93,664 square miles. But of this area over 24,000 square miles, or more than half, are occupied by the ramifications of several mountain chains, which contain here and there a few clearings and villages of the wild Karen tribes; but the greater part of the lower and all the higher ranges are pathless and impenetrable jungle, without sign of human habitation. These mountain ranges run up into peaks, from 3,000 to 6,000 feet high. The highest point in British Burma is the 'Nát-Toung' Peak, which attains an elevation of near 8,000 feet. The Tenasserim division touches the Shan States of Siam, to about the latitude of Maulmain (16° 25′ N.), and thence runs down the northern part of the Malayan

Peninsula to the Isthmus of Kraw, being divided from Siam Proper by the great mountain chain that cuts the peninsula longitudinally into two nearly equal halves.

The Salween River, which empties itself into the sea at Maulmain, rivals the Irrawaddy in length but not in importance. Owing to the rapids in its bed, at a comparatively short distance from its mouth it ceases to be navigable; and, as far as is known, it flows for nearly the whole of its course through a narrow, thickly-wooded valley, very sparsely populated by semi-savage tribes.

The great Pegu and Martaban plain forming the sea-coast is barely above the high-water mark of spring tides; in some parts, in fact, the face of the country sinks away from the river banks, until it is actually below the level of high water. Its formation is comparatively recent, and the coast line has in some places advanced twelve miles within the memory of living man, and is every year gradually stretching itself into the shallow waters of the Martaban Gulf. Strange to say, although the great drainage rivers yearly bring down with them vast quantities of detritus, and the whole country is flooded, the interior plains are not in the slightest degree affected nor silted up by it. The cause of this has been thus graphically explained:—

'The first showers of rain fill the numerous "engs" or depressions scattered over the country, and these, gradually enlarging, submerge the country before the turbid floods of the rivers have risen to a similar height (forty feet above their summer level). In default of any effective drainage, the ground adjoining the rivers being higher than the flooded interior, the ordinary rainfall is usually adequate to produce this effect; but the low land skirting the hills receives in addition considerable though irregular supplies through streams which, pouring out from the hills, diffuse themselves over the country, and lose themselves in the plains. The turbid waters of the Irrawaddy (or other rivers) now rising, top their banks; but their course is soon arrested by the limpid water of the plains, which opposes a perfect barrier to the spread of the river water, charged with sediment, over the low country.'[1]

This regular and complete inundation of a whole country from one range of hills to another, not as an accidental occurrence, but as a yearly recurring event, affords one of the most singular phenomena of Burma. With the exception of high knolls standing up here and there, and a strip of high ground at the base of the hills, the whole country, fields, roads, bridges, are under water from one to twelve feet or

[1] Theobald, *Geology of Pegu.*

more in depth. Boats are the only means of locomotion for even a few yards. You sail across the country, ploughing through the half-submerged long grass, piloting a way through the clumps of brushwood or small trees, into the streets of large agricultural villages, where the cattle are seen stabled up in the houses, sometimes twelve feet from the ground; the children are catching fish with lines through the holes in the floor; the people are going about their everyday concerns, if it is only to borrow a cheroot from their next-door neighbour, in canoes; in short, all the miseries and laughable *contretemps* sometimes pictured in the illustrated papers as caused by floods in Europe may be seen—with this difference, that every one is so accustomed to them that they never create a thought of surprise.

Though in some ways unpleasant, this heavy monsoon is the great blessing and source of prosperity to British Burma. There may be too much or too little rain in certain districts to ensure a good, full crop, but we have no fear of famine; nothing but an absolute blight passing over the whole land could produce it. The rice fields are not prepared, as in China, Italy, and elsewhere, in terraces carefully levelled for irrigation; but the grass and weeds are raked and pulled out with a huge harrow, and the young plants from the nurseries are set in the soft ground a foot deep in water. In a large plain there are of course inequalities, if even of only a few inches, in the surface, so that if the waters subside too quickly the crops on the higher ground are more or less injured; if the monsoon is a late and heavy one, the paddy plants in the low grounds are rotted while the outturn of the higher land is increased. In ordinary years, the high lands being first planted, the danger on both sides is guarded against.

There are three seasons in Burma—the rains, which begin about the middle of May (sometimes in the end of April) and cease about the middle of October; the cold weather till about the middle of February, though the really cold months are December, January, and February; and the hot weather, from February till the rains set in.

As may be supposed, during five months of almost constant rain, the rainfall in Burma is very large, but there is a wide difference between that of the inland and of the littoral zones, ranging from forty inches in the season at Thayetmyo, our west frontier military station, to 184 inches at Maulmain, or even, in an exceptional year, to 228 inches at the latter place. The commencement and the end of the rains are both unpleasant and unhealthy; there is a great sultriness and an oppressive electricity in the air, and fevers are prevalent, while (except for the universal moisture and damp) the rainy months, when the monsoon has well set in, are pleasant.

The thermometer in July, about the middle of the rains, ranges from 76° F. at sunrise to 84° F. at midday. In May (the hottest month) the average temperature in the shade at midday is 90° F.; in December, at the same time of day, 81° F. Of course these approximate figures vary in different years. The climate is equable, and there are no specially sickly localities, excepting the dense forests upon the mountains during and for some time after the end of the rains. But this might be expected, and few are called on to face this danger; and about January, the thermometer registering 29½° F. on the hills, the cold clears off all malaria even there. Though free from serious maladies, the European finds the very equability of the climate, with the thermometer standing at so high a range, to be enervating and depressing. As with a machine constantly at work without rest or intermission, although each part of the system may be radically sound and without a flaw, the constant vibration loosens and disorganises their action. To this may be added outside the seaport towns the want of a varied and nourishing diet for Europeans, who consequently, after some years, without actual disease, suffer much from weakness and nervous depression, requiring a change to a bracing climate. On the question of a sanatorium for Europeans many proposals have been made; but stations on the high mountain ranges in Burma, however pleasant in summer, would have to be abandoned to the jungle beasts and the elements during the rains, for not even natives could remain to take care of the buildings, and so incredibly rapid and luxurious is vegetation there that the very next year a forest would have to be cleared away to find the houses again.

The excellence of the Burman climate is, I think, clearly shown by comparing it with that of any other country in the same latitude. The inhabitants of Burma are robust and healthy looking; they attain the average length of human life, and children especially thrive in the country. The infantile diseases —measles, chicken-pox, whooping-cough—which cause such a mortality among the young in England exist in Burma in so mild a form as to excite little or no apprehension. The registration returns show that in Burma the deaths of children under five years of age are in the proportion of 27·85 of the total deaths at all ages, whereas in England they are 40 per cent. The percentage of children under twelve years of age is 35·8 of the whole population. The proportion of persons over sixty years of age to the whole population was 4·40 according to the census of 1872. All these facts prove that Burma is not, as it was once considered, one of the most unhealthy climates in the East.

Mention has been made of the great alluvial plain which forms the southern seaboard of British Burma. Without going too deeply into scientific details it may be interesting to explain how this plain, together with the three great valleys of Burma, afford an instance of the extensive growth of fluviatile deltas in historic and even recent times. If any one will take the map of Burma, he will at once observe the three great mountain ranges that run north and south through the country, the Arracan, Pegu, and Salween ranges. Let him imagine the plains covered with water, and it will be seen that these three ranges would form long peninsulas, enclosing between them two great estuaries. This was doubtless the condition of the country in not very remote times, according to the threefold evidence of ancient tradition, scientific investigation, and the analogy of existing facts.

The Burman Radza-win, or history, states that when Gaudama visited the Upper Burman country, he arrived at a hill on the west bank of the Irrawaddy, nearly opposite Prome; before him to the south stretched out the sea. He looked upon it, and prophesied that 100 years afterwards a violent earthquake should shake the whole land, and then the sea covering it should be dried up. In the time of Dwottaboung, the founder of the city of Prome, 544 B.C., the history afterwards relates that these events occurred, and that the country around Prome and to the south formerly beneath the sea became dry land. The prophecy without doubt is as mythical as Gaudama's visit to this region; but is it not most probable that the actual occurrence of such a convulsion of nature was the origin of the prophecy? In fact, across the whole breadth of the delta, from Cape Negrais to Martaban Point, every local village tradition, every fairy tale, points to a time when the sea covered all the country of Martaban and of Lower Pegu.

History affords us the following facts, which there is no reason to suppose untrue.

At least 600 years after Christ, Thatone, now twelve miles from the sea, was a seaport, and ships traded thence to the Coromandel Coast and Ceylon. In 1191, Narapadiseethoo, King of Pugán, in Upper Burma, came down with a fleet of war boats to Rangoon, and, going *round by the sea*, he sailed up the Sittang River and founded the city of Tonghoo. He then returned down the river and sailed across to Martaban. No montion is made of the dreaded 'bore,' which would effectually prevent such an expedition in the present day; and this shows that the mouth of the Sittoung must have then been under different conditions to those of later times. The geological evidence, as given in the Government Geological Survey Report, is even stronger and more complete.

The older alluvial clay deposit comprises the entire level plains of Pegu within the valley of the Irrawaddy, and the alluvial plans of the Sittoung Valley also, the two deltas so blending to the south that no distinction can be made between the deposit in either. I am not aware of any fossils having been found in the alluvium of Pegu.

During the south-west monsoon the whole of the Gulf of Martaban opposite the mouths of the Irrawaddy and Sittoung is a sea of muddy water, from which at the subsidence of the monsoon a considerably widespread and homogeneous deposit must take place. All, then, that the supposition of the marine origin of the older clay of the Irrawaddy Valley requires is, that a gradual elevation should have taken place, whereby the sea was forced to recede to its present limits, and the estuary to yield to the encroachments of the land.

'The now deserted military station of Sittoung was situated on a steep bluff of rock overlooking the river. This rock is *laterite,* and runs with a slightly sinuous and somewhat indented outline to Kyketo and thence to Martaban. At the time of its formation the waters of the Gulf of Martaban stretched up what now forms the Irrawaddy, Sittoung, and Salween Valleys. The coarse gravels which underlie the clay towards the frontier in the upper portion of the delta (above Prome) are clearly of marine origin.'

Thus the scientific conclusions drawn from the present geological features of the country concur with native tradition and history in pointing to *a* time when the great plains of Pegu and Sittoung to Martaban were still submerged beneath the waters of the Gulf of Martaban, which at that time extended far inland, even above the latitude of Prome, and formed deep estuaries between the three great mountain ranges.

But it may be said that the phenomena here presented are not unique, and that the upraising and extension of low coast lines is going on at present in many other parts of the world. This is true; but perhaps no other locality shows this process in operation on so recent, so extensive, and so rapid a scale.

An old phoonygee of my acquaintance, about eighty years of age, remembers, when a lad, the whole of the plain south of Kyketo about fifteen miles from the sea, and now covered with villages, being then, as he expressed it, the 'pinlay gyee,' or broad sea; that is to say, at every high tide the whole land was covered, except high knolls that formed islands here and there, while the receding tide left exposed a vast expanse of miles of mud and sand flats. This old man also remembered, some sixty years ago, seeing the timbers of a foreign-built ship, which had been found buried at the foot of a bold rocky bluff on which formerly stood the ancient town of Tike-kolah, which is now twelve miles in a straight line from the present sea-coast. He could give no intelligible description of the vessel: the timbers, of course, have long since vanished, but the trench, out of which they were dug, still remains.

In two cases which happened within my own knowledge, when digging for wells, large pieces of coir cable have been found at fifteen and twenty feet below the surface. The localities were near Poung Village, in the Thatone subdivision, and at Shwegyeen, in both cases near the foot of the laterite range, and in the sandy talus or bank which formed the shore line of the ancient sea. As the alluvial deposit in these places is marine, and not fluviatile, these cables must have been buried while the spots, where they were found, were still underneath the sea, and receiving fresh accumulations of alluvial deposit;

consequently the elevation took place after the occupation of the country, unless we suppose the ships came to uninhabited places.

In the Martaban plains the cultivation is still every year receding from the foot of the hills, and following the extending high ground along the seacoast. Large tracts that still show the ridges of the old rice fields have become impossible to cultivate, and been abandoned during the last twenty years, from the depth of the water deposited during the monsoons, and which finds no escape, the land always sloping down from the coast line to the interior, thus forming a low basin towards the foot, as shown in the following diagram.

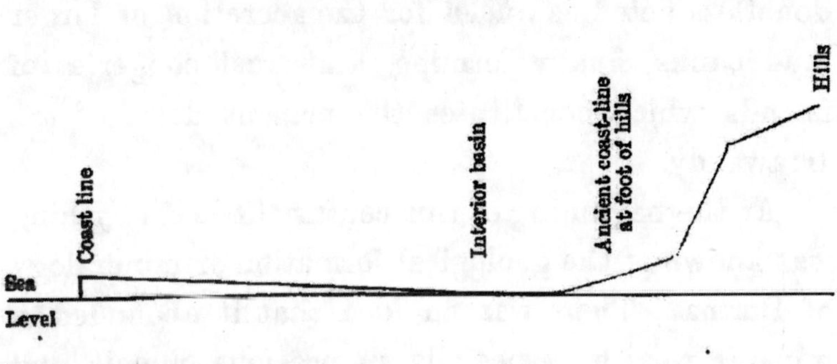

There are thus thousands of square miles of most fertile and once cultivated land, only awaiting the appliances of modern science in the shape of embankments and drainage, which will certainly come as soon as the world's consumption of rice so increases as to ensure the expense incurred on such works being met by a profitable return.

It may be fairly stated that the plains extending along the foot of the mountain range running from Martaban Point to the Sittoung River have been finally abandoned by the sea waters only at most within the last hundred years.

With regard to the still wider plains of Pegu and Rangoon, west of the Sittoung, these would appear to have been formed in a similar manner but at an earlier date. Syriam, Dalla, Twantay, Engtay, are all in their earliest history mentioned as islands; and these, scattered amidst the shallow sea then existing over what is now the Province of Pegu, doubtless acted as nuclei for the accretion of larger mud banks, finally forming that vast congeries of islands which constitutes the present delta of the Irrawaddy.

At the beginning of this century little if anything was known of the geological formation or mineralogy of Burma. There was an idea that it abounded in mineral wealth, especially in precious metals and stones. Most people, and even writers, were content to take their ideas from the expressions of the old travellers. 'There be great riches in this country,' says De Cruz in 1550. 'For people, dominions, gold and silver, the King of the Bramas far excelleth the power of the Great Turk in treasure and strength,' writes Cæsar Frederick in 1569.

After our annexation of Arracan and the Tenasserim Provinces in 1826 strenuous efforts were made for some years both by Government and by private individuals to develop the vast treasures believed to lie hidden in our new possession. 'Few countries in the world are so rich in minerals as Burma,' writes Dr. Mason; 'in none, perhaps, do those riches lie so dormant. Mergui has tin equal to that in Cornwall; in Tavoy iron could be made equal to the Swedish; the copper and antimony of Maulmain are good; the gold of Shwegyeen is not inferior to the Australian; and the lead of the Tounghoo Mountains has no superior in the hills of Missouri. In Burma Proper are the petroleum wells, the amber mines, the precious serpentine, the Bandwen silver mine (supposed to be one of the most extensive mines in the world), and the Capelan mines of precious stones.' A truly glowing vision of wealth, but alas! like the *Fata morgana*, it fades away on too near an inspection. Except some small petroleum wells in Arracan and the upper portion of the Irrawaddy Valley, and the traces of gold sands in some spots on the banks of the Irrawaddy, all the mineral wealth exists on the east side of the Sittoung River. The ancient name of the country lying there was in the old Pali books 'Suvānna

Chúmi,' 'the Land of Gold,' and some enthusiastic scholars have identified it with the Aurea Chersonesus of Ptolemy, and with the 'Ophir' of Solomon. The gold is there certainly; at the present day gold washing is carried on to a certain extent in the district of Shwegyeen (literally 'Shwekyin,' *i.e.* 'gold-sifting'), and I possess specks of gold washed from the earth in my own garden in that town; but unfortunately the golden treasure is so diffused through the soil, that it does not pay to extract it. Australian and Chinese gold diggers have prospected it; a practical mining geologist employed by Government has examined the best localities; but all have gone away disappointed. Yet the gold, as it is found, in small rounded or flattened flakes, is of great purity, proving on examination to contain in 100 parts 92 of gold and 8 of silver. This gold is valued by the Burmans for making amulets or charms, and fetches four or five shillings per ounce above the price of ordinary gold. It therefore pays the Karens and some of the poorer Burmans, when they have no other occupation, to wash for a few grains at a time. The process is very simple: the earth is washed in a wooden dish about two feet in diameter, having the centre sinking to a point, so as to be something like a very broad flat funnel, but without any hole. This is dexterously twirled in the hands round and round, every now and then ejecting the water and coarser earth to one side, adding fresh water, and so continuing the process till there only remains in the funnel-like centre a little fine black sand containing a few flakes of gold. They say that they never take, and that it would be dangerous to do so, any nugget that is more than a 'tickal's' weight ($\frac{100}{3\cdot65}$ lbs. av.). I have never, however, met with any one who had had the temptation thrown in his way. These larger nuggets are called 'Shwé má,' the 'Mother of Gold.'

In the same way as gold, tin, lead, iron, and copper are plentifully scattered over the mountains between the Salween and the Sittoung and in the Southern Tenasserim Provinces, but, with the exception of the first mentioned, none of these mineral deposits are of any avail; the difficult nature of the country in which they are found, the want of labour, of coal for working, and of communications of any kind, render them practically useless.

The tin mines of Mergui, however, seem to have been long known and worked; whether any of the tin which the early Phœnician traders drew from the East was thence derived, we cannot say; but in A.D. 1586 Ralph Fitch, the first Englishman who visited Burma, writes: 'I went from Pegu to Malacca, passing many seaports of Pegu, as Martaban, the Island of Tavi (Tavoy), whence all India is supplied with tin, Tenasserim, the island of Junkselon, and many others.'[1] For many years these mines were in the hands of a Chinese speculator, who paid a small rental to Government, and who merely picked, as it were, at the surface, confining his operations to washing the gravel and extracting the sand (or binoxide of tin) by the process called, in Cornwall, 'streaming.' The once washed ore contains about 70 per cent. and the twice washed about 75 per cent. of tin. The mines are now, however, in the hands of an enterprising European firm, who have brought out machinery and English miners, made communications between the mines and the landing places, and appear determined to make a fortune, if it can be made by energy and enterprise, out of Burman mining.

The ruby, amber, and jadestone mines belong exclusively to Upper Burma, and some account of them is contained in Colonel Yule's 'Embassy to the Court of Ava.' With these, therefore, we have nothing now to do. It may, however, be mentioned as an instance of error continued in spite of available information, that in the last edition of Dana's 'Mineralogy' (1868) it is stated that 'the best ruby sapphires are found in the Capelan Mountains

[1] Purchas, vol. ii.

near Syrian, a city of Pegu, and in the kingdom of Ava.' Syrian, or Syriam, is a village (once a large town) nearly opposite Rangoon across the Pegu River, and one would think a scientific writer seven years ago might be aware that rubies were not found in British Burma. 'Kyat-pen' (query, Capelan?'), whence the rubies *are* obtained, is situated near Momiet, about seventy miles south of Bamaw, or Bhamo, as we have named it.

Coal of an inferior and almost useless kind is found rather extensively throughout the Tenasserim Province, and sanguine expectations have been several times raised of the discovery of beds of a valuable quality. When that fortunate event shall happen, we may hope to see the hidden mineral wealth of Burma developed, and the former ideas respecting it to some extent at least realised.

CHAPTER II.

THE RACES OF BRITISH BURMA.

As the purpose of this book is not only to amuse the reader, but also to give him as far as possible a faithful and comprehensible account of the Province of British Burma—to describe its people, their manner of life, their religion and habits—it is clearly necessary that he, the reader, should have some idea of who those people are, whence and how they arrived in their present localities. I would therefore ask my readers to bear with me, if, at the outset, I present them with a dry chapter of ethnological details, but have at the same time a hope that the present popularity of such studies will ensure some interest in the subject. It is with a due sense of modesty, but with a firm conviction of their truth, that I have ventured to advance opinions not quite in accordance with the theories of such distinguished scholars in all matters relating to the Burman Peninsula as Sir A. Phayre and the late Dr. Mason.[1]

[1] Every one connected with British Burma must bear his testi-

It may, however, direct the attention of other Orientalists to the subject.

In the official report of the first regular Census taken in British Burma in the year 1872 it is remarked: 'There is possibly no country in the world whose inhabitants are more varied in race, custom, and language than those of Burma. It would be easy to suppose it a disputed spot in the earlier days, and to expect that in the collision of great races, through a long period of history, many ethnological fragments should people the middle land; and although the Mongolian element has been, and is, the predominant race, it appears under very numerous forms, and in races who among themselves reject the connection of a common stock.'

The statistical tables of the Census Report give eighteen divisions of the indigenous races of so-called Mongolian origin. Dr. Mason enumerates four *national* and thirty-nine *tribal* divisions, together with eight more unclassed or 'miscellaneous' tribes, making a total of forty-seven varieties of the human

mony to the talent and worth of the late Rev. F. Mason, D.D., M.R.A.S., one of the able and devoted men whom the American Baptist, or, as it was better known in early days, the Serampore Mission, has furnished to the East. His comprehensive work on Burma, its *Nations, Fauna, Flora, and Minerals*, published in 1860 by Trübner & Co., although more a scientific catalogue than a popular description, is a treasure house, on which to draw in every subject relating to Burma.

race within the area of the tract of country which lies between the Bay of Bengal and the Province of Eastern Bengal on the West, and China and Siam on the East, comprising British and Independent Burma.

It may be as well to give Mason's classification of the different tribes.

1. *Mōns.*

No Tribal divisions.

2. *Burmese Tribes.*

Burmese.
Arracanese.
Mugs.
Kanyans.
Tonghooers.
Tavoyers.
Yaus or Yos.
Yebains.
Pyūs.
Kadōs.
Danūs.

3. *Karen Tribes.*

a. Sgau tribes.
Sgau.
Maunepgha.
Paku.
Wewa.

b. Bghai tribes.
Tunin Bghai.
Paut Bgai.
Laymay ?
Manu-Manau.
Red Karens.

c. Pwo tribes.
Pwo.
Shoung.
Kay or Ka.
Taru or Khu-ta.
Mopgha.
Hashwie
Toungthoo.
Khyen or Chin.

d. Shan Karens.
Yen or Yein.
Yenseik.
Yingbaw.
Pandung.
Toungyo.
Black Karens.

e. Miscellaneous tribes.
Ka-khyeus or Kakoos.
Kamis or Kumis.
Kyaus.
Koons.
Sak.
Mru.
Shendoo.
Selung.

4. *Shan Tribes.*

Shans or Taï.	Paloungs or Paloas.
Lao or Laus, or Lawa or Wa.	Phwons or Mwoon.

How useful soever this detailed list may be in an historical point of view, as showing the sub-divisions of the various races from time to time, it has only so much reference to their ethnological or linguistic history, as a similar classification of the English people would have if it were made according to the dialects of their counties. As we should not (except for some special purpose) describe the English nation as being divided into Northumbrians, Devonians, Kentish-men, &c, so there seems no good reason for such a confused description of the people of Burma. In the same way that a classification of the inhabitants of Scotland two centuries ago according to the various clans, thus giving the idea that Campbells and Gordons, Forbeses and M'Dougals were distinct tribes of the Scottish race, would be fanciful and untrue, so is a scientific discrimination as '*tribes*' of the petty *accidental clan* divisions of the Burmese and Karen nations.

We find four great races occupying the Burman Peninsula—the Mōn, the Karen, the Burman, and the Taï or Shan; and we shall endeavour to give a probable account of the route and order by which they arrived in their present localities.

Though there are still some dissentients,[1] the general consensus of the ablest ethnologists agrees in placing the starting point of the present inhabitants of the globe in that 'hive of nations,' the mountainous region bordering the Caspian Sea. From thence, says the oldest ethnological record in existence, 'they journeyed from the East, and found a plain in the land of Shinar (Babylonia) and they dwelt there.' From this place began that migration which was to 'people the whole earth.' It is clear that in the early ages of the world the Hamitic family were the most powerful and energetic, and the earliest civilisations were those of the Cushite and Mizraimite Empires of Babylon and Egypt. The Cushite races appear to have been the foremost in extending themselves east and west over the then 'void spaces of the earth.'

Without meaning here to raise the question of the actual meaning and extent of the facts related

[1] Oscar Peschel's revived theory of the primæval but now submerged continent of 'Lemuria' in the Southern Indian Ocean is an ingenious and poetic idea, but is not confined to the minds of European speculative philosophers. Discussing once with an intelligent Buddhist monk the difference between the geography of his sacred books and that which his own knowledge taught him now existed, he advanced the theory that his books referred to a primæval world in which Nāts and spiritual beings walked the earth with man, but which had gradually sunk beneath the sea as the present world was formed. This was not in accordance with his creed, and he certainly had never heard of European speculations on the subject.

in the Mosaic account of the 'Dispersion,' it may be suggested that there is nothing there recorded which opposes the idea that the extension of the human race had been previously and gradually going on. There is no reason for believing that at the time therein alluded to the whole of mankind, although 'of one language and of one speech,' were actually collected together in a mass in the plain of Shinar. The fact that many important branches of the human family are entirely omitted in the Mosaic list, favours the idea that these were absent.

The next event in the history of the world seems to have been the great migrations of the Turanian families who overran not only Asia, but the farthest parts of Europe before the advent of the Aryan race. We have some knowledge of the successive order of the migrations of the Indo-Germanic families that now people Europe, and, judging by analogy, we conclude that similar successive waves flowed from the central region round the Mesopotamian plains into Eastern Asia. The precise order and route of each family cannot certainly be accurately ascertained, but we have still some landmarks to guide us.

According to the Chinese histories, that nation formed their earliest settlements in the North-

Western provinces of Kansu and Shensi about 2000 B.C.[1] Everywhere they found possessors of the land before them, whom they pushed southward and eastward in their advance. These aboriginal tribes exist to the present day as the Miau or Miautze, the Nung, Lolo, Yau, and other wild inhabitants of the mountain ranges of South-Western China.

The route taken by the Chinese race in their migration from the common hive would seem to have been the Northern part of Turkestan or Chinese Tartary, and across the Southern portion of the Great Desert of Gobi into Kansu.

Singular is the confirmation afforded by two traditions of the Karens, a people whose connection with the Chinese will hereafter be considered. They say 'the Karens and Chinese in two companies, as elder and younger brother (the Karens the elder), wandered together from the West. The journey was long and continued for a long time. The two companies were finally separated, as the younger brother went in advance of the other. The company of the elder brother ceased to follow, and founded cities and a kingdom of their own, but were conquered and scattered by others, who followed them

[1] Edkins's *China's Place in Philology.*

from the same quarter from which they themselves came.'

Again, 'we anciently came from beyond the river of *running sand*, and, having marked out Zimmay for ourselves, returned. Afterwards, when we came to dwell there, we found the Shans occupying the country. Then the Karens cursed them, saying, Dwell ye in the dividing of countries.' Both Dr. Mason and Sir A. Phayre have clearly pointed out, that this 'river of running sand' can be only the great Mongolian Desert of Gobi. We find then that at a date at least 2,000 years before the Christian era certain tribes, whose descendants exist to this day, occupied South-Western China. According to the oldest Chinese record (the 'Shooking'), the San Mian or aboriginal tribes were finally subdued in the reign of Shun B.C. 2255.[1] As the Chinese traditions hint at no contact with any other people on their long journey eastward until they found these barbarians *in situ* in the South-West provinces of the present Empire of China, we are led to presume that these latter found their way thither by a different route. As far as has been ascertained, these aboriginal tribes of South-Western China belong to the Himalaic family, having the greatest affinity to the Eastern or Mon-Anam branch.

[1] Legge's *Shooking*.

The route of all the Himalaic tribes seems to have been from the Western side of Tibet. Physical geography comes in to our aid. Looking at the Map of Asia we find south of the great highway leading through Bokhara and Cashgar into Central Asia, there is to the eastward an impenetrable barrier presented by the Hindoo Koosh, the Bolor Tagh, and Karakorum ranges, until we come to the famous Khyber Pass opening into the valleys of Cashmir and the Panjáb.

Through these passes then it is probable the Himalaic races poured into Tibet, the Eastern 'Mon-Anam' branch occupying the vanguard and yielding gradually to the pressure from behind of their Tibeto-Burman brethren, and finally making their way into Ultra-India, where we now find them.

What has been called the 'Mon-Anam branch' in Dr. Logan's phraseology, comprises the Mons or Peguans, the Anamites, the Cambojans, and some of the wild tribes in the South-Western part of the Chinese Empire. All these appear to have characteristics so similar to each other, and so distinct from the Western Tibeto-Burmans, as to warrant our classing them for the present as one family, and assuming their arrival in their present localities at about the same period. We have seen that the Miau tribes occupied the South-Western provinces of China before the arrival of the Chinese, and we conclude that the countries to the south, Pegu, Laos, and Cambodia, were also occupied by kindred but more civilised races of the same family.

The Mōns of Pegu have not existing among them the *slightest trace* of any tradition of their having ever occupied any other locality than their present one. The Burmans, who lie above them to the North, and who have preserved accounts more or less reliable of their first wanderings from the West, and of the tribes they encountered in their migration, make no mention of the Mōns or Taleins until some time after their own occupation of the Upper Valley of the Irrawaddy. The Mōn traditions represent themselves as having been a wild, uncivilised race at the time of the advent of Gaudama six centuries before the Christian era.

It must, therefore, be remembered, when speaking of British Burma and Burmans, that we really possess a very small portion of what is really Burma; but what we do possess is Arracan and the ancient kingdom of Pegu, the majority of the inhabitants of which are Mōns and not Burmans.

These two nations, though so closely connected by position and by their mutual history, are as distinct in origin, in blood, and in language as the Welsh and English. Nevertheless in manners and customs they have now become so assimilated by centuries of close mutual connection, as well as by the identity of religion, which in the East is the great moulder and former of national life and habits, that to describe one people is, except in some trivial details, to describe both. While, as has been mentioned, the traditions of the Karens point to an exodus from the North, the national histories of the Burmans assert that the progenitors of their nation came into their present seats from the West, from the Upper Valley of the Ganges, and claim a Rajpoot origin for the people; while the royal family pretend to trace their descent from the Sacred Solar and Lunar dynasties of Hindustan.

This myth has been generally ascribed to national vanity, and completely ignored. Sir A. Phayre is quite opposed to it, and says in his 'History of the Burman Race:' 'The supposed emigration of any of the royal races of Gangetic India to the Irrawaddy in the sixth century B.C., or even later, will appear very improbable. I see no reason for doubting, that they (the Burmans) found their way to the Valley of the Irrawaddy by what is now the track of the Chinese caravans from Yunnan, which track debouches at Bamo on the river.' With all deference to such an authority as Sir A. Phayre, this is a theory opposed to all probability and evidence, for according to it we must seek the original domicile of the Burman race in the South-Western provinces of China! whereas everything points to a route from the westward as that followed by them in their migratory journey.

In the dim mists of prehistoric times we can only take as our landmarks the facts that loom out here and there, themselves faint and unconnected, but affording the only helps to our ignorance. Thus we know that before the Aryan invasion of India, the Gangetic Valley was occupied by tribes of Turanian origin. The great Hindu epic, the 'Maha Bharata,' is generally accepted as a mythical account of the conquest of India by the Aryan races, and of their wars with the people they found in possession. These non-Aryan tribes are described under various names, several of which have been identified with those so-called aboriginal tribes of the present day. Among these were the Nágas, who are described as having been a powerful and partly civilised people. We cannot certainly clearly connect these Nágas with those tribes of the same name which now occupy the East of Bengal, and belong to the Tibeto-Burman family, but we may mark the coincidence.

It has been often observed that the features of the sculptures among the Buddhist ruins at Sánchi, in Lower Bengal, even those of Gaudama himself, are Mongolian and not Aryan.

We cannot fix the dates of the successive advances of the Aryan conquerors from their first colonies west of the Sutlej River, nor of the establishment of their power in the various ancient capitals on the banks of the Jumna and Ganges. But there is good reason to believe that, in the time of Megasthenes, who has left us so precious an account of the Aryan Empire and capital of Pataliputra (B.C. 312), the country to the east (*i.e.* Lower Bengal) was still more or less occupied by unconquered non-Aryan races. The rude tribes, the Chepangs, Kusunda, and Vayus, in the west corner of Nepál, between the Kali and Gunduck Rivers, whom Mr. Hodgson classes as aborigines, exhibit close affinities to the Hill tribes of Arracan, and would appear to be a fragment left behind in the eastward advance of the main body of their kindred.

There seems, then, no good reason why we should peremptorily reject as false the Burman national tradition in so far as it traces their migratory march from the Gangetic Valley. Their assumed Rajpoot origin is, of course, an invention of courtly historians of a date subsequent to their conversion to Buddhism, which is fully disproved by their language, their physiognomy, and by every point of their national characteristics. It is true that, as has also been supposed, the Burman and kindred Lhopa tribes of Bhután *may* have come round from Tibet, through the Eastern passes, into the valley of the Brahma pútra. But in the absence of any evidence to the contrary, it appears more reasonable to follow the lines of ancient tradition as far as they agree with probabilities.

With the Burmans we may, for the present, class the various Hill tribes of the Arracan Yoma,[1] as scattered and uncivilised clans of the same race. It is impossible to decide who were the earliest arrivals. Sir A. Phayre inclines to consider the Hill tribes as the earliest—a view which is confirmed by the Burman traditions, that when they penetrated into Arracan they found the seaboard occupied by savage monsters, termed by them 'Beloos,' whom they expelled; probably a mythical account of these wilder tribes whom they found in prior possession of the land.

The Karens appear to belong neither to the Eastern nor Western branches of the Himalaic family; that is, they are closely related neither to the Mōns of Pegu nor to the Burmans of Burma Proper. Their own traditions point, as we have seen, to a connection with the primitive Chinese; and many things seem to confirm this idea. Their language,

[1] A bone, ridge, or range as applied to mountains.

both by its glossarial and structural characteristics, is allied more to the Chinese than to the Himalaic class. Their present locality seems to indicate a migration southwards from the Chinese province of Yu-nan. The most civilised tribe, the Sgaus, which has been long in contact with races superior to itself, has partly made its way into the plains of Pegu, and a few scattered families are to be found on the eastern slopes of the Arracan Hills, but these are recent and very unimportant settlements. The real home of the Karen people is the vast series of lofty mountain ranges that lie between the great Irrawaddy and Menam Rivers, and from the south of Yu-nan Province to the extremity of the British district of Mergui, in lat. 11° N.

We still find the wilder and fiercer tribes to the North continually attacking and pressing southwards their more civilised brethren. All the clans agree in pointing due north as having been the direction of their wanderings. Their tradition of their first intended location near Zimmay having been preoccupied by the Shans has been mentioned. Shan history informs us that their oldest city, Labong, which lies a little south of the present town of Zimmay, was founded about A.D. 574.[1] The Chinese annals state that a powerful kingdom was established in Yu-nan

[1] Dr. Richardson, J.A.S.B.

about the beginning of the eighth century of the Christian era by the Taï or Shan race, which was finally subjugated by Kublai Khan in A.D. 1253–54. May not the establishment of this Shan kingdom of Nan-chao have a connection with the expulsion and southern migration of all the Karen tribes from their ancestral home in Yu-nan? Finding themselves then, as at the present day, hemmed in on the East by the Laos race, and on the West by the Burmans in the Upper Valley of the Irrawaddy, the fugitive Karens could only follow the watershed east and west of the Salween River into their present mountain homes.

Here they have remained ever a wild, uncivilised race of mountaineers, broken up into many petty clans and communities, jealous of and ceaselessly at war with each other. Surrounded by Buddhist nations, they have retained their primitive nature-worship, leavened with singular traces of a purer but forgotten faith.

The great Taï or Shan race completely envelope Pegu and Burma on the East and North from the Gulf of Siam to the upper waters of the Brahmapútra, and are found scattered in such numbers over our province that they may claim to rank as one of the races of the soil. They, according to their own account, originally occupied the province of Yu-nan, and the country east of the Salween. Chinese history tells us that Kublai Khan's armies conquered Yu-nan and invaded Burma about A.D. 1272. Marco Polo confirms this, and we also learn from Burmese history that at this period the Burman Empire in the Upper Irrawaddy Valley was destroyed, and divided among several Shan princes, one of whom in A.D. 1365 founded the city of Ava. Bishop Pallegoix, following the native annals, places the commencement of the present Shan kingdom of Siam in A.D. 1350, and at the beginning of the thirteenth century the Ahoms, a Shan tribe, invaded and conquered the present British province of Assam. We see therefore that the movement of the Shan race into its present localities is quite modern, and was the last great wave of migration that swept over these countries. I would also remind many of my readers that the Siamese, whom we all now know well, are the same race as the Shans of whom we read in such books as Anderson's 'Mandalay to Momien,' and poor Margary's 'Journal.' Previous to the middle of the fourteenth century, Siam (a name unknown to the natives) was occupied by a race kindred to the Mōns of Pegu.

To summarise what has been said, in popular if not strictly scientific language, the races occupying the Burman Peninsula, and of whom we have been speaking, belong to the same family of the human race as the Tibetans, the Chinese, and Siamese, and have no affinity or connection with the nations of Hindustan, who belong to the Aryan or Indo-Germanic stock.

We shall perhaps better understand the foregoing remarks by glancing at the map, showing, generally of course, the ethnological divisions of the country. It must be remembered that the population has now become so intermixed in British Burma, that these divisions now merely show in what parts the different races are still predominant, and also what we may term their original habitat.

It will be seen that in our province the Burman race (or rather a branch of it) occupy Arracan, and others, pure Burmans, the upper portion of the Irrawaddy Valley. They appear again at Tavoy and Mergui, in the Tenasserim Peninsula. The Mōns occupy the sea-coast and lower valleys of the great rivers, the Irrawaddy, the Sittang, and the Salween. The Karens and wild tribes are scattered everywhere over the mountain ranges, which they hold as their fastness and heritage. The Shans surround the others as with a fringe, and, without gaining footing anywhere, form an important element in the population of many parts of the country.

CHAPTER III.

SOCIAL LIFE AND MANNERS.

'UNLIKE the generality of Asiatics, the Burmese are not a fawning race. They are cheerful and singularly alive to the ridiculous; buoyant, elastic, soon recovering from personal or domestic disaster. With little feeling of patriotism, they are still attached to their homes, greatly so to their families. Free from prejudices of caste or creed, they readily fraternise with strangers, and at all times frankly yield to the superiority of a European. Though ignorant, they are, when no mental exertion is required, inquisitive, and to a certain extent eager for information; indifferent to the shedding of blood on the part of their rulers, yet not individually cruel; temperate, abstemious, and hardy, but idle, with neither fixedness of purpose nor perseverance. Discipline or any continued employment becomes most irksome to them, yet they are not devoid of a certain degree of enterprise. Great dabblers in small mercantile ventures, they may be called (the women especially) a race of hucksters; not treacherous or habitual perverters of the truth, yet credulous and given to monstrous exaggerations; where vested with authority, arrogant and boastful; if unchecked, corrupt, oppressive, and arbitrary; not distinguished for bravery, whilst their chiefs are notorious for cowardice; indifferent shots, and, though living in a country abounding in forest, not bold followers of field sports.'[1]

Such is the character drawn by one well acquainted with the people, and it is in the main correct. On the whole amiable and pleasing, but with no noble points; the character of a race which is not destined to advance far on the path of civilisation, nor to profit much by intercourse with the superior genius of their European conquerors.

Twenty odd years of British rule, while it has materially increased the external well-being and happiness of the people, has, we fear, not by any means improved the picture above drawn; if anything, the reverse. Though still, to a great degree, in the agricultural districts, 'temperate, abstemious, and hardy,' the Elders tell with sorrow the common tale, that English spirits and opium are gradually destroying their native good qualities in the rising

[1] Major Allan Yule's *Embassy to Ava*, p. 251.

generation. A feebler constitution, greater arrogance, disrespect of parents and elders, and disregard of religion, are fast becoming the characteristics of young Burma in the British province.

We do not intend to discuss this point here, but to give some account of the customs, ideas, and superstitions of the people of Burma, under which head we shall include both the Taleins, the inhabitants of Pegu, and the Burmese of Burma Proper. Except, however, in so far as is necessary to give a complete view of the subject, our descriptions will chiefly apply to the people of our own province. To describe the social system and life of Burma, so as to be intelligible to the European, is as difficult as, on the other hand, it is for the Burmans to understand ours. In both cases all the familiar ideas of social organisation must be abandoned. In India the Aryan feudal system, or a semblance of it, established and supported an aristocracy; a landed gentry was created by a continued series of 'sunnuds,' or grants from the supreme authority, while the strong bands of caste kept the blood of the higher race pure from intermixture by marriage. The Chinese, again, have an hereditary aristocratic class, and are most careful in preserving their family pedigrees. In Burma, as it exists under its native rule, we find below the absolute sovereign, not an aristocracy, but a bureaucracy. There are, it is true, good families who can trace their pedigree some generations back, in spite of all the intestine convulsions of society in these countries: there is also a certain class of revenue officials, called 'Thoogyees,' in whose families their offices are hereditary; but the only real social position universally acknowledged is that of official Government employ. The King's cook may be one of the chief ministers of the realm to-morrow, and rank superior to all but the blood royal, but he sinks back into his original insignificance the moment the *office* is lost. Excepting the members of the royal family, every Burman outside the circle of officialdom is socially the equal of another. Slavish and cringing to those having official power over him (the natural result of centuries of despotic oppression), he is free and *dégagé* in his bearing towards all others. Men of property and standing have, of course, the influence that wealth always confers; but what I wish to convey is, the entire absence of the subtle yet powerfully defined division between the working man and the middle class, between this latter and the gentry, that constitutes the foundation of our social system. The coolie working for his daily wage by the sweat of his brow, and the rich trader or forester, who has just spent his thousands on some pagoda or other meritorious work, meet on neutral ground as equals. There is no social distinction to prevent the coolie marrying the rich man's daughter, if the want of wealth is overlooked; and, as regards the wife, no union with any woman is deemed a *mésalliance*, except in the case of the descendants of pagoda-slaves—unfortunate captives in former wars, dedicated to perpetual servitude to the pagodas. Of course, in British Burma the servitude has ceased, but the social ban still remains.

The present King's mother was of very mean extraction, and while he was only Prince of Mendoon he was obliged, according to Burmese etiquette, whenever he met his half-sister, who is now the present chief Queen,[1] to kneel and make obesiance, addressing her as 'Phra,' 'Lord,' she being the daughter of his father by the chief Queen. The people laugh and tell how the King, after he had obtained the throne and married this princess, at first from old habit used to fall on his knees, whenever his wife appeared, to her intense amusement, and doubtless satisfaction. In attempting to describe the social life and system of Burma, it will be best to give some slight account of the present branch of

[1] The law enforcing the marriage of the Burman kings with their eldest half-sisters is said to be derived from the ancient custom of the so-called Lunar Royal race of Hindostan.

the royal family, with domestic particulars not found in any written history.

To go back to the uncle of the reigning sovereign, Noungdangyee, or Bágyee-daw, who succeeded his grandfather in A.D. 1819. This prince, while heir-apparent, was married to Tsin-byoo-maia, a princess of pure royal blood. Some time after, however, he met a fish-girl, Mai Noo, with whom he became perfectly infatuated. The Burmans, with their love of the marvellous, relate that long before she met the prince, while bathing, in company with her brother, some say lover, Moung Oh, a kite flew away with her cloth, which was drying on the bank. Overjoyed at this omen of future greatness, she promised Moung Oh that he should share whatever good fortune was in store for her.

The prince devoted himself to his new love, to the neglect of his royal wife, who died giving birth to a son, called the Tsekya-min. His old grandfather the King threatened to put Mai Noo to death, and turned her out of the palace, but without lessening the prince's devotion to her. On the accession of this latter to the throne, he at once made her the Chief of the Four Queens (the legitimate wives of a Burman sovereign), and Moung Oh, her brother, the fisherman, was made a prince. Her influence and power now became boundless, her word was law to the monarch, and she indulged in all the vulgar insolence of the *parvenue* towards all the princesses of the royal blood, making some of the younger ones, it is said, pound pepper for her meals in mockery. She gave birth to a daughter, the Allay-nan-ma-daw, or third Queen of the present King, who, inheriting her mother's pride, affects to consider herself superior to her cousin, the chief Queen, because the latter was born not in the palace, and before her father ascended the throne.

One curious instance of Queen Mai Noo's absurd pride is her prohibition of the use of the word 'noo,' which means soft, tender, as applied to vegetables, &c., and substitution of the similar word 'twut.'[1] The only person who would not succumb to her was the King's brother, the Kongboung Prince. The Queen and her brother, Moung Oh, plotting to murder this latter prince, he fled from the city (in Burma the sign of rebellion on the part of one of the royal family). The King sent to him, asking why he had fled, adding that if his brother wished the throne he himself was quite ready to resign it. The Kong-

[1] This incident is worthy of note in connection with the customs of more uncivilised nations, as mentioned by Max Müller, in *Lectures*, vol. ii. p. 37-41, and Tylor, *Early History of Mankind*, p. 147; also the Burmese objection as a matter of etiquette to mention the *name* of any person of position, always designating him by some title.

boung Prince replied, demanding that Moung Oh and some other nobles should be given up, and they were put to death. Noungdangyee saw his power was gone, and sent again to his brother to come and take possession of the throne, and, according to the Burman royal custom on abdication, he left the palace by one gate as his successor entered it by another.

Kongboung Min solemnly promised his brother not to adopt the White Umbrella, the mark of supreme sovereignty, during his lifetime. After a little while he demanded the surrender of Queen Mai Noo. The unfortunate King reminded him of his promise, and begged him to assume the crown, but to spare his wife, who was, moreover, *a consecrated* Queen. His prayers were disregarded, and Mai Noo, who, at the news, had embraced her husband's feet, and implored his protection, was led away to execution, and beaten to death with clubs, the mode of its infliction on members of the royal family. The eldest son of the dethroned King, the Tsekyamin, was also murdered soon afterwards.

Kongboung Min, or King Tharrawaddy as he is generally called by English writers, went mad after a reign of about eight years. His chief Queen and her son, the Prince of Pagán, determined to seize him, and, followed by several others of his sons, entered the monarch's chamber, and found him lying on the sofa in a semi-lucid interval. They pretended they had brought some medicine; but the King told them plainly he knew that the throne was what they wanted, and seeing the Prince of Mendoon (the present King) hanging back behind the others, he praised him as the only good one among his sons. He was secured, and the Prince of Pagán assumed the sovereignty, only to be in turn deposed and succeeded by his brother, the present reigning monarch.

We have here a fair picture of life in the highest native circles of Burma; those of the lowest grade raised to the highest pinnacle of grandeur and fortune, and again as suddenly cast down. Truly the King is the 'fountain of all honour:' outside the royal family there is no hereditary dignity or nobility.

The Queens, Princes, and Princesses receive each certain towns and districts 'to eat'—a most expressive and characteristic phrase—and the great ministers and officials have similar appanages while in office; but there are no large private estates, and the position of a great English landed proprietor is a mystery to the Burman mind. The only allodial right they know of is that which a man has to the ten, twenty, or more acres, which his father or ancestors actually ploughed and paid tax on; all else belongs to the King.

Besides the actual holders of official position, there are certain possessors of various honours and privileges conferred by the sovereign. Among these the chief is the right to be attended by one or more followers carrying golden umbrellas with long handles (the emblems of rank), to use vessels of gold, and with the fair sex to wear necklace, rings, or earrings of diamonds, all which is forbidden to any except members of the royal family, without the King's permission.

Although sometimes betraying the mingled *gaucherie* and arrogance of the man of low-born origin suddenly exalted, the natural adaptability and grace, which seems peculiar to Eastern races, combined with the system of easy social intercourse before described, render it easier for the Burman to fit himself into a higher position, than it would be for the European in similar circumstances, and this is especially the case with the women. But there, as regards the higher official and wealthy class, with rare exceptions, praise must end; indolent beyond conception, when without some potential motive for exertion, and, as regards the women, with little or no education, the higher class of Burmans find their sole occupation in endeavouring to kill time. With the men there is of course a certain amount of public or private business, that must be got through; but the women are left to the cares of the toilet, visiting, gossiping, and attending feasts and plays wherewith to get through the day. Comparatively few can read, and those who can are too lazy; and even should they while in a humbler sphere have exercised the domestic arts of needlework and cookery, these are abandoned in a higher position, while their daughters know no other accomplishments than dressing their hair and powdering their faces. Of course there are exceptions, as has been said, and, at least in British Burma, there are some notable housewives among the ladies of the native officials.

The intelligence and activity displayed by their sisters among the trading and working classes prove that these habits arise, not from a want of natural talent, nor perhaps are they wholly a fault of disposition, but are more owing to the great blot in the Burman educational system. Although occupying a far higher position in some respects than among any other civilised Eastern race, woman is almost entirely neglected in the matter of education. There are a few who can read and write, having been taught by their fathers, or in the small lay schools that lead a feeble existence. But they are completely debarred from the privileges of general education open to their brothers in the monastic schools, which form the real educational system of the country. In British Burma the Government is striving to remedy this evil, and, as a rule, the European officers heartily support and encourage the cause of female education; but progress must be slow, owing to the utilitarian light in which the Burmans regard the question, urging, 'What is the use of it? women cannot become officials, or Government *employés*, or clerks?' and also to the early age at which, among the middle class, girls become useful, and are withdrawn from school, when sent there, to help in the shops or in the household. The mere development of the mind is never thought of.

Though the inferiority of the softer sex is a point that has never yet been disputed, in Burma women enjoy a much freer and higher position than elsewhere in the East; indeed, in some matters they have attained rights that their sisters in England are still seeking to obtain, or have only lately gained. The fortune that a woman brings on marriage is (by law at least) carefully kept separate for the benefit of her own children or heirs; she can acquire separate property during coverture, by inheritance, or by her own industry, without any deeds of settlement. In case of ill-treatment or other just cause, she can divorce herself from her husband, in the presence of the Elders, taking all her separate and a certain portion of the jointly acquired property.

Among no class in Burma is exclusion of females practised; those of the highest rank have the same freedom of action as the ladies of Europe. Indeed, it may be said that from the easy, indolent disposition of the men, and their own energy and natural *savoir faire*, the women rule the roast in Burma.

Some writers, judging on matters of morals from a Christian and European standpoint, have formed a wrong conception of the actual position of the women socially. Thus, an intelligent observer like Symes remarks: 'In their treatment of the softer sex, the Burmans are destitute both of delicacy and humanity, considering women as little superior to the brute stock of their farms. The lower class of Burmans make no scruple of selling their daughters, and even their wives, to foreigners, who come to pass a temporary residence amongst them. It reflects no disgrace on any of the parties, and the woman is not dishonoured by the connection.[1] Now first, one part of this charge is as true as to say, that the lower orders of English are in the habit of selling their wives, because one or two such cases occasionally appear in the newspapers. Secondly, as Father Sangermano observes, 'in concluding a marriage,

[1] Symes's *Embassy to Ava.*

the customs of the Burmese are somewhat different to ours. With us it is the woman who brings the dowry . . .; but in this country the man, on the contrary, must take with him a dower according to the resources of his family.'[1] In fact, a distinct survival of wife-purchase exists among the Burmans, as in all countries of Islam, as formerly among the Romans in the rite 'co-emptio,' and the traces of which prevailed among ourselves in the old marriage ritual till A.D. 1549. It is true that under Burman rule, where slavery is lawful, parents hard pressed by poverty sell not only their daughters, but their sons also, to procure food or to free themselves from debt; but this is not the point in question.

That the system of morality which allows of marriage as a temporary arrangement, merely binding at the will of the parties, is of a low and debased type must be granted, but it does not necessarily affect the legal position of women in the social scale; if anything, it rather tends to add to their independence, of which the state of society in Rome under the Empire offers another instance. And, in fact, we find such to be the case here. Indeed, Symes himself in another place says: 'Women in Burma are not only good housewives, but likewise manage the more important mercantile concerns of their

[1] Sangermano's *Burman Empire*, p. 129.

husbands, and attend to their interests in all outdoor transactions. They are industrious to the greatest degree, and are said to be good mothers, and seldom from inclination unfaithful wives.' If this description be true, as it undoubtedly is, women, who are not merely household drudges, but are allowed the management of their husbands' most important business and other concerns, can scarcely be justly characterised as occupying a very subordinate social position. As with us, the husband raises the wife to his own status; even more so perhaps, as in Burma the wife popularly shares her husband's official position to a certain extent; for instance, a revenue official's lady will receive tax money and give the receipt; while a native police officer's wife, in his absence, will order out in pursuit of a criminal the 'posse comitatus' of the village, arrest, and send him off to Court, quite as a matter of course. Inferior as they may be deemed according to Symes's view, no Burman would venture to use the coarse familiarity towards his female acquaintances that is common among our own lower order. Without pretending to the gallantry, supposed to be characteristic of Western nations, the Burman men treat women and children in a crowd with a consideration that more civilised races might copy.

A recent writer on Burma, among many other errors arising from a want of acquaintance with the people, writes: 'As a people, they are thoughtless about the future, without the desire to accumulate fortune, without "family," in the sense understood among Occidentals.'[1] True, they are thoughtless, but so are other nations; the Irishman, for instance, is popularly so described. They formerly had no desire to amass wealth, because under native rule its possession only led to extortion and oppression; but it will be found that the natives of British Burma are now not behind others in the race for gain. But in what sense the word 'family' is here used it is difficult to say. If to imply pedigree and lineage, then the Burman is as fond, if he can do so, of tracing these as any Celt or Gael. If it means that they are without family feeling and family ties in a social aspect, there cannot be a greater mistake. No people can be more careful in preserving and acknowledging the bonds of family relationship to the remotest degrees, and that not merely as a matter of form, but as involving the duty of mutual assistance. A general reverence for age is one of the pleasing traits in the Burman character, and the respect for the venerable head of a family of two or three living generations is very great among his

[1] *Our Trip to Burma.* Dr. Gordon, C.B.

descendants. Parents are as fond of, and as affectionate towards, their children as with us, and where the natives still preserve their old ideas and customs, the children are dutiful and obedient, although it is sadly true, that, as the Elders say, respect for parents, together with all old fashions, has been much weakened by the influence of a new civilisation and new manners.

Courtships are managed among the young people very much in 'the old, old way,' until they have made up their minds; but 'courting' deserves to rank as an *institution*, for it even designates a particular time of the day, known as 'loo-byo tay thee achyrin,' or 'the time for young men to go about,' meaning, *to court*. This time is about nine o'clock at night, when the old people are supposed to have gone to bed. A suspicious character found by the police lurking about the streets after dark, will almost always answer when questioned, 'I am only loo-byo tay-ing.' As soon as it is dark the young men, dressed in their best, wander about in twos and threes, and loiter near the houses of their sweethearts. Having ascertained, by listening, that the old people have retired for the night, the lover and one or two of his intimate friends enter the verandah, and find the young lady nicely dressed, flowers in her hair, and a liberal amount of cosmetic powder on her face. Cheroots and betel are provided, and flirting and conversation go on in a subdued voice, for custom supposes that the parents are in bed fast asleep; although, in reality, the mother at least is carefully keeping watch in the next room, that no rudeness or improper conduct occurs. Having paid their visit, they perhaps proceed next to the house of another young lady, in whom another of the party is interested, where a similar scene is repeated. The solitary evening walks of our middle class would be considered by the Burmans highly improper.

The Taleins, however, have a curious custom by which the lover, having ascertained whereabouts on the floor his mistress is accustomed to sleep (which, if he is a favoured one, she generally indicates to him by letting her handkerchief hang through the bamboos forming the floor), goes below the house after dark, and, putting his hand through the interstice, tries to find, and hold the young lady's hand. After some visits, in which the hand is first allowed to be seized, and then coyly snatched away, he is permitted to retain possession of it as long as he likes, and this may be considered equivalent to a 'yes' on the part of the maiden. Occasionally, however, an unlucky wooer, finding no favour, or perhaps mistaking one sister for the other, is seized by the hand, his wrist tied fast to the bamboos, amidst the half-smothered laughter of the girls, and he is kept there till they take pity upon him. A case occurred, in which the joke was carried a little too far, as, not content with tying up the unfortunate wight, two sisters cut off with a pair of sharp betel-nut nippers the first joint of his little finger. However, he was so laughed at by all his companions, that he was ashamed to make any complaint in Court. It is probable the girls did not really intend to inflict any serious injury, but nipped rather harder than they thought to do.

When a young man intends to ask for a girl in marriage, he first sends some old people to propose the matter to her parents. The negotiations may be long or short; but as a general rule the bridegroom, when accepted, goes quietly to his father-in-law's house, takes possession of his wife without any further ceremony, and lives there as a son for a year or two. After this he may take his wife away, especially if he has a child, and set up house for himself. Sometimes on the marriage a feast and 'pway,' or theatrical performance, is given. On this occasion a custom is sometimes still kept up, and is the cause of complaints in Court, which is mentioned by Father Sangermano in A.D. 1782. He says: 'There is a curious custom observed on the night of the marriage, of which I have never been able to discover the origin. A troop of lads will, on these occasions, assemble round the house, and throw upon it such quantities of stones and wood as to break the roof and the utensils in the rooms, and sometimes to do considerable injury to the inmates. The sport continues till morning, and there is no way of escaping from it, but by observing the greatest secrecy in celebrating the marriage. It is difficult to conceive any reason for this extraordinary practice.'

Another custom at marriages, but only at those of officials or wealthy persons, is that of barring the road of the marriage procession with gold cord and silver cord, as it is termed, and has the same reason as the extraordinary practice of throwing stones which puzzled the good Father. It is simply a piece of horseplay on the part of the mischief-loving young fellows of the village to raise a little money for their own entertainment. On the morning of the marriage day the bridegroom's party set out from his to the bride's house, carrying trays with the indispensable 'letpet' or pickled tea (the accompaniment of every Burman ceremony), betel, handkerchiefs, and all the presents intended for the bride, often including the whole domestic paraphernalia, as a mattress, mosquito curtains, looking-glass, &c. On the way, here and there, parties of young lads, or sometimes women, sometimes little toddling children, stretch any cord across the road and demand silver or gold from the bridegroom; hence the phrase. If it is refused, they threaten to cut the cord as a curse, that unhappiness may be the lot of the young couple. Sometimes three or four earthen pots are placed on the road, and threatened to be broken with a similar signification. In the case of wealthy persons large sums are often demanded; but there is always a respectable Elder charged with arranging the matter, who decides what is fair, and this is always given and received without demur.

Polygamy is legal, but except among officials and the wealthy is seldom practised. In ordinary life a man with more than one wife is talked of as not being a very respectable person. This seems also to have struck the early European travellers in Burma, for we find many of them, like Nicolo Conti in 1430, remarking, 'This people take onlie one wife.'

With regard to the morality of the Burmans, it would not be fair to judge them by our standard. The legal marriage tie is easily formed, and as easily dissolved. Openly living together as man and wife, and *eating out of the same dish*, is as perfect a form of marriage, as a whole string of ceremonies could make it. Divorce may be obtained by going before the village Elders and signing an agreement to separate. Except in the large towns, where there is a mixed population, prostitution and its frightful evils are unknown. Illegitimate children, at least those having the status of such, are by their easy marriage customs rare, and wives are as generally faithful as with us.

Even where polygamy is indulged in, the general feeling may be said to be against it, for any native official or wealthy man, in which classes it is more common, who contents himself with one wife, is looked on with much greater respect for so doing. Though all the wives are equally legitimate, there is always one chief wife, generally the first married, whose house is the family home; the lesser wives being provided each with her own house, perhaps living in another town or village, but never under the same roof as the head wife. As regards inheritance, the families of these wives are quite distinct; the children inherit any property belonging to their own mother, and also that acquired by the joint industry of their parents, for a man often carries on a separate business in partnership with each wife. Among the agricultural and trading classes two or three families are often found under the same roof-tree, as the sons-in-law take up their abode with their wives' parents for two or three years, being in all respects as sons of the family, and working for the common benefit.

Burman women age very soon after the birth of

one or two children, but this is chiefly owing to the barbarous treatment which custom prescribes in childbirth. Directly the child is born, a large fire of wood is made upon a hearth about six feet long, and in front of this at a couple of feet distance the wretched woman is laid and literally scorched and baked for seven days or more, the fire being kept up night and day. That they survive the ordeal is wonderful; but outraged Nature asserts herself by drying up all the natural juices as well as those noxious humours, which it is the object of the torture to eliminate from the body. The custom is not, however, universal, many families never practising it, and it will probably fall into disuse in time, first becoming obsolete in the large towns under the influence of the example of women of European and other nationalities.

Strange to say, the idea of the efficacy of a child's caul is found also among the Burmans, only, instead of preserving the wearer from drowning as our sailors imagine, it is supposed to assist in gaining the goodwill of any person he addresses in order to ask a favour, and the child so born is deemed sure to be fortunate in after life.

A prettier idea is, that when newborn infants laugh and cry, the 'Nát thanāy,' or 'fairy children,' are teasing them, saying, 'Your mother is dead;' on which the little thing laughs back the answer, 'I have just been at her breast;' or sometimes, 'Your father is dead,' and the child not having yet learnt to know its father, believes this to be true and cries because he shall never see him. Children are named with no particular ceremony, though sometimes a name is given, when the child's head is first washed, or when the ears are bored, if that is done at an early age; otherwise a name is simply acquired by use.

The first ceremony named above is called 'kin-bwon tat,' because a decoction of the pods of the 'kinbwon' tree, or Soap acacia (*Acacia rugata*), is used for washing the infant's head and the guests' hands. It properly takes place seven days after the birth, and has been supposed by some to be a kind of baptism. But it has no religious meaning, at least as connected with Buddhism (though the particular Nát that the family reverence is always duly propitiated with the usual offerings of fruit and flowers), and it is probably a survival of some forgotten ancestral custom. The relatives and intimate friends assemble to congratulate the parents, bringing their presents in kind or in money; the midwife washes the head of the child with the decoction mentioned above, with which also the guests wash their hands, and a name may then be given to the child or it may not. There is a feast and perhaps a 'pway,' or theatrical performance, to close the affair.

Burman names are peculiar. There is no such thing as a surname; indeed, they cannot understand the idea. A man has only one name, often derived from some apparent or supposed peculiarity, or sometimes without any meaning. Politeness prefixes the epithet 'shwé,' 'golden,' though in Upper Burma no man of the lower class would be allowed to use this, and every name is prefaced by either 'moung' (literally 'brother'), showing equality or condescension; with 'ngā,' implying superiority in the speaker; with 'kōh,' denoting friendship or esteem; or with 'pōh,' showing respect for one much older. These last three terms can hardly be translated by any English equivalent. A man whose name is 'Pan,' 'flower,' may thus be addressed as 'Moung Shwé Pan,' Mr. Golden Flower, or as 'Nga Pan,' or 'Koh Pan,' or 'Koh Shwé Pan,' or 'Poh Shwé Pan.' Other names of men are, 'Shwé Tee,' Golden Umbrella; 'Shwé Tsin,' Golden Elephant; 'Moung Gouk,' Mr. Crooked; 'Moung Pyoo,' Mr. White; 'Moung Nee,' Mr. Red; 'Moung Wet-galay,' Mr. Little Pig—(I know a most respectable magistrate of that name); 'Moung Taw,' Mr. Forest; 'Moung Leip,' Mr. Turtle; 'Moung

Kywaai,' Mr. Buffalo. A great many of these names may be also applied to women, but a female is addressed as 'Mā,' respectfully, or to inferiors 'Mee;' the rule respecting 'shwé,' 'golden,' being the same as to a man, as 'Mā Shwé Pan,' Mrs. or Miss Golden Flower; or 'Mee Pan,' Mrs. or Miss Flower, there being no distinction between married and single women. Other ladies names are 'Mā Ein,' Mrs. or Miss House; 'Mā Ein Tsoung,' Mrs. or Miss Housekeeper; 'Mā Tso,' Mrs. or Miss Naughty; 'Mā Kway,' Mrs. or Miss Dog; 'Mā Hla,' Miss Pretty; Mā Pāh-oo,' Mrs. Frog's Egg.

The Burmans have no gestures of salutation, except the ceremony of prostration before officials of certain rank, which hardly falls under the head of social civilities. Two relatives or friends meeting, begin a conversation by the expressions, 'Are you well?' 'I am well,' if they have been some time separated; otherwise, those daily accustomed to meet, say, 'Where are you going?'—just as among ourselves; but they have no such phrases as 'Good morning,' 'Good night.' A visitor when leaving a house says, 'I am going;' and the host *politely* responds, 'Go.'

Kissing is unknown to them, as well as to the cognate Karen and wild tribes of Arracan, and also to the Shan race; the corresponding word literally expresses the act of 'smelling.' The mother covers her baby's little face and body with 'smells' or sniffs; the lover puts his arm round his fair one, and *smells* her cheek. I am not aware whether husband and wife practise similar olfactory endearments; I rather think not; at all events, a Burman lady would think herself shockingly disgraced, were her spouse publicly to salute her, even if *he* would *condescend* so to do. A wife generally addresses her husband by name, or as 'moung,' 'brother,' and similarly a husband calls his wife by her name, as 'Mā Poo.' Amongst the better class, when they become elderly, and have sons and daughters growing up around them, husbands and wives address each other by some honorific title referring to some pious deed, such as 'kyoung tăgá,' or 'kyoung ămá,' 'supporter of a monastery;' 'yaydwin tăgá,' or 'ăma,' 'builder of a well.' Officials, however, always use their title, when husband and wife speak to or of each other, as, 'Myo-woon,' 'Governor of the city;' 'Myo-woon kadaw,' 'Governor's lady.'

After what has been mentioned of the free and open position held by the women among the Burman races, it need hardly be mentioned that the men have no hesitation in speaking of their wives and families, such as exists among the Mussulman nations of the East, with whom the only inquiry the most intimate friends can make respecting each other's family is by some such phrase as, 'Is your house well?'

One of the most important points in Burmese etiquette, as indeed it is generally throughout the East, is the use of the proper phrases and words according to the relative positions of the speaker and the person addressed. Thus there are not only different forms of the personal pronouns for the male and female, and for the superior and the inferior, but also completely different and circumlocutory phrases to express the ordinary actions of life as regards superior personages: thus it is said,

The king	sleeps,	'set dau moo thee,'
The phoongyee		'kyein thee,'
The man		'eip thee,'

each phrase meaning to sleep, to repose, but it would be a most absurd solecism to apply them indiscriminately. Again, the phoongyee does not 'die,' but 'pyan dau moo thee,' that is, 'returns' (to the state of blessedness). The King also, does not 'die,' but 'nát yua tsan thee,' that is, 'ascends to the Náts' village.'

A superior uses the *actual* personal pronoun, 'nga,' I; but an inferior says, 'kyun daw,' lit. 'the royal slave.' A superior addresses an inferior, as 'moung min,' 'you,' politely; or as 'nin,' 'thou,' contemptuously; but the inferior uses a periphrasis, as 'kō daw,' lit. 'the royal self,' or 'kō daw ashin, 'the royal lord's self,' or 'kyay zoo shin thăkeen,' 'the lord, the benefactor.' In all this, however, the Burmese resembles most other Eastern languages.

Although horology is unknown except as a modern European introduction, the people manage to define accurately enough for all practical purposes the different times of the day. The principal divisions are: 'Noon;' 'past noon' (between noon and 1 P.M.); 'nay-kin,' lit. 'the expanded or broad day,' which lasts till 'towards sunset;' then 'sunset;' 'mō chyōp,' lit. 'sky shutting in;' dusk, sometimes expressed as 'brothers would not know each other time;' 'lamp lighting time;' these last three vary of course slightly at different seasons of the year. After dark comes, 'children feel sleepy time,' about 7 P.M.; 'grown-up people lay down their heads time,' about 10 P.M.; 'midnight;' 'past midnight;' 'the red (or morning) star rising;' 'the sky lightens,' or the dawn; 'sun-rise;' 'morning meal,' about 7.30 A.M.; and 'the morning,' till noon. Subdivisions of these periods can of course be easily explained by a few words. The common mode of expressing short durations of time is by saying, 'the boiling of one pot of rice,' about fifteen minutes, or, 'of two pots of rice,' half an hour; 'the chewing of a betel,' about ten minutes; 'a holding of the breath,' a moment. All these are the native measures of time, used everywhere except in the large towns, where clocks and gongs, beaten each hour at guard-houses, have led to the adoption of European expressions.

As a rule, I have found the lower class of Burmans much better judges of distance than our own peasantry, whose idea of 'a mile and *a bit*' is well known. The ordinary measure is a 'teing,' equal to about two miles. Among the Hill tribes, however, the estimation of distances is made in a much vaguer way; they say 'two hills,' 'three hills distant,' meaning that two or three hill ranges will have to be crossed.

CHAPTER IV.

SOCIAL LIFE AND MANNERS (CONTINUED).

I SHALL now endeavour to convey to the reader some idea of the ordinary life, and household economy of the people, and must ask him to bear in mind, that in this matter there is no very striking difference between the various classes of society. The rich man may excel his poorer neighbour in having a large house built of teak-wood, instead of a small one of bamboos, in always wearing silk waistcloths, in his wife and daughters possessing more gold ornaments, in the number of his cattle, or the amount of his stock-in-trade; but it is a mere question of quantity; the marked distinctions that civilisation, art, and refinement have introduced among ourselves are wanting. The mass of the population being engaged either in agriculture or in trading on the numerous rivers, the towns and villages are built along the banks of the rivers or in the low flat plains favourable for rice cultivation.

Owing to the heavy floods, which during the monsoon place the whole country except the hills more or less under water, the houses are *all* built on piles, the height above the ground being regulated by the local depth of the inundation. Ralph Fitch, the old English merchant and traveller, A.D. 1586, notices this, though he gives another reason for it. He says: 'The houses are high builte, set upon great high posts, and they goe up them with long ladders for feare of the tigres, which be very many.'

In all the purely native villages the houses are built on the same model, only differing in size and material, from a shanty nine feet long, built entirely of bamboos, to a good-sized wooden dwelling, thirty feet or more in length. It consists of an upper and lower part. The upper portion has generally planked gable ends, the other walls being of mat or woven bamboos, and is the part of the house private to the family; the roof is of grass, forming a thatch. The lower part, or verandah, about two or three feet from the ground, is a general reception, eating, and working room. It is sometimes entirely open, but often a portion, or even the whole, is enclosed with mat walls, so as to form a room. If the houseowner is a petty trader or dealer, this part forms the shop. The floors are of bamboos tied down; oftener the upper floor only is made of bamboos, and that of the verandah is roughly planked. The upper part is six or seven feet above the ground, and affords shelter (in the dry weather) for the carts, sometimes for the cattle at night, and generally serves as a store-place. The hearth or fire-place is movable, being only a strong square wooden frame, or box filled with earth, about six inches deep, which may be placed anywhere, but oftenest occupies one end of the verandah. In dry weather the cooking is generally carried on out of doors; and should a dish require frying in oil, it would have to be done *outside the village*, as the natives have the greatest aversion to any rancid smell, imagining it causes, or at least augments, disease. The best class of house is built on the same model, except that it is larger and entirely of wood, the roofs in some few being of shingles or tiles; but in the towns some of the wealthier traders and native officials' houses exhibit an awkward compromise between Burmese and European styles.

One striking feature in all the Burman villages is the number of petty shops for eatables. Almost every house has something displayed for sale in a corner of the lower verandah. One wonders who the buyers are, where all seem sellers. The amount of stock, however, in each shop, if we may call it such, is but small, consisting of a little dried fish, 'nga-pee,' or pressed fish, oil, salt, dried capsicums, a basket or two of rice, and a few little condiments, all which find a ready sale among the Karens of the hills, and also among a large passing class of boatmen, carters, and other travellers. These petty speculations are, moreover, in such cases only a little source of pocket-money to the women, and an occupation to the little mites of girls who sit in charge of the stalls in their mother's absence, and sell the halfpenny worths with all the precocious gravity that seems peculiar to these miniature editions of the softer sex, and is never found in boys of the same age.

In many houses, either in the verandah or under the house, is to be seen the loom of the thrifty housewife, to which in spare moments she or her grown-up daughters sit down and give a few throws of the shuttle. There is nothing peculiar about the loom; it is rudely made on the common principle. The cloths woven are silk or cotton, but for home use generally only the latter, as silk goods are chiefly brought from up-country, which sets the fashion in patterns. They consist of 'putsoes,' or men's cloths, 'tameins,' or women's petticoats, and 'tsoungs,' or wrappers. The cotton goods are almost always woven in checks and plaids of dark, serviceable colours. It is in his holiday silk garment that the Burman blazes out in all the glories of the rainbow.

The 'putsoe' is woven in a piece eighteen yards long and three-quarters of a yard wide; these are the sizes of the best sorts. The patterns are either plain variegated stripes, checks, and plaids, or, in the most fashionable and expensive, a series of zigzag lines of varying breadth and colours, with sometimes a leaf-like pattern between. These last, from the intricacy of the pattern and the number of the shuttles employed for the different coloured threads, require great skill and a large amount of labour. In some of the best cloths one hundred shuttles are used, and cloths are distinguished on this account as fifty-shuttle, eighty-shuttle, hundred-shuttle 'putsoes.' The prices of cloths of the best manufacture, as above described, run up to 200 rupees (twenty pounds), or even more. The piece is fashioned for wear by cutting the length of web in half, and then stitching the lengths together, so as to form a double width. One end is closed so as to make a kind of wallet. The 'putsoe,' now nine yards long and one-and-a-half wide, is girt round the waist in an ingenious manner without any belt, by a twist and a hitch of the cloth. It thus forms a kilt, with a long spare end in front; this is sometimes tucked in at the waist, and allowed to hang low in front in heavy folds; but the most graceful way of wearing it is to throw it loosely over the shoulder. A white cotton jacket (of English longcloth) reaching the waist, and a handkerchief (of Manchester manufacture) wound round the head, complete the costume. A Burman thus arrayed, with a headkerchief of the brightest crimson or yellow silk, a spotless white jacket, and his flowing kilt of colours, various and gorgeous as the hues of the peacock, is a resplendent being. Some officials and old men still adhere to a more national style of head-dress; the hair, long and soft as a woman's, is gathered up in a knot on the crown of the head, and a small piece of white muslin twisted in a roll about an inch wide is tied round the brows, the two stiff ends or points sticking up a couple of inches behind the head.

The 'tamein,' or female dress, is difficult to describe. It consists of three pieces joined: the 'upper,' of English red or black cotton stuff; the 'body' of the dress, three-quarters of a yard deep and a yard and a half wide; and a lower 'border,' about half a yard deep. These parts sewn together form an oblong cloth a yard and a half wide and about two yards long. This is simply wrapped round the body and securely fastened by a hitch in the edge of the cloth in some mysterious manner, over the bosom below the armpits, and again at the waist; the fold remaining loose downwards displays in walking rather more of the lady's leg on one side than would be considered quite proper with us. It would perhaps simplify the explanation, if the reader took a bath-towel six feet long and four and a half feet in width, and endeavoured to put it on as a garment, covering the body from the armpits to the feet. This singular dress attracted the notice of all the early European travellers in Burma, and is described in quaint old Purchas thus: 'It was also ordayned that the women should not have past 3 cubites of cloth in their nether clothes, which they bind about them; which are so straight that when they goe in the streets they shew one side of the legge bare above the knee.'[1] Over the 'tamein' is worn a long open jacket of rich velvet or of figured muslin, or else a shorter one down to the top of the hips of long cloth, loose, but having no opening in front, being put over the head, like a jersey; in all cases the sleeves are made some inches longer than the arm, and so tight about the wrists that the hands can with difficulty be inserted, and to get the jacket off, the sleeves must be turned inside out and stripped off the hands; the extra length causes the sleeves to form puckers above the wrists. The centre portion,

[1] Fitch's *Travels*, A.D. 1586; Purchas, vol. ii.

or body, of the 'tamein' resembles the men's 'putsoe,' except that the patterns are smaller, and one cloth costs four or five pounds. No head-dress is worn, except flowers, either natural or artificial. When going abroad, a gaudy silk handkerchief of European manufacture is lightly thrown over the shoulders as a shawl, and to an end of this is generally fastened a bunch of keys, a little silver earpick, and a pair of tweezers.

The ornaments of rich Burmese ladies are often very handsome and valuable. They consist of diamond or ruby necklaces and earrings, heavy gold bracelets, and gem rings. The middle class content themselves with these articles in gold, and some of the necklaces of filigree work in red or yellow gold are very pretty. A family must be poor indeed, the females of which possess no gold ornaments. It is the ordinary investment of all spare money, banks being to the natives unknown. They, moreover, only use the purest metal, and consider our 18-carat gold much as we do electro-plate.

Always sitting and sleeping on mats, the Burmans have little furniture in their houses. Officials and head-men generally have a table and a chair or two to produce on the visit of a European, and in some houses there is at one end of the verandah a large wooden couch or divan, which is used as a lounge or as a strangers' sleeping-place. Occasionally, in passing a native house, a Burman may be seen sitting on a chair, but then he has his heels up on the seat; and in the Courts in our province presided over by native magistrates, in which the use of a chair and table is imperative, they may often be caught in a similar easy position.

Their beds consist of a mattress made of wild cotton, spread on a mat, with rugs of strong cotton woven in the country, and mosquito curtains of the same.

The culinary utensils consist of round earthen pots, and the meal is served in a large round lacquered wooden tray, the rice being heaped up on it, and the different curries and condiments contained in small cups or basins of European crockery. Sometimes among the poorer classes a large wash-hand basin forms the rice bowl. The better class use a large lacquered three-legged tray, which answers as a table, on which the rice and cups are placed, and round which all sit dipping fingers into the same dish according to Eastern custom.

The cooking is not of the most savoury kind to our taste; the different curries, whether of flesh, fowl, fish, or vegetable, being little better than tasteless stews, deriving any piquancy in eating from the pounded 'nga-pee' and chillies, which forms the invariable condiment of every meal as salt does with us. 'Nga-pee' means simply pounded fish, and differs in quality, from the best, made of shrimps, being the same as the 'balachong' of the Malay Straits (a kind of shrimp paste) to the rankest filth used by the mass of the population. This latter is really fish in a certain state of decomposition, pounded up into a mass with coarse salt, rendering in its preparation the fishing villages perfectly unbearable to a European. Yet the favourers of this high relish find the smell of an English cheese disagreeable. The chief article of food among all classes being plain boiled rice, a highly flavoured condiment of some sort is required to counteract its natural insipidity, and perhaps its bad effects on the stomach, when eaten in such quantities, often cold, as a Burman will get through at a meal.

In the houses of the working class the preparation of rice for the family use forms an important part of the woman's work. The 'paddy' (unhusked grain) is first husked in a hand mill, one or two women holding by each of the handles in the upper part, and giving it a half-turn backwards and forwards. The two parts, made of hard wood, are grooved where they work on each other, the upper part being hollow and containing the supply of grain, which falls between the grooved surfaces as the machine is worked, and the husk is thus rubbed off, the grain and husk falling on a mat below. This does not, however, completely clean the rice, as an *inner* skin still adheres to the grain, which, having been sifted from the husk, is pounded in a mortar, the friction taking off the inner skin, and the rice, being again sifted, is turned out clean and fit for cooking. For this second process a different implement is sometimes used. The mortar is buried in the ground up to the lip, a short pestle is fixed in one end of a long heavy lever placed on a fulcrum, and the operator works the pestle by treading on the other end of the lever, thus raising and letting it fall. Both these are very laborious but very effective processes. A good deal of rice is in this way cleaned in the agricultural villages, and brought in by the women to the larger towns for sale, at a rate giving them a profit of about fifty per cent., or in the rains much more, on their labour. Even in Rangoon rice cleaned in this manner is considered by the Burmans far superior to that from the European rice mills, which is cleaned by machinery.

The universal drink of the people is water, and they never drink at meals, but, having finished eating, rise, go to the water jar, which is provided with a ladle (generally a cocoa-nut shell with a long carved handle), and, having rinsed out their mouths, take a copious draught. A few puffs at a cheroot act as a digestive.

Tobacco and 'betel,' or 'pān,' as it is termed in India, are two of the necessaries of life to a Burman. Latterly, and especially in the towns, they have taken to cheroots of tobacco-leaf rolled after European fashion, but the true Burman cheroot is made of an envelope formed of a certain leaf dried, or of the inner husk of the maize plant; this is filled with a mixture of tobacco and finely chopped wood, either of the stalk of the tobacco plant itself, or of certain trees, and is about *six inches* long and an *inch* in diameter at the thicker end. A Burman seldom or never smokes a cheroot out at once, but takes a few whiffs, and lays it down, or passes it on to his friend. All classes and ages and both sexes smoke continually, and a mother may be seen to take the cheroot from her mouth and put it to that of the child at her breast; but then they suckle their children till over two years old, and I cannot say I ever saw what we should call a sucking babe under six or nine months old pulling at a cigar.

The preparation of the 'betel' deserves a word. Every Burman carries about with him a small round lacquer-ware box with two or three trays in it, containing the materials for this delicacy. This box also serves him as a purse to hold cash, or any small valuables, and out of doors is carried in a shoulder bag, or in a fold of his 'putsoe' tucked in like a bag at his waist. With high Burman officials the box is a mark of dignity, being of gold, and is carried by one of their nearest attendants. To prepare the 'betel,' a leaf of the betel vine (*Piper betel*), being taken from the box, a little slaked lime sometimes coloured pink is extracted from a small silver or brass box with the finger, and laid on the inside of the leaf, a morsel of 'cutch' (the extracted sap of the *Acacia catechu*), a pinch of tobacco, and perhaps a clove, are wrapped up tightly in the leaf so as to form what a sailor would call a quid; a betel *nut* (*Areca catechu*) is then split with a pair of nippers, and a piece about the size of a small filbert placed, together with the little leaf packet, in the mouth, and for a quarter of an hour the Burman is supremely happy in chewing the morsel. This in itself would be of no consequence, but the effects are disgusting; in old people who are especially given to the habit, its constant use hideously blackens the teeth, and stains the lips a dirty red colour, while a dribble of red saliva marks the corners of the mouth, and the constant working of the jaws contorts the face. Every public building in Burma open to the natives, and their own houses among the poorer class, are disfigured by the broad red stains of the ejected fluid, which is so strangely like blood, that in several cases of trial for murder articles stained with it had to be submitted to chemical or other scientific tests for determination. These effects of betel chewing necessitate in any respectable house the use of a spittoon, generally of earthenware, but a golden spittoon is one of the paraphernalia of a Burmese dignitary. The reason given by themselves for this practice is, that it corrects all acidity and flatulency in the digestive organs. There is no doubt that the aromatic qualities of the betel leaf may be useful as a corrective, but whether the bitter astringency of the catechu is equally so, doctors must determine.

The use of opium and spirits is forbidden the Burmans by their religion, as one of the five deadly sins; but unfortunately here, as everywhere else, civilisation has introduced its vices, and both opium-eating in its worst form and the use of European liquors, are gradually gaining ground among the young generation, especially in the towns.

A great deal of nonsense has been written about opium-smoking, either from ignorance, or with an object, perhaps a good-intentioned one, in view. That the use of opium in any shape except medicinally is a vice, and a most dangerous and often fatal one, cannot be denied; but there are many men eminent for talent and virtue who hold the use of spirituous liquors as equally vicious, and though this latter idea may be an extreme, it is not more so than that which pictures every opium smoker as the miserable and degraded wretch shown in sketches or descriptions of Chinese 'opium dens.' As one well capable of forming an opinion says: 'A confirmed smoker may go a day or two without his smoke and only feel incapable of eating or performing his daily work, but within a week or ten days he would probably die from want of it. Yet while his supply is regular he is little affected by the indulgence, if not carried to excess, and is to all intents and purposes as well able to go about his daily work as a man who does not use it. Indeed, the opium smoker can bear a much greater amount of fatigue than the man who does not smoke, while, as far as I can judge, the habit does not shorten life, unless, as already stated, the consumer be deprived of his drug.'[1]

It is when the drug is *eaten*, not smoked, that its baleful effects are surely felt, and this unfortunately is the mode in which the Burmans and other native tribes habitually consume it when they adopt its use. As in all cases of similar indulgence, the habit once formed is most difficult to eradicate. In our jails,

[1] T. T. Cooper's *Mishmee Hills*, p. 104.

the medical men are obliged to administer the drug to those accustomed to it, and to wean them from it gradually. In some few cases a permanent cure is effected. I once ordered a man of respectable family, but a confirmed opium eater, opium seller, and harbourer of thieves and bad characters, to find sureties for his good behaviour for a year, as he had no ostensible means of livelihood; in reality he lived on his share of stolen goods which he disposed of. Not being able to furnish sureties, as his relatives would not come forward, he had to go to jail. One day long afterwards, sitting in my house, a respectable looking, well-dressed man came in with a fine little boy. Not recognising him, I asked his name, on hearing which, I exclaimed, 'What! of such a village whom I sent to jail for bad livelihood?'

'Yes, sir,' he answered; 'and I have come with my little son to thank you for sending me there. I have been out now three months, and am busy cultivating my land, and find I can live without opium, which I will never touch again. Look at the difference between me now and when you last saw me.'

And certainly there could hardly be a greater contrast than between the dirty, sodden-looking wretch, half crippled from some disease in one leg, that I remembered, and the spruce, smiling, active man

I saw before me. As long as I knew him afterwards, more than a year, he was still persevering in his new life. In another similar case also I received a grateful message to say that the sender was out of jail, and had been cured of opium eating there, which he could never have accomplished by himself outside.

Yet some, who have lived long among them, brand the Burmans as a race with ingratitude, and urge as proof, that they have no *abstract* name for gratitude in their language. No more have they for *hunger* or *thirst*; do they therefore not experience those sensations?

Another condiment in great request, and which we often have occasion to mention, is 'letpet,' or pickled tea. This is prepared from the leaves of a shrub, not the true tea-tree of China, but which Dr. Anderson names *Elæodendron persicum*. The leaves are brought down from Upper Burma in large baskets, and are kept constantly moist by wetting them, or immersing them in water. When used they are mixed with a little salt, oil, fried garlic, green ginger, and parched sesamum seeds, so that it may be conceived what a delicacy it is. A small saucer of this mixture is the invariable accompaniment of any ceremonial, whether it be a gift, an invitation, a feast, or an important agreement, and always forms part of the little luxuries provided for any entertainment.

The Burman peasant thus leads an easy, contented life; his wants and his luxuries are simple, and abundantly supplied by nature. The daily cost of food for an average family of five persons of all ages may be roughly put down as—

	d.
Rice	3
Fish	$1\frac{1}{2}$
Chillies, garlic, grapes	$1\frac{3}{4}$
Oil, salt, &c.	2
Turmeric, vegetables	$\frac{3}{4}$
	9

Add to this $1\frac{1}{2}$*d.* for the indispensable 'betel' chewing, and we have a total of $10\frac{1}{2}$*d.* as the day's subsistence of a family. Of course, there are other little luxuries, such as tobacco, habitually indulged in, but $1\frac{1}{2}$*d.* will buy a man as much as he can smoke in a day; and the object is to show the *necessary* expenses of living, to provide for which the *lowest* rate of unskilled labour is one shilling a day. But the labouring class, such as ploughmen and boatmen, often live for days on rice, a little broiled fish, and a chillie, or some other little condiment, the whole day's food costing threepence. The well-to-do classes, such as traders, petty officials, and the higher artisans, spend from one shilling to one-and-sixpence on the day's house expenses, the difference being caused by their eating more fish, or in the towns meat. Even this is not a very extravagant rate of living, but yet it is double or more than double that of twenty-five years ago, before the English conquest. Then 'paddy,' that is, unhusked rice, sold for 10 to 15 rupees the 100 bushels; now the price ranges from 50 to 80 rupees the 100 bushels. Chillies, which sold for 5 rupees the 100 vits, or 10 shillings for 28½ lbs. avoirdupois, have risen to five times that price; onions the same, and all other eatables in a similar proportion. But, if the prices of provisions have thus increased, the wealth of the people and the value of labour have progressed in an equal ratio.

There is in Burma no class of regular bankers and money lenders like the *shroffs* and *bunniahs* of India. Every trader, indeed, everyone who has a little spare cash, endeavours to put it out at interest, the rate of which is generally, for small sums, 5 per cent. per mensem, that is, 60 per cent. per annum; on tangible security, such as gold ornaments, cattle, houses, &c., it is often as low as 36 per cent., but 60 per cent. may be taken as the general rate in the country. This may mean either that money is very scarce, or that the profits it returns by use in trade are large, and the prosperity of the country and the people show that the latter is the case.

I have endeavoured thus far to pourtray the salient points in the social life and customs of the Burmans, so as to give a general idea of the character of the people; to enter further into petty minutiæ would, I fear, be only tiresome to the reader, without being even instructive.

The funeral ceremonies of various nations form one of the most important and interesting chapters in anthropological science. We often find in them traces of a more ancient religion than that now professed by the people, or of customs which enable us to ally them to some kindred race, from which they are in all else completely separated. So the Burmans in their funeral rites retain several customs, which have no connection with their Buddhistic faith, but are clearly survivals of an earlier belief.

When a Burman dies, the moment the breath has left the body the female relatives begin to beat their breasts with dishevelled hair for an hour or so. The body is then washed, the thumbs and toes are tied together with a cotton thread, the corpse wrapped in white cloth, and a piece of gold or silver money placed in the mouth. This last is called 'kădō ăkāh,' 'ferry toll,' a most singular custom, the analogies of which the scholar will at once discern, but of which the Burmans can give no explanation, save that it is 'Nibban kădō,' which can only be rendered the 'ferry of Death,' for 'Nibban' is used here in a popular and not philosophic sense. The corpse is placed on a bench or bed, the face, unless there are any sanitary objections, being left exposed. A band of music is hired, and night and day continues with short intervals of rest, to give forth melancholy music. Directly after the death all the fires in the house are extinguished, and fresh fire to light them must be *bought*, and that not with money, but with some betel nut, tobacco, or something of that kind; a formality of which also they can give no explanation. The body remains generally for two or three days in the house; with very old and respectable persons, or those in a superior position; it is often kept much longer; of course, the season of year and other circumstances influence the arrangements. During this time, refreshments in the shape of betel, cheroots, and pickled tea are provided for all visitors; in some cases, where the house of the deceased is small, the body lies there and the music and visitors occupy the next-door or opposite neighbour's verandah.

All the relatives and acquaintances of the deceased and most of the neighbours repair to the house, bringing with them a present of money or rice, tobacco, betel, &c., to assist in defraying the funeral expenses; each village or quarter thus forms, as it were, a mutual benefit society. In front of the house the coffin and bier are constructed, the former being generally made of a very light and porous wood resembling deal, and is covered with tinsel paper; the bier is made of a framework of bamboos forming a kind of pinnacled canopy of pasteboard and tinsel, within which the coffin is placed and carried on men's shoulders by means of the bamboo staves at the bottom, or sometimes, where it is very large, as in grand funerals, it is borne on a four-wheeled truck drawn by oxen. On the day fixed for the funeral the phoongyees are invited to the house of mourning, where they rehearse to all present the teachings of Gaudama on the misery and instability of life.

On the conclusion of their address the coffin is brought out and placed in the wing-like part of the bier. While this is being done every vessel in the house containing water is emptied out. The funeral procession is now formed. First come a procession of men carrying the offerings intended for the phoongyees, such as have been before described; then come the phoongyees, behind them a band of music; next, the bier carried as above mentioned (sometimes in the rear of the bier is another band of music); then follow the relations, friends, and general company. The procession starts; and then comes, to the European observer, the most singular and inexplicable part of the ceremony. The bearers are generally the young men of the village or neighbourhood, and as they proceed they every now and then halt and *dance* with the bier on their shoulders, singing to give the time to the movement of their feet. No other explanation could I ever get for this than that 'the lads were amusing themselves,' or that it was 'to prevent too sorrowful feelings;' it is doubtless the survival of some forgotten allegorical usage. Nothing delights them so much as to obtain permission to fire off muskets as the procession advances, this being a privilege reserved in Upper Burma for the funerals of officials and great men.

On arrival at the cemetery the coffin is taken from the bier and placed on the ground; the phoongyees sit down near it, the offerings are placed in front, and the relatives and near friends of the deceased gather round again to hear the law preached; meanwhile, those who have followed merely as a matter of compliment, or from curiosity, partake of refreshment, such as betel, pickled tea, cheroots, sherbet, provided in one of the 'zazats' near. While the sermon is proceeding, an Elder keeps pouring water slowly from a cup (termed 'yay set chyā,' 'pouring out drops of water'), which is the ceremony of dedicating a religious offering. As the phoongyee concludes, the cup is emptied, and the congregation call out, 'May we share the merit—Thā-doo! thā-doo!'—that is, 'Well done! well done!' The phoongyees' attendants then take up the offerings, and the phoongyees leave the place. The 'tsandalas,' or 'grave-diggers,' who are deemed an outcast and degraded class, then take the coffin and place it on the funeral pyre, formed of some large logs, and heap more firewood upon it. The nearest relatives then each apply a small light, and the 'grave-diggers' superintend the consumption of the body. Sometimes the relations remain till this is accomplished, but generally they retire as soon as the pile is fired. As they leave the cemetery the nearest relative calls out, mentioning the deceased's name, 'Oh! so-and-so come! come! let us go home! do not remain behind in the cemetery.' Unless this notice was given, say they, the spirit of the deceased might remain, and not be able to find its way home alone. Then all return home. The bamboos, ornaments, or anything that is worth taking from the bier, belong to the grave-diggers.

Although cremation is the general mode of disposing of the dead, there are certain cases, in which interment is usual, if not imperative.

Such is the case with those who have died from cholera, small-pox, or other malignant disease, and with all children under fifteen years of age. If a person die just before the full moon, the body must not remain *in* the house over the day of the full moon, but must be deposited outside. In the case of a child, who has no younger brothers or sisters, the body must not be kept for a night, but buried at once.

After the body has been burned, the relatives collect the remains of the bones and the ashes, and place them in an earthen pot, which is buried in the cemetery, or other suitable place, and sometimes a tomb is erected over it.

Seven days after the funeral the phoongyees are again invited to the house, the friends and relatives assemble, the law is again recited, and offerings of food made to the phoongyees. Then the 'leip-bya,' the 'butterfly,' the soul of the deceased, is expelled by the house Nát from the house, in which up to this time it has been sheltered. It is singular to meet here the trace of the beautiful old Greek legend.[1]

What a contrast to all this was a little scene, a little natural idyll, I once witnessed! Riding along through some dense elephant-grass jungle, I passed a little hamlet of about three houses, and a short distance beyond, heard in front of me a sound of lamentation. Turning a corner of the road, I suddenly came on a small clearing on one side. At the end of this were a man and woman, and something laid on the ground. The man was digging, and I guessed his occupation—making a grave for his

[1] The same poetic myth is found among the wild Karens.

child. The woman ceased her cry as I passed, but after I had gone a little way her sorrowful wail, 'Oh, my daughter! oh, my little one! why have you gone?' rang in my ear. And often as I have heard the sounds of mourning, nothing ever so thrilled me, and I have that little scene of the high grass jungle round, the solitary father and mother, and the little bundle on the ground, before me now, as plainly as when I saw it ten years or more ago.

Dr. Mason says: 'The "psyche," or soul, of the Greeks, represented by the butterfly, was the life, the perceptive principle; and not the "pneuma," or spiritual nature. So the Burmans regard the butterfly in man as that principle of his nature which perceives, but not that of which moral actions are predicated.'

The 'leip-bya,' or butterfly, may be temporarily separated from the body without death ensuing. Thus when a person is startled by some sudden shock and is for the moment unconscious, they say the 'leip-bya,' or butterfly, is startled. In deep sleep it leaves the body and roams far and wide. A sleeping wife dreams of her absent and distant husband; their two 'butterfly' souls have met during their wanderings in the land of dreams.

If a mother dies leaving a little suckling baby, the two souls are supposed to be so intimately united that the 'leip-bya' of the child has followed the departed one of the mother, and if not recovered the child also must die. For this purpose a woman who has influence with the Náts (not a witch) is called in. She places a mirror near the corpse, and on the face of it a little piece of the finest, fleeciest, cotton down. Holding a cloth in her open hands at the bottom of the mirror, with wild words she entreats the mother not to take with her the 'leip-bya' of her little one, but to send it back. As the gossamer down on the smooth face of the mirror trembles and falls off into the cloth below, she tenderly receives it, and then places it with some soothing words on the bosom of the infant.

The same ceremony is sometimes observed, when one of two young children, brothers or sisters, that have been constant playmates and companions, has died, and, as is thought, attracts the soul of the survivor to follow along the dark path to the land of spirits.

In his interesting work on the 'History of India,' Mr. Talboys Wheeler has made a mistake in saying of the Buddhist monks, 'They take no part in the rites . . . of funerals; the burying or burning of a dead body has nothing to do with their religion.' [1]

[1] Vol. iii. p. 128.

In Burma the funeral of no respectable man, however poor, takes place without the attendance of one or more phoongyees. At the same time we must remember, that though they thus visit the house of mourning, accompany the funeral to the cemetery, preach the law to those assembled, and then receive the offerings made to them, their ministrations or presence in nowise affect the state of the departed, or even in our sense hallow the ceremony. It is the merit obtained for the deceased by the offerings made on his behalf out of *his own* late possessions, that will go to his benefit in his next state of existence, and all that the phoongyees do is to afford the opportunity of his obtaining this merit by attending and accepting these offerings; but, except to give more *éclat* to the ceremony, these might just as well be presented privately in the monastery. If we may venture to use the comparison, it is as if in the Catholic Church it were not the mass for the dead, but the mere payment for a mass that benefited the soul of the deceased.

The reader has doubtless himself remarked in these funeral rites some singular and interesting points of resemblance with the ideas of ancient Greece and Egypt, such as the ferry and toll of the dead, the personation of the soul ('psyche') by the butterfly, the libations to consecrate offerings, all which, as before remarked, belong not to Buddhism, but to the long-forgotten ideas and beliefs brought by the ancestors of these Indo-Chinese races from the primæval cradle of the human family.

CHAPTER V.

AGRICULTURE, TRADES, AND MANUFACTURES.

BRITISH BURMA is pre-eminently a rice-producing country, and its rice crop has made it the flourishing province it is. It should be remembered, that in the East the term 'rice' is only applied to the husked and cleaned grain; the plant itself and the unhusked grain is always called 'paddy.' The general aspect and character of the plains in which rice is grown during the monsoon has been described. After the first heavy rains, when the ground has been thoroughly saturated and softened, it is ploughed, an English farmer would probably say scratched, for the plough is merely a large wooden rake about five feet long, with hard wooden teeth about an inch in width and nine inches in length. This process clears the ground of weeds and old roots, all which are drawn to the sides and ends of the fields to form the small bunds, from six inches to two feet high, according to circumstances necessary to regulate the water supply. The ploughman occasionally adds his weight by standing on the beam, as the plough is drawn along by the oxen or buffaloes, which are used in the lower parts of the province, where the rainfall is greatest, rendering the land very heavy. The first land ploughed is that in the higher parts, for the purpose of forming nurseries, in which the seed is sown broadcast, about one bushel to an acre. After the rains have well set in, the whole of the 'paddy' fields are ploughed in the same manner. In some few instances the seed is sown broadcast on the whole of the land, and left to come to maturity without further care or trouble. But the yield in such cases is very small. The young plants in the nurseries having attained a height of about eighteen inches, are easily pulled up out of the soft mud in which they grow, and made into bundles. If the cultivator, for any reason, has not been able to form his own nursery, he purchases seedlings elsewhere when his fields are ready. The transplanting is performed principally by the women and children; sometimes neighbours help each other in turn at this work, as also at harvesting. A bundle of seedlings being laid across the arm of each person, all standing in a row, a couple of the young plants are disengaged from the bundle with the right hand and stuck in the ground, or rather mud, in rows about a foot apart, with the same distance between the plants. Sometimes a forked stick is used, with which the plants are deftly drawn from the bundle and planted with a slight thrust into the soft soil; this obviates the fatigue of the stooping posture when the hand only is employed. The operation proceeds at a rapid pace, the seedlings being put down almost as fast as one can count. After the transplanting no further care is given to the crop until it begins to ripen; no weeding is thought of, nor is any manure ever applied to the ground before planting; all is left to nature.

The fulness of the crops depends on the character of the monsoon rains. As is well known, the rice plant requires water up to a certain point to grow in; but, as in Burma no means are ever taken to regulate the supply, beyond the slight bunds to keep a sufficiency of water in each field, it happens, if the rains are heavy the lower fields are flooded and the plants drowned, or in a short rainy season, the rains ceasing before the plants have attained their full strength, and the waters drying up, the crop is weakly and meagre.

When the grain is beginning to ripen, about December, it becomes necessary to guard the fields against the attacks of myriads of birds, especially the black-billed parrakeet, which sometimes settle down in a flock so thick, that the ground looks as if covered with a bright green carpet. Small stages are erected of bamboos fifteen or twenty feet high, and about four feet square at the top; all over the field bamboos are stuck up connected with each other by strings from which are hung shreds of cloth, feathers, &c., all leading to the watchman's stage, where he sits or coils himself up, giving every now and then to the leading strings a pull which sends the whole of the elastic bamboos quivering, and with an occasional shout creates a most effectual scare among the little depredators. This is an occupation well suited to the *dolce far niente*-loving Burman; seated aloft with his cheroot, a little cold boiled rice, and a jar of water, he will spend the whole day happily in a half-dreaming state.

The crop, when ripe, is reaped with sickles, but only a foot of the stalk is cut off with the ears. The corn is stooked somewhat after English fashion, and, when dry, is carted home to the threshing floor, which is a carefully levelled piece of ground near the cultivator's house, covered with a hardened coating of mud; though sometimes the farmer threshes his crop in the field, erecting a small shed in it, to which he betakes himself for the time with all his family.

The 'paddy' is laid in a circle on the floor, the ears inwards, and is trodden out in the old Eastern fashion by oxen or buffaloes walking round and round; and it may be mentioned in favour of the Burmans, that they fully obey the Scriptural injunction, 'thou shalt not muzzle the ox that treadeth out the corn.' I have often explained to them the English process of threshing with a flail, but they failed to see the sense of such unnecessary labour on their part. The grain is next winnowed by being poured with baskets from a small height, so that the wind carries away the chaff, though in the more civilised districts a rude wooden fan is getting gradually into use among the weather agriculturists. The granaries are made of bamboo and mud wattle and daub, raised about two or three feet from the ground, and thatched; in these the grain is stored and the labours of the harvest are ended.

As a large portion of the straw is left in the fields, the cattle are turned loose in them to pick up what they can, and about February or March the remaining stubble is burnt, really, merely to clear the ground, but unintentionally affording the land, in the ashes, the only manure it ever gets. There is no rotation of crops, and the land is seldom left fallow, which of course sooner or later lessens its productiveness.

The average quantity of seed required for an acre is about a bushel, and the yield of ordinary land about forty bushels an acre, though in new land, especially near the sea-coast, it runs up to seventy and eighty bushels. A pair of oxen or buffaloes will plough about seven acres, which has been ascertained to be the average of the holdings in British Burma. The carts are always drawn by oxen or buffaloes, and are singular from the cant upwards of the body of the vehicle, the solid wooden wheels, and the curious and sometimes elaborately carved figure-heads with which the pole is ornamented. In and near the towns iron-tired spoke wheels are now general, but in the country for the large and heavy buffalo carts the solid wheels are still in use. These wheels, if of a large size, are very expensive when made of a single piece. I remember a pair of extraordinarily large diameter, for a buffalo cart, that had cost the owner 400 rupees (40*l.*) in the rough, and which he would not have sold under 80*l.* These wooden carts and wheels make a most horrible creaking noise, which may be heard in travelling half a mile off, but which the people, the Talines especially, consider so musical, that this quality adds greatly to the value of a cart.

Although rice-cultivation is the principal agricultural pursuit of the people in the province of British Burma, there is also a large amount of cultivation along the banks of all the rivers and on the small diluvial islands in them, which are completely submerged, or nearly so, during the monsoon floods. The crops raised here consist of vegetables of all sorts, tobacco, and in some places cotton in small quantities.

Another great branch of industry is the working the vast number of inland fisheries in certain parts of the province. During the rains, when the whole of the plains are more or less under water, fish ascend by the innumerable streams and water ways, to spawn in the comparatively still waters and shelter of the flooded lowlands, so that the whole country is one enormous fishpond. When the floods retire, large bodies of water are left in all the depressions in the surface of the country, forming lakes and ponds, some of which last through the year, while others dry up soon. All, however, now swarm with fish, to prevent the escape of which weirs are erected across all the outlets. These fisheries are leased from Government, and are the source of a large revenue, and of considerable profit to the lessees. The fish taken are dried, or salted, or prepared as 'nga-pee,' which has been explained to be pounded and pressed fish. Immense quantities of preserved fish are exported to Upper Burma, where the absence of any large fisheries renders this necessary of life to a Burman scarce.

The third principal employment of the mass of the population is trading. Besides the petty vendors of eatables to be found in every village, there is a large class of regular shopkeepers pursuing no other occupation than that of trade, generally joined to what we would term retail business speculations more or less extensive in rice, preserved fish, betel-nuts, sugar, salt, &c., which they receive from the producers either for cash or on commission sale, and convey to Rangoon and other centres of trade.

The stock-in-trade of a well-to-do shopkeeper in one of the towns or larger villages, such as form the stations of the European officers, would make an amusing exhibition in itself, forming a heterogeneous assemblage of European 'imports,' mixed up with native productions of all kinds. Unlike the Hindoo, whose caste rules prescribe not only what he shall eat, but also how and in what vessels he must eat and drink, and so keep him to the brass pots of his fathers, the Burman, untrammelled by any such prejudice, readily adopts any useful objects of Western civilisation within his reach. Hence in these shops or stores we find English crockery, plates, basins, teacups and saucers, jugs, &c., glass tumblers, wine glasses, decanters, small plates, dishes, salt cellars, and such-like articles of common moulded glass, plated candlesticks and shades, small kerosine lamps, looking-glasses, cutlery, Peek and Frean's biscuits, Bryant and May's matches, in company with white and printed calicoes, coarse broadcloth, and silk handkerchiefs, &c. It may perhaps puzzle some of my readers to appreciate the suitableness of some of these items, after what has been said of the Burman *ménage.* But although not in every-day use, such things as plates, tumblers, and a decanter or two, to hold water or milk, are kept in every respectable house, to be produced for any distinguished visitor, as a European, or a native official or a phoongyee. Small glass dishes, sugar basins and pickle glasses with covers, are in great request to hold the pickled tea, the sweets, or fine sugar, that are sent round as complimentary notices of family feasts, or accompany more substantial offerings to the monasteries. Plated candlesticks and glass shades, and small lamps, are favourite articles to present to the phoongyees; and every native official and well-to-do trader or farmer has one or a pair to produce with candles on grand occasions. Boxes of biscuits are largely sold, a box being a common present when paying a ceremonial visit to friends or to a superior, or to the phoongyee; while matches are found in use even among the hill Karens, in villages, where a European has never been seen.

In addition to the regular settled traders there is a numerous class of itinerant vendors, who live with their families and stock of goods in boats, travelling up and down the great rivers, and turning into their various smaller branches, visiting the interior villages which lie out of the regular route of traffic. The people of this country are, as they were described at the beginning of this chapter, eminently a race of hucksters. Petty trading is the occupation most agreeable to them, and they seem always to have had the same characteristic. In A.D. 1586 Fitch writes: 'We went from Cosmin to Pegu in paroes or boats, and passing up the rivers we came to Medon, which is a prettie towne, where be a wonderful number of paroes, for they keep their houses and markets in them, all upon the water. They have a great sombrero or shadow over their heads to keepe the sunne from them, which is as broad as a cart wheele made of the leaves of the coco trees and figge trees, and is very light.'[1] The above is an exact description of the wandering boat traders of to-day in Pegu province, and of the enormous sun hats worn by the boatmen and agriculturists, which are sometimes truly as big 'as a cart wheele,' and not more than a few ounces in weight, but are made not from the leaves of the coco, but from the sheath surrounding the joints of the giant bamboo, and sometimes of a double framework of very thin bamboo strips interlaced, with the leaves of the 'thaloo,' a species of wild palm, enclosed

[1] Purchas, vol. ii.

between, so that the old traveller is not very far wrong after all.

Burmans seldom, if ever, make any bargains, at least of any value, without the intervention of a broker, either amateur or professional. Under the native rule, these men were appointed, or at least approved of, by the Government, and were under very stringent regulations. We have, however, preferred to leave all such matters to the people themselves.

These brokers were, it seems, an ancient institution among the people, for they are mentioned by nearly all the early European traders to Pegu; and one of their customs at this day is so accurately described by Cæsar Frederick (A.D. 1569), that I cannot find better words than his. He says: 'In selling, the broker and the merchants have their hands under a cloth, and by touching of fingers and nippinge the joynts, they know what is done, what is bidden, and what is asked. So that the standers-by know not what is demanded, although it be for a thousand or ten thousand duckets. For everie joynt and everie finger hath his signification.'[1]

The Burmans are most expert boat-builders. The lines of all the boats, from the smallest canoe up to vessels of eight tons burden and sixty or more feet long, are the same. I should, however, except a

[1] Purchas, vol. ii.

peculiar heavy barge, that is built in quite a different way. The first-mentioned boats consist of a lower part or keel, hollowed out of a single log, which thus forms the body of the vessel, and on the sides of which bulwarks are built up. The immense logs are brought down from the forests with merely the centre roughly hollowed out so as to make them lighter in the water, and thus floated down to some boat-building village. In order to open the log a number of wooden crooks are hooked over the sides firmly lashed to a cross bar or fulcrum on each side; levers are fixed to these cross bars, and fire is applied underneath the whole length of the log. As the partially hollowed log expands under the heat, the levers on each side are brought into use and the sides forced outwards as far as possible, and then the crooks are lashed tight to the pegs. The carpenters then set to work with adzes, hollowing out as much more as they can of the wood. Fire is again applied beneath, the levers again used, and the sides forced open a little more, the adzes again brought into play, and the same process repeated several times until the log has been opened out to the desired breadth, and the thickness of the sides reduced to about two inches. Thwart beams are of course inserted to keep the log from collapsing. These holes are made of the wood of several trees, but the most valuable as well as the largest boats are made from the 'thingan' (*Hopea odorata*). Teak boats are of course still more valuable, but that timber is now in too great demand to admit of very large logs being used in boat-building, but the sides or bulwarks of the large boats are made of long single teak planks.

The lines of the Burmese boats are beautifully fine and graceful, but of course the absence of any keel gives them no hold of the water, and they can only sail with the wind. They carry a single square sail generally, but the largest boats used on the Irrawaddy have a peculiar mast, if it can be called so, consisting of two bamboo spars separated by the breadth of the boat at the bottom, and lashed together at the top, with cross bamboo ratlines, making it look like a gigantic ladder. The mainyard is formed in three pieces firmly spliced together, the centre of a tough wooden spar, and the outer pieces of bamboo, and the whole is sometimes over 130 feet in length. This would give an enormous spread of canvas for the size of the vessel. The sail in these large boats is generally in three pieces, and I have sometimes seen smaller canvas carried in addition above the mainyard. The cloth used is very light country cotton stuff, like coarse unbleached calico. On these boats are erected houses, either of thin wooden planks or of matting with thatched or matted roofs, and the steersman occupies a high chair of state, often elaborately carved, at the stern. The rowers generally row standing, the long oars being hung on pivots; in shallow water they use long bamboo poles, one end of which being stuck into the hollow of the shoulder, they push the boat forwards by walking along the sides, the whole weight of their bodies being thrown against the poles; where the nature of the bank permits, they use long tracking ropes.

There is, as was mentioned, another description of boat, differing in shape and construction from those alluded to above. This is a kind of flat-bottomed barge, unwieldy and ugly in appearance, looking very much like an enormous barrel cut down lengthwise, with a house built on it. There is no single hull in this, but a broad, thick slab with the ends turned up having been laid down as the bottom of the vessel, the sides are built up on it with ribs and planks. This style of boat belongs more to Upper than to British Burma, and is, I think, falling into disuse, except for carrying earth-oil or petroleum from the wells in Upper Burma.

There are not many native manufactures, and those that they possess are entirely for home use.

Their silk and cotton hand-loom weaving has already been described; the others are lacquer ware, gold and silver work, carving and gilding, pottery and iron work.

The lacquer ware comes principally from Upper Burma, but a small amount of the coarser kind is made at Prome. This ware includes round boxes, cups, dishes of all shapes and sizes, made not like the Chinese and Japanese lacquer work, with wood or papier-maché, but with thin strips of woven bamboo. The boxes are all made on the same pattern, namely, an inner case in which are two or more trays, and a cover that fits over the whole; they are made from three inches diameter and four inches in height (betel boxes) to two feet in diameter and three feet high or even larger, to serve as trunks for clothes; but all of the same material, bamboo.

Colonel Yule had the opportunity of seeing this manufacture as carried on at its principal seat in Upper Burma, and I therefore take the liberty of quoting his interesting account:—

'The men and women were busy, either splitting and cleaning the bamboos, or weaving them into little basket-like boxes, forming them all of assorted sizes, on regular mandrils of wood. These are then passed on to others, who smear them over with well-tempered mud, mixed (in the better class of boxes, but not in the coarser) with the black varnish which they use so abundantly. These are put out to dry in the sun, and when dry, are again put on the lathe, and polished down to a smooth surface by the use of bits of soft earthy sandstone and water. After thorough drying again they are coated with a mixture of the ashes of burnt bones and varnish, and rubbed down again. Next they receive another coating of the same composition, in which the varnish is mixed in somewhat larger proportion, and again they are smoothed down. Varnish alone is then put on and polished. The box has now a smooth and brilliant black surface, and is in a sense complete. The subsequent processes vary with the pattern and the colour that may be desired. For instance, the ordinary kind, in which the prevailing colour is red with black markings, is produced in an extremely simple but most ingenious way. The bands or lines passing round the box are laid on by a kind of style or point, fixed in a bit of wood or bamboo, and projecting from it a little. This point being charged with the varnish the box is put on the lathe, and the bamboo held firmly with the hand against the end, with the point on the proper line. The box being now turned, a line of the black varnish raised slightly from the general surface is thus laid on. When all the required lines have been thus drawn, the box is entirely covered with a coating of red paint, made of vermilion ground with a peculiar oil. This is not laid on very thickly, but sufficiently to conceal all the black varnish below. When this coating is dry, the box is again put on the lathe, and the workman, taking a handful of the husks of rice and a little water, applies them firmly to the surface, causing the box at the same time to revolve rapidly. This friction rubs off all the red paint from every point which projects in the slightest degree from the general surface. By this means the black lines on the box are rendered clear and continuous, and over the general surface a peculiar small chequer-work pattern is produced by the slightly projecting edges of the bamboo in the plaited work of the original basket. When more colours are to be used, they are successively applied, and subsequently removed down to the black, by which the pattern is produced. This is done by a steel style, pointed at one end and slightly flattened at the other. The portion of the coloured layer to be removed is marked round by an incised line, and then lifted off by the flat end of the style. In this way the most elaborate patterns are produced, and in no case is any preliminary sketching or drawing used. When the surface is partitioned into regular divisions or panels, these are measured off and rudely marked, but the whole of the detail is put in without any first outline or drawing and without any pattern to copy.'

The value of these boxes depends on the fineness of the lacquered pattern, and on their elasticity. The best will bend until the edges almost meet, without the lacquer cracking. A small betel box of this kind about three inches in diameter and the same in height sells for from fifteen to twenty rupees (1*l.* 10*s.* to 2*l.*)

There is also another variety of lacquer on wood used for bowls, large flat dishes, vases, &c.

Connected with lacquer-work are the rude but richly ornamented boxes in which the phoongyees keep their palm-leaf books. These are made of teak, and covered with devices and ornamentations in a low relief, formed of 'thitsi' lacquered and gilded over. The mouldings of some of these boxes are also ornamented with a mosaic of tinfoil, mirror and coloured glass.

The gold and silver smiths are not equal in point of finish and delicacy of work to their Indian brethren of the craft; but the style is highly effective and characteristic. Their best designs are large silver bowls, embossed in high relief with the signs of the zodiac or other fanciful figures. The process of embossing the pattern is singular and yet simple. The plain cup or bowl, having been fashioned to the required shape, is filled with a resinous composition, in the centre of which a wooden pin is inserted; so that when the resin cools the cup is fixed as on a lathe, the pin forming a handle. The workman then proceeds with a graving tool and hammer to mark out slightly the pattern on the cup, having no guide but his eye and his fancy. The pattern having been thus delineated, he raises or embosses it by *sinking* the surrounding metal with hammer and graver into the yielding matrix, which of course brings out the details of the pattern in relief. Thus, when the bowl is finished and the resin cleared out, the inside surface is the reverse of the outside. It is, in fact, like die-stamping, except that every line and dot is laboriously made by hand, and without any other guide than the eye. The gold work consists chiefly of necklaces, earrings, and bracelets, and a few other female trinkets. The design of some of these is elegant, but the workmanship fails in finish. One form of necklace, called 'băyet,' is especially pretty. It consists of several strings or chains of filigree work joined together and sewn with little figures in red gold of the mythical 'henza,' or sacred goose. This hangs low down on the breast, and at a short distance has a very good effect.

The earrings are more properly ear cylinders of gold, hollow, with a pointed top either set with precious stones, or having the gold cut in facets. These cylinders are thrust through a hole in the lower lobe of the ear, so that the reader may imagine a Burman maiden's ear is not of fairy-shell-like shape. The bracelets are generally what are called 'torques,' in form hollow, and filled with gum lac.

Another species of silver work, but not common (I know of only three good workmen in the province), is a 'niello,' like the Russian work. The pattern having been embossed in a manner similar to the ordinary silver work, but not in such high relief, the whole is coated with a black enamel, which thus fills in every hollow. The surface is then rubbed and polished down on a lathe until the silver of the relieved parts appears, leaving the ground of black enamel.

Connected with the jeweller's art is that of the lapidary. The Burmans know how to cut and polish stones, but in a rude and inartistic manner.

It is in their wood carving that they display the greatest talent and artistic feeling. The material being teak, a coarse-grained and brittle wood, there is not room for nice finish, and this is perhaps an advantage in rendering their style bolder. The best carvers are of course to be found in Mandalay, where the work of decorating the royal palaces, and the monasteries that are constantly being built by the King and nobles, afford them employment, which they only occasionally obtain in our province. The talent for free-hand drawing of some of these men is wonderful. I have seen one half sitting, half lying, on the floor with a sheet of atlas drawing paper before him, and a black crayon, produce in half an hour an elaborate design of intricate and graceful tracery. Colonel Yule's book gives some beautiful drawings of the royal monasteries and their wealth of carving, far surpassing, of course, anything to be seen in British Burma, where such works are only the efforts of private individuals. His description of one of these monasteries may give some idea of the effect produced:

'From post to post run cusped arches in open filigree work of gilding, very delicate and beautiful. The brackets or corbels from the outer posts, which support the projecting eaves of the platforn above, were griffins or dragons with the head downwards, the feet grasping the post, and the tail rising in alternate flexures, which seemed almost to writhe and undulate as we looked. No art could be better of its kind. The outer range of posts rose as usual through the platform, forming massive props or stanchions for the balustrade above. The tops of these posts were gorgeously carved, and hollowed into the semblance of an imperial crown, with various figures under its arches. The successive roofs were sheeted with zinc, that glanced in the sun like silver, and the panelled walls which rose in diminishing area from roof to roof were set round with half columns, diapered with a mosaic of mirror, which looked like silver covered with a network of gold. The balcony balustrade is quite unique. Instead of the usual turned rails, or solid carved panels, it is a brilliant open work of interlacing scrolls, the nuclei of the compartments into which the scrolls arrange themselves being fanciful fairy-like figures in complete relief, somewhat awkward in drawing, but spirited in action. Below this balcony is an exquisite drooping eaves board, in shield-like tracery, with interlacing scrolls cut through the wood like lace work.

'The staircase parapets (gilt masonry) are formed in scrolls of snakes scaled with green looking-glass, and each discharging from its mouth a wreath of flowers in white mirror mosaic. The panels of the walls in the upper stories are exquisitely diapered and flowered in mosaic of looking-glass, whilst the eaves-crests and ridge-crest (the latter *most* delicate and brilliant) are of open carving in lattice work and flame-points tipped with sparkling mirror.'[1]

The glass mosaic work above mentioned is, I believe, a peculiarity of Burmese ornamentation. It is made by laying small pieces of mirror and coloured glass, backed by tinfoil, in a coating of very strong

[1] Yule's *Ava*, p. 165.

gum or resin from the *Melanorrhœa usitatissima*, mixed with bone ashes. Although very coarsely executed, it has a most rich and effective appearance at a little distance. Unfortunately, under the extremes of heat and damp common to the climate of Burma, the resinous bedding soon becomes affected, the glass falls off, and the once rich and glowing decorations look poor and shabby. The broken pieces and strips of mirror and coloured glass are pretty largely imported from England; another instance of the many little petty objects of the world's inter-trade unsuspected by the general public.

The pottery manufacture is rather an important one, being extensively carried on in those places where a suitable earth is found. Every variety of utensil, from enormous glazed jars capable of holding twelve bushels, to little plain earthen saucers two inches in diameter, for illuminations, are made. Cooking pots, water pots, water-goglets porous and rather elegant in shape, thick pots for salt cooking, bowls of various sizes, spittoons, ornamental vases, lamps for petroleum, of the old classical form, and many other articles, are largely manufactured. Boats laden with piles of earthenware of all kinds may often be met on the rivers going from village to village, the arrival of one causing a little welcome excitement among all the good housewives, who will pleasantly spend an hour or so in examining and sounding all the pots in the boat, to choose one for twopence.

There are very fair blacksmiths among the Burmans, but the Shans far excel them in this industry. The latter are really first-rate workmen, who can smelt their own iron ore, and make their own steel, although in British Burma at least they now find it easier and cheaper to use English iron and steel for their work. The Shans say, that their best steel, made by those who possess the full mysteries of the craft, surpasses the European metal in toughness; this I will not quite vouch for, although I have seen some very good blades from the Shan states. The bellows used by the blacksmiths, and on a smaller scale by goldsmiths, seems to be common to all the races east of the Bay of Bengal, for Tylor's description of that used by the Malays exactly answers to the Burmese apparatus: 'It is a double-barrelled air forcing-pump. It consists of two bamboos, four inches in diameter and five feet long, which are set upright, forming the cylinders, which are open above and closed below, except by two small bamboo tubes, which converge and meet at the fire. Each piston consists of a bunch of feathers or other soft substance, which expands and fits tightly in the cylinder, while it is being forcibly driven down, and collapses to let the air pass as it is drawn up; and a boy perched on a high seat or stand works the two pistons alternately by the piston-rods, which are sticks. Similar contrivances have been described elsewhere in the Eastern Archipelago, in Java, Borneo, New Guinea, and Siam, the cylinders being sometimes bamboos and sometimes hollowed trunks of trees.'[1] A similar, but smaller and more delicate apparatus, engraved with mystical sentences and signs, is also used by the Burman alchemists.

But perhaps, considering their want of scientific knowledge and of appliances, their metal castings reflect most credit on the native skill and ingenuity of the people. The largest castings that exist in the country are the colossal brass image of Gaudama at Amarapoora, and the great bell of Mengoon, both in Upper Burma. The former is a sitting figure about twelve feet high and the limbs in proportion. It was once regarded as the palladium of Arracan, and was brought from that province on its conquest, A.D. 1784, by the Burman monarch.

The great bell of Mengoon is said by Colonel Yule to be probably the biggest in the world except one at Moscow. It is twelve feet high, the external

[1] E. Tylor's *Early History of Mankind*, p. 170.

diameter at the lip is sixteen feet three inches, the thickness of metal from six to twelve inches, and the weight on a rough calculation eighty tons.

Perhaps a description of the casting of an image of Gaudama, about five feet high, in a sitting posture will serve to show the rude method by which such large works are executed.

The event of casting an image or a bell of large size is made a quasi-religious ceremony, that is, it gives excuse for a festival. In this case the money for the work had been gradually collected by a highly respected and venerable phoongyee. A previous attempt to cast it had been made the year before, which ended in failure and the flight of the master workman. I cannot pretend to give either the value or weight of metal employed, as I made no notes at the time, and shall briefly describe the method of casting. There being an assemblage of some thousands of people, any amount of labour, which it will be seen was a very important point, could be commanded. A space in a wide field was carefully smoothed about twenty feet square, and thickly strewed with sand, a slight ridge of earth about six inches high marking it out. In the centre of this square the figure of Gaudama was modelled of clay in the usual crossed-legged posture; when this was properly fixed, the whole figure was covered with a coating of beeswax of the thickness which it was intended to give to the metal casting. Over this again was laid an outer skin of mixed clay, and finely chopped straw, a couple of inches thick. This outer coating had a series of rows of funnel-like holes pierced through it at intervals of about four inches above each other; it also had a number of air holes formed by straws put in as it was built up. The use of these will be seen presently. The model and mould, and hundreds of earthen crucibles about six inches diameter and three in depth, having been prepared, numbers of simple mud furnaces were erected just on the outside of the square on all four sides.

All this had taken some days, during which the usual festivities of a Burmese gala time had been going on. At length, when I arrived, everything was complete, and an auspicious day found for the ceremony. Early in the day hundreds of men were told off in regular gangs to the different circles of furnaces, and the fires of charcoal were lighted and kept up at a fierce steady heat. The metal was distributed among the assistants of the artist, each of whom had so many furnaces under his charge. The actual casting is performed at night for the sake of the coolness during such fiery work. All being ready, towards evening the operations began: the metal was placed in the crucibles to melt, and when properly liquefied the workmen stood round the furnaces, while the expectant thousands formed a vast ring around. It should have been mentioned that the crucibles had a lip for pouring out the metal, and simple but effective cradles of bamboo for carrying and handling them had been provided. At length the master workman, standing by his model, gave the signal, the appointed number of men from the nearest furnaces on each side rushed forward with their crucibles, and poured in the molten metal through the lowest series of funnel-like holes in the mould before mentioned. The wax in the mould of course melted under the glowing heat, running out at the bottom through holes provided for that purpose. Thus a ring of metal, as it were, was formed all round the mould; quickly another gang came forward with more metal, the process was repeated, and a second ring formed above the first, homogeneous enough in the interior, but showing plainly, before the figure is smoothed and polished, the marks of each successive ring. Thus the casting was built up in layers of metal, the excitement of the crowd increasing as the work progressed, when suddenly consternation fell on them, as the master announced his fears that not enough metal had been provided. A few moments of surprise, and then off rushed to their houses the inhabitants of the town, and speedily returned laden with brass bowls, salvers, drinking cups, and anything of the kind they could find, which were speedily broken up and put into the crucibles.

The excitement now became intense, as the work proceeded towards completion, and the upper part of the figure was reached; women rushed forward and threw into the crucibles of molten metal their gold earrings and rings, men tore off their rings and cast them in, parents made their children take off their little silver anklets or bracelets and devote them to the same pious purpose; while the clashing of music, and the enthusiastic shouts of thousands, as the mould was completely filled, and the work triumphantly finished, awoke strange and undefinable feelings even in the breast of the Christian who stood looking on.

So far all seemed well; but unknown flaws might exist within the core of the mould. As it would take some time to cool, I did not stay to witness the breaking of the outer mould, but came back after a few days. The casting was then exposed to view, and was a very fair one: there were two or three holes and flaws at the back of the figure, but those would be neatly patched; and the whole surface more or less showed the marks of each ring of the metal as it had been poured in, which would, however, disappear in the smoothing and polishing.

The people were very proud of their success, as it was the largest work of the kind that had been undertaken in the Province, I believe, since the English annexation. The large bells are cast in a similar manner, except that the moulds are generally sunk in the ground.

Besides these great works, the brass-founders produce gongs of all sizes, basins and dishes, weights, and a variety of smaller articles. Of the gongs, the most pleasing is the flat triangular one peculiar to Burma, but a modification of which is found, I believe, in Siam; it is impossible to express in words the singular mellow, surging vibrations of sound given out by these little instruments. They are all thinned away from the edges to the centre; whether this has any effect or not on the sound I must leave to those learned in acoustics. These gongs are only used in the monasteries, or in religious processions, or when going to the pagoda to worship.

The weights are all made in the supposed form of the 'henza' or sacred goose, the Sanscrit 'hansa,' whence the Latin 'anser.' These weights are made in sets up to a 'viss,' that is, 3·65 lbs. avoirdupois, and are used in all the bazaars. The weights above one viss are made of marble, in shape something like a Scotch curling stone, and are brought from Upper Burma.

I think I have now described all the principal manufactures of British Burma: perhaps paper umbrella making, though borrowed from the Chinese, may be added; but these oiled paper umbrellas are now so well known in England through the Chinese and Japanese curiosity shops, as to need no description. There are of course many other little manufactures of articles in use among the people, to enumerate which would require a walk round the bazaars, note book in hand. A few may be mentioned for example.

Artificial pith flowers delicately cut out of the pith of the 'solah' plant, used in India for making the 'solah' hats.

'Parabeiks,' or note books, made of a coarse thick paper from a certain kind of bark, which having been thickly coated with a charcoal paste, and cut into long strips of the intended width, varying from 3 inches to 18, is then folded alternately backwards and forwards to form the leaves, something like a folded paper fan. These books are written on with a steatite pencil, and, when the writing is no longer required, it can be rubbed out as on a slate. They are used by traders, and others, for noting down their transactions; and before our annexation, every record, every money or other agreement, was written in this perishable manner, and to this day the records of the native Courts in Upper Burma consist of piles of these books, each containing one case.

Mat and basket work; the former from the coarsest kind of thin bamboo strips to the finest and softest, made from a species of 'maranta;' the baskets are of all shapes and sizes, made of cane, strips of bamboo, and the leaves of a screw-pine or 'pandanus.' Some of them are covered with a thick coating of black varnish, which renders them waterproof, and they then form light and convenient basket trunks.

It will be seen from the above sketch, that the Burmans are a people by no means deficient in natural ingenuity and a certain amount of taste. If it were asked, what is the most characteristic handicraft of the people, it might be replied, *carpentry*, for every Burman is more or less naturally a carpenter; and indeed they seem in a sense to recognise this themselves, for whilst other trades are designated according to the material they work in, the word for carpenter is 'let-thama,' a handy man, or 'one skilled in (the use of) hands.'

CHAPTER VI.

AMUSEMENTS.

ONE of the most salient points in the Burman character, by which he is most widely separated from the Aryan, is his love of sports and social amusement, as well as his intense appreciation of the ridiculous. Much of this is owing no doubt to the different idiosyncrasies of the two races, but even more is due to the genius of the two religions which they profess, Buddhism and Brahmanism. Religion dominates over the acts and the inmost lives of the Asiatic nations in a degree uncomprehended in the West, although it may be seen in a modified extent among the more fervid people of Southern Europe.

In India, caste, which rules supreme, and crushes out some of the holiest and noblest impulses of our nature, forbids the existence of any free, hearty social intercourse. As Mr. Talboys Wheeler has felicitously expressed it of the Hindus, 'their religious life, so far as it finds expression, is one of inflated ostentation, accompanied by settled gloom. Whether on pilgrimage to sacred shrines, or gathered together in hundreds of thousands at the great religious fairs, or sacrificing to the village gods with all the paraphernalia of flags and garlands, the people of India seem on most occasions to take their pleasures with sadness of heart. They are virtuous and contented; but their aspirations are stifled by priestly repression, and their contentment is little better than a helpless resignation to their destiny.'[1]

Not so with the Burman. Free from all caste or priestly influence, all classes seek the society of their fellows freely and without restraint. Their social gatherings are enlivened by the presence of their wives, sisters, and sweethearts, not merely tolerated, or taking advantage of the licence allowed on certain occasions, but mixing with them on as equal terms as can be found in woman's history anywhere in the East.

Added to the natural temperament of the people, or perhaps in great measure inducing it, is the quality of their diet. Although forbidden by his creed to take life, the Buddhist is not, like the Hindu, debarred from the use of flesh. Indeed, the death of Gaudama himself is attributed in the legends

[1] *History of India*, vol. iii. p. 96.

to indigestion from eating a rich dish of pork. Therefore the Burman is almost omnivorous; any animal that has died by accident, or of a disease not infectious, or that has been killed by some other person, he eagerly devours. Fish forms part of his daily food in some shape, and consequently the whole physical organisation of the man is totally different to that of the simplest rice-eating native of Hindustan.

Placed in a country whose food-producing resources are practically boundless; free from the fears of seasons of drought and consequent famine, which oppress the Indian cultivator, the peasant of Burma pursues his light and easy toil, suiting the amount of it to his own pleasure and convenience. As may be supposed from the description given of them, the Burmans are a lively people, fond of amusements. Horse and boat racing, and 'pooëys' or dramatic performances, are the greatest attractions. The young men and boys may often be seen of an evening playing football in the village streets, and the elders engaged at chess in the verandahs. These two games are not quite the same as with us; football is played with a hollow ball of cane work rather larger than a cricket ball. The players stand round, and the ball is sent from one to the other, but only struck with the knee and the *sole* of the foot, and it is amusing to watch the dexterity with which they will turn their backs to a descending ball, jump off the ground, and kick it up again behind with the sole of the foot.

The chessboard in similar to ours, but the men have not the same names or moves; pawns, for instance, are 'tigers,' but their variety of the game could not be explained except on a board.

All classes and both sexes are inveterate gamblers. Under his native rule, which allows debt slavery, a Burman will gamble away his wife, children, and finally his own liberty. This, of course, cannot take place under English laws; but the owner of a fine trading boat of three or four tons has been known at the end of a journey to step on shore with only the cloth round his waist, having gambled away boat and everything he owned on his trip up the river. Their games of chance are various: cards; a kind of rouge-et-noir; a game of odd and even with cowries; tossing heads and tails, and many others. English cards are now universally used; formerly they had wooden ones of their own make resembling dominoes, but twice the size. These, of course, were not painted like ours, but had the values otherwise expressed on them.

Horse-racing consists more of what we should term matches, being bets between the owners of two ponies, the public betting among themselves, and are generally run in quarter-mile heats. The Burman ponies are stout little animals, averaging about 11¾ hands high, and seemingly capable of carrying almost any weight. It would, I think, be a most amusing sight to watch an English jockey's face, if he could be suddenly put down to witness a Burmese race. Putting aside the difference of dress and appearance of the people, the course is very similar to one at home; an excited crowd rushing over it aimlessly from side to side bellowing, '3 to 2 on Kyay Nee' (Red Star), or 'Who wants to back Kya Gon?' (Lily Necklace), &c. There are no betting books, but the money laid is deposited with some third party as stakeholder. But here come the ponies, two wiry little animals without a superfluous ounce of flesh, but yet not showing any of the signs of fine training that an English racer exhibits, rough coated and perhaps dirty. There are of course exceptions to this rule. But what shall we say of the jockeys? Naked but for the cloth girt tightly round their loins, their long hair gathered into a knot on the top of their heads and tied with a bit of string, their knees and thighs in a horizontal line, and the great and second toe only thrust into the stirrup, they present a picture that would make a racing-man stare. They are led down by the owners or backers to the starting point. There *they start themselves*, which of course gives rise to apparently endless false starts and alterations. At last, they are off! and here they come, followed by the yelling crowd. About half way they are close together, and there is evidently something wrong, a cross perhaps. However, along they come, slashing the ponies right and left with their long canes, the foremost man dancing in his saddle with body and arms. But both speedily appear with their respective backers before the umpire, and loud and bitter charges and countercharges are made. It seems, after inquiry, that about half-way, No. 2 ranging up, No. 1 cut his pony with his whip, which No. 2 revenged by stooping over and seizing hold of the tail of No. 1's horse and holding on by it for some seconds. After any amount of wrangling it is decided to run the heat over again. It is not meant that this is the usual manner of riding a race, but such an occurrence did happen under my own eyes.

The great national sport of the Peguans is boat-racing, induced, no doubt, by the facilities offered by the great bodies of water in the country during the rainy season. The racing boats are long canoes paddled, not rowed, the number of men being from four to twenty-four, though some boats hold even more. Their rules are more complicated than ours, and the drift of some of them does not seem obvious to our ideas. Heats are also the rule in this, as in horse-racing; the water is changed each time, but unless the first two heats are won by the same boat, the affair is generally drawn. The principle is, that as one side of the stream is always easier work than the other, unless a heat in *each* water is gained it is no real test, and the men are generally too exhausted for the third. The boat-races occur generally in October, and a few years ago those of certain localities were in their degree as celebrated as our 'Derby' or 'St. Leger.' The boats belong to certain towns or villages, and are rowed, or rather paddled, by the men belonging to them; and sometimes, when a match occurs between two localities that have long been rivals, the enthusiasm, the wild excitement, is almost incredible, certainly indescribable. The whole population nearly, men and women, have laid every farthing they are worth, and even mortgaged their jewellery and often their houses, to obtain more money for the purpose; and while the race is going on, the partisans of each boat in turn, on the slightest advantage gained, give way to the most ludicrous and frantic demonstrations of joy. But when the contest is decided, no words can fully picture the scene presented by the wild, yelling, roaring, dancing, laughing, crying crowd. The losers all seem to have disappeared, and the winners all to have gone mad. Here you see a grave, respectable, wealthy, corpulent elder who in ordinary times would consider anything beyond a smile unsuited to his dignity, with his 'putsoe,' or kilt, tucked up round his thighs, his headkerchief torn off and waved wildly in his hand, his few long grey hairs streaming in the wind, dancing and giving vent to his feelings in the most frightful whoops. Sometimes the farce is heightened by the imperturbable and exaggerated gravity of his countenance during this absurd performance. Here is a woman, the wife of an official, an old respectable lady, who in natural manner and good breeding might pass muster anywhere, with her handkerchief tied round her waist, dancing wildly to the music that adds its din to the uproar. To a stranger it would seem at first to be a vast crowd of furious drunkards; but I will be bound there is not one really drunken man among the thousands, though they do seem to be *mad* for the time. I have often laid my hand quietly on some old man, whom I did not like to see thus making himself absurd; he has sat down with a look as if thanking me for recalling his senses, and remained looking on quietly for some minutes, then suddenly jumped up again, as if unable to control himself, and joined in the wild 'sabbat.' This is not owing solely or chiefly to the sordid pleasure of gaining the money staked, though thousands of rupees change hands on a great race, but to the excitable and irrepressible disposition of the Burman. Simple and thoughtless as a child, he has all the child's passionate temper and unbounded fund of pure animal spirits; as easily excited, he as easily forgets one impression in the next following.

To the sports above mentioned must be added buffalo fights, which are, however, principally confined to the two districts of Tavoy and Mergui, in the Tenasserim province, the northern portion of the Malayan Peninsula; but they are brutal in character, and as they only consist of two animals butting and goring each other, till one runs away, a further description would be uninteresting.

One of the characteristics of the Burman race is their intense love of dramatic performances. After the Lent, when the rains have ended, they rush to every 'pooëy' they can find, and you will hear the expressive phrase, 'I am hungry for a pooëy.' There are two kinds, the drama proper and the puppet plays; but the latter are, strange to say, considered to represent high dramatic art. No festival, public ceremony, or private rejoicing, is complete without a performance of this kind. The Burman cannot understand paying to see a theatrical performance, which with him is always a gratuitous exhibition by the hirer of the troupe. Indeed it would be rather difficult to collect entrance money to a performance in the open street. There are professional actors, the best being from Upper Burma. The general plan for forming a company is for a manager to enter into a written engagement with the actors, male and female, for the season, which lasts from November to May. He makes all arrangements, and as a general rule takes up his head-quarters in some town or large village, from which engagements in the surrounding villages can be easily carried out. They do not give performances themselves on the chance of the house filling, but are hired for one, two, or three nights. In some large villages the youths and maidens form an amateur company, but of course only perform occasionally in their own or in neighbouring villages.

It is amusing, the celerity with which the whole thing is got up. An officer arrives in a village; while at dinner perhaps, the wife of the headman presents herself and requests permission to give a 'pooëy' (performance). For police reasons the sanction of the highest authority is always required for these gatherings. The good lady's request having been granted, in a few minutes the village band may be seen passing towards the lady's house, or to some open space in the village suitable for the purpose, and soon after the clang of music rouses up the whole village, old and young, into excitement. Women and children hasten to the spot with mats to spread on the ground, and secure good places; the former often with a babe under one arm, a roll of mat under the other, and a bundle of rugs on the head. Others, more sensible, pass, carrying baskets and trays of all the delicacies they can muster, such as fruit, cakes, 'letpet,' cheroots, &c., for sale on the outskirts of the crowd, for a 'pooëy' would be nothing without its 'night bazaar,' or market. By the time dinner is done, the officer strolls down and finds the performance ready to begin.

Colonel Yule, in his 'Mission to Ava,' gives a very good account of the Burman pooëy, as it strikes a European unacquainted with the language or customs of the people, and this we quote:—

'Each performance is attended by a full Burmese orchestra. The principal instruments belonging to this are very remarkable, and, as far as I know, peculiar to Burma.

'The chief instrument in size and power is that called in Burmese "patshaing," and which I can only name in English as a drum harmonicon. It consists of a circular tub-like frame about 30 inches high, and 4 feet 6 inches in diameter. This frame is formed of separate wooden staves fancifully carved, and fitting by tenon into a hoop which keeps them in place. Round the interior of this frame are suspended vertically some eighteen or twenty drums or tom-toms graduated in tone, and in size from about 2½ inches diameter up to 10. In tuning the instrument, the tone of each drum is modified as required by the application of a little moist clay with a sweep of the thumb in the centre of the parchment drumhead. The whole system then forms a sort of harmonicon, on which the performer, squatted in the middle of the instrument, plays with the natural plectra of his fingers and palms, and with great dexterity and musical effect.

'Another somewhat similar instrument consists of a system of small gongs arranged and played in a similar manner. The remaining instruments consist of two or three clarionettes with broad brass mouths and a vile penny-trumpet tone, cymbals, sometimes a large tom-tom, and invariably several clappers of split bamboo, which make themselves heard in excellent time but always too liberally.

'The stage of the Burmese theatre is the ground, generally spread with mats. On one, two, or three sides, are raised bamboo platforms for the more distinguished spectators; the crowd press in and squat upon the ground in all vacant spaces. In the middle of the stage arena, stuck into the ground, or lashed to one of the poles supporting the roof, is always a small tree or rather large branch of a tree, which like the altar on the Greek stage, forms a sort of centre to the action. I never could learn the meaning of this tree. The answer usually was, that it was there in case a scene in a garden or forest should occur. But there is no other attempt at the representation of scenic locality, and I have a very strong impression that this tree has had some other meaning and origin now probably forgotten. The footlights generally consisted of earthen pots full of petroleum, or of cotton-seed soaked in petroleum, which stood on the ground blazing and flaring round the symbolic tree, and were occasionally replenished with a ladleful of oil by one of the performers. On one side or both was the orchestra, such as it has been described, and near it stood a sort of bamboo horse or stand, on which were suspended a variety of grotesque masks. The property-chest of the company occupied another side of the stage, and constantly did duty as a throne for the royal personages who figure so abundantly in their plays.'[1]

The whole stage management is of the most primitive style, but perhaps not more so than to

[1] Yule's *Embassy to the Court of Ava*, p. 15.

our present ideas would be the scene presented by the stages of Paris and Londen theatres in our great-grandfathers' times, when the boards were lined at the sides with stools, on which sat the critics. While the audience is assembling, the actors are quietly making their toilet in the presence of all; the ladies have indeed assumed their dresses before they arrived, but they proceed to arrange their hair, pencil their eyebrows, powder their faces, and perform sundry other mysterious rites, without themselves or the beholders seeing anything extraordinary in the matter.

During the performance one of the actors sometimes interrupts a long speech, or takes advantage of a break in his dialogue, to kindle his cheroot at the flaring light, and after a puff or two goes on. Small boys are constantly bolting across the stage, between the legs of the performers, for the same purpose, or to get a draught of water from a large earthen pot which stands near the centre tree and lights. In spite of all this, I have seen the passions as forcibly depicted on these rude boards, as in the splendidly appointed theatres of Europe. One of the best, I think, and certainly the most interesting performance I have seen in Burma, was that of a small children's company in a village of about 200 houses. The eldest performer was about fourteen, the daughter of the headman, a slight, pretty girl; the others, boys and girls, younger. The parents and villagers generally were very proud of their talents, and they were regularly trained by an old man as stage manager, prompter, &c. Their principal piece was the 'Waythandara,' the story of one of the previous existences of Gaudama, in which he exemplified the great virtue of alms-giving, and in itself one of the most affecting and beautifully written compositions in Burmese.

The Prince Waythandara having distributed in charity all his treasures, jewels, and everything else, at last wishes even to give away the sacred white elephant to those who beg for it, which so enrages the people, that they insist on his banishment by his father, who is forced to yield to the popular outcry. His wife refuses to separate from him, and with her two children, a boy and girl, Zālee and Ganāh, they set out amid the pathetic lamentations of their relatives in a chariot for the far-distant wilds. On the way the mendicant Brahmins meet him, and, having nothing else, he offers them his chariot and pursues his journey on foot, he and his wife carrying the little ones. Some time after they have reached their retreat in the forests, a Brahmin, who is the villain of the piece, finds them out, in order to beg the last object the generous Prince has left, viz. his beloved children. He times his approach, while the mother is absent, works on the charitable disposition of the Prince, who, after sundry struggles with his paternal feelings, gives his two children to the greedy Brahmin. It must be remembered that Waythandara is himself conscious that he is the coming Buddha, and must practise to the very utmost the law of self-abnegation to attain that lofty position for the benefit of all human beings. With a bleeding heart he sees the Brahmin drag off the children, silencing their piteous entreaties with blows. Then the mother returns to find her little ones gone. Her agonised appeals are beautiful in their simple pathos, and I have seen men moved to tears by a good representation of this play. The plot ends happily, the children being restored to their parents, and the Prince to his country.

The little village company used to perform this piece capitally, but the acting of the little maid of fourteen in the part of the Princess could not be surpassed; she seemed really to have lost herself in her part, and her natural and graceful attitudes heightened the effect. The first time I witnessed the performance, in going round and saying a word to the tiny actors, when I came to the little fellow of ten or eleven, who had acted the part of the surly and greedy Brahmin, I pretended to be disgusted with his cruelty to the two poor infants. This the little man took in earnest, so much to heart, that, as I learnt on my next visit, nothing would induce him to act the part again; and it was not till his father almost forcibly brought him to me, and I had soothed him by what was deemed most condescending kindness, and excited his vanity, that I could obtain a repetition of the play.

In the ordinary performances the dancing, or, as we should say, the incidental ballets, form a principal attraction, and are supposed to be performed by the ladies of the Palace for the amusement of the King and Princes. The style is much more animated than that of the Indian dancing-girls, but still is rather posturing than European saltation. Indeed, the dress prevents any free play of the limbs, being the ordinary oblong cloth of the women, which, to prevent the fold in front opening, is sewn or pinned down the length, so that the dancer is as confined as if in a narrow sack eighteen or twenty inches wide with her feet through the bottom. Some of these girls are wonderfully supple, and from an erect position will bend the whole body over backwards till the head touches the ground, and pick up rupees from the mat with their mouths. Another of their accomplishments is very singular, namely, the power of moving certain muscles only, while the remainder of the body is at rest. Thus one will hold out her arm, and, while it and the whole of her body seem in perfect quiescence, the muscles of the arm alone will work and play so as to be visible yards off, or the bosom will rise and fall in an extraordinary manner without a sign of movement elsewhere. There are generally four to six female performers, including one or two of ten years or even less. Two clowns or jesters also play an important part in providing amusement by jokes and ridiculous imitations of the other performers.

It is, however, singular that, according to Burman ideas, the legitimate drama of high Art is contained not in these plays, but in the puppet-shows or marionettes. The figures are from two to three feet in height, and are very cleverly manipulated on a bamboo platform some thirty feet long. In these pieces the action is much more complicated than in the live drama, as there is the facility afforded for introducing elephants, horses, dragons, ships, and supernatural beings of all sorts; the dialogue is much loftier and in more polished language, while the *operatic* portion is much larger, and a company often acquires an extensive reputation from the possession of a 'prince' or 'princess' with a good voice and pleasing recitative. The performers—that is, those who work the puppets and speak for them—are always men and boys. These puppet-plays are almost always founded on the story of one of the many previous existences of Gaudama, such as the 'Waythandara,' before described, or else are historical dramas taken from the actual national history, but always with a very large proportion of the fabulous and supernatural. Some of them take six or seven days, or even longer, for complete representation, the performers being relieved from time to time.

Conjurors and snake-charmers are often met with, but they are not so numerous as in India, nor generally such skilled adepts in legerdemain. It has frequently been asserted, that the snake-charmers of the East deprive the animals of their fangs, or give them pieces of woollen cloth to bite, so as temporarily to exhaust the poison before exhibiting them. This, as a rule, is not the case; the snakes are in full possession of their deadly powers, and the only wonder is, that more accidents do not occur. In ten years of magisterial work I have had five cases brought before me of deaths caused by dancing snakes; in three cases spectators, in the other two the snake-charmers themselves, were the victims. This is pretty clear evidence against the idea that the animals are always rendered harmless.

One day, sitting in my tent in a small village, I saw two men and some boys hastening past with a peculiar-looking basket. Calling to them to know what they had got, they said they were snake-charmers, and were going to catch a large snake that the lads had seen in an old tree in the fields. They were told to bring it for inspection, if they caught it; and about half an hour afterwards they appeared again with a small crowd following, and turned out of the basket a large python about eight feet long, which they had just caught. This was an innocuous snake. One of the charmers, squatting on his hams before it, and moving about his body, waving his hands, made the animal follow all his motions; occasionally, when it made an attempt to dart at him, checking it with a 'Hey! hey!' and a rapid wave of the hand. According to the natives, these charmers when they proceed to catch a cobra, or other *venomous* snake, for the purpose of exhibition, first make an offering, such as a little rice or plantains, to propitiate him, and then enter into a solemn covenant to release him at the end of six months or a year, as they may choose to state, in a safe place in the jungle; and they firmly believe that, if this agreement were broken, and the animal kept a day beyond the appointed time, he would revenge himself on his master.

Dr. Fayrer's elaborate experiments on the various snake poisons, and the native antidotes for them, would seem to prove, that there really is no effectual antidote against the poison, when it has been thoroughly planted in the blood by the bite of a full-grown snake. And yet these men, whose business and profession it is to expose themselves daily to this deadly risk, have firm faith in the usefulness of their remedies. They allow that they may not be applied in time, or that there may be something in the patient's system rendering them powerless, as with ordinary medicinal treatment in diseases. As I write there lie before me a snake-stone and two pieces of some roots. These latter are at once lightly and quickly passed round above the part bitten to prevent the poison ascending, and the stone is applied to the wound, to which it adheres, and after half an hour drops off, having, it is supposed, absorbed the poison. I cannot say what the roots are, as they, as well as the snake-stone, were procured from Indian snake-charmers, who occasionally make their way over to Burma. The stone appears to be similar in substance to those brought from Ceylon by Sir Emerson Tennent, and which were pronounced by Professor Faraday to be bone, or horn, charred in some particular manner.

The Burmese charmers do not use these means, but rely on inoculation of the body and limbs with a secret medicine. Whenever bitten they immediately prick in this medicine afresh with a tattooing needle freely all over the body. I knew a case which, although not witnessed with my own eyes, rests, for my own satisfaction, on as good evidence. One of the most celebrated masters of this art was exhibiting his snakes, and ordered one of his pupils to take out a certain cobra from its basket. The man, on looking in, saw the snake was sullen and disinclined to move, and wished to leave it undisturbed; but the master desired him to pull it out, which he did, and while playing with it was bitten by the animal. He laid down and gave himself up for lost, laying all the blame on the master; but the latter immediately set to work and speedily introduced with the needle a quantity of medicine in differents parts of his body. The man turned quite black and remained for an hour shivering and groaning, then gradually recovered, to the relief of all present, who had made sure of his death.

These men profess to have two kinds of medicine—one which attracts and the other instantly repels the snake, and they tattoo one hand and thigh with the figure of a snake, with the former medicine; and the other hand and thigh with the figure of a 'Galong,' or eagle, with the latter. What truth there is in their assertions I do not pretend to say; but I have repeatedly seen snakes, following and dancing to the motions of the snake-marked hand, instantly crouch as it were to the dust on the 'Galong' being presented to them, and remain motionless as long as it was held over them. We know the influence that certain substances have over some animals; and it seems not impossible, nor, I may add, improbable, that a race of men who for centuries must have closely and anxiously studied and experimented on this one point, may have discovered some nostrum having great effect on the ophidian tribe. The 'Galong,' or eagle, of course refers to the bird 'Garuda,' the sacred bird of Vishnu, in the Hindu Pantheon, which was the mortal foe of the Nágas and all the snake race.

To the oft-repeated objection, that if there be anything in these antidotes of the Eastern snake-charmers, how is it they ever themselves fall victims, I would venture to reply that as the vaccine lymph is not a certain safeguard against, but a palliative of, the virus of small-pox, so these remedies may be often useful, though they are ineffectual under certain conditions.

In speaking of their amusements, it should not be omitted that the Burmans are passionately fond of cock-fighting. In our Province it is prohibited by law, but is a good deal carried on in secret. The cocks are armed with steel spurs, and, as the contest is necessarily much the same in every part of the world, it needs no description. Boxing may also claim to be a national diversion, and often takes place at a great festival or at the boat-races. Some one, an official probably, offers to give a 'let-pway pooëy,' or boxing-match show. A large shed is erected, and a ring formed by the people squatting down, and kept by several men armed with canes, which, however, they never use. The person present highest in rank having taken his seat, and given permission to open the proceedings, two elderly men, who have the reputation of having been champions in their day, are appointed masters of the ring. As a general rule the young men of the different divisions of the country, or, as we should say, of parishes or counties, assemble together on opposite sides. The umpires begin exciting them to come forward, and first one, then two, then half-a-dozen, spring into the ring, with their 'putsoes,' or waistcloths, girded tightly round their loins and between their thighs, naked all else, and begin to jump, shake their fists, and defy all the world, chiefly by slapping the left arm held tight into the breast with the open right hand, exclaiming, 'Youkya bā thā,' which really means 'Man son of a father,' but may, I suppose, be interpreted 'Hurra!' The two umpires seize a couple of these boasters, drag them forward, and place them side by side. Perhaps they are friends and decline to fight, or otherwise, after glancing out of the corners of their eyes at each other, one laughingly stoops and makes himself shorter by some inches than the other, for equality in height is one of the chief things observed in forming a match. We will suppose all objections overruled and the match made. Each champion retires among his friends to prepare for the combat, which consists in changing his silk putsoe for an old one girded as tightly as possible, his long hair is tied up in a knot, and probably fastened with a bit of string. They then enter the ring, kneel down and make an obeisance to the chief person present, and the same to the audience on each side. Having rubbed their hands on the ground to make them clench more firmly, they advance towards each other and make little mutual arrangements, as that the hair is not to be pulled or caught hold of, the face not to be punched—for these are merely the village lads playing for the amusement of the people, and not professional bruisers. The umpires then take possession of them, and set them to work. The sparring is generally with the open hand, but it is allowed to *jump off the ground and kick with the sole of the foot.* I have seen a man jump straight up, kick his opponent down by striking him on the *top* of the shoulder, and alight on the other side, or rather behind him. The several contests do not last long; the least scratch, or one of the combatants saying he is hurt, puts an end to it. Then each approaches the official present, if any, or the giver of the entertainment, and kneels while a piece of white muslin for a headdress is thrown on his shoulder, or, if there has really been a good round or two, a silk handkerchief is given to the victor, or even, in cases where the loser has boxed well but has been hurt, a handkerchief is given to both. Other matches are made in a similar manner. All the while the music has been clanging and clashing, especially during the fights, to inspirit the combatants. At the end the umpires each receive a silk handkerchief in return for their exertions. It should be added that no women are present at these performances.

The constant mention of music shows, that the Burmans are fond at least of their own music, for no festive gathering of any kind is complete without a band, as before described; and even in the house of mourning, from the moment the last breath is drawn till the funeral pile is fired, the melancholy strains of wailing music continue to sound night and day almost without intermission.

Having unfortunately no knowledge of the science of music, I cannot say anything myself on the subject; but I have been told by a friend who tried the various instruments according to European notes, that they proved to contain a full octave.

Besides those which have been described as forming an orchestral band, they have a harp, guitar, harmonicon, fiddle, and flute, and in almost every village is found an amateur performer on one or other of these instruments, whose verandah is sure soon to fill with appreciative visitors as he begins to play in the evening twilight. Women seldom learn to perform, although here and there is one who can play a little on the harmonicon.

This latter instrument deserves a description, and Colonel Yule's is so clear that I again quote from him. 'The bamboo harmonium, or staccato, is a curious example of the production of melody by simple and unexpected means. Its use, though unknown in India, extends throughout the Eastern Archipelago, and something similar is, I believe, possessed by the negro slaves in Brazil. Eighteen to twenty-four slips of bamboo, about an inch and a half broad, and of graduated length, are strung upon a double string, and suspended in a catenary over the mouth of a trough-like sounding-box. The roundish outside of the bamboo is uppermost, and, whilst the extremities of the slips are left to their original thickness, the middle part of each is thinned and hollowed out below. The tuning is accomplished partly by the regulation of this thinning of the middle part. The scale so formed is played with one or two drumsticks, and the instrument is one of very mellow and pleasing tone. Though the materials are of no value, a good old harmonicon is prized by the owner like a good old Cremona, and he can rarely be induced to part with it.'[1]

The Burmese singing is to our ears very unmusical and monotonous, being more a recitative than a song, and it would be very difficult to adapt the words even approximately in an English version. I give, as a slight illustration of their songs, two little lover's ditties and a child's lullaby. The Burmese in Roman characters is not intended as a transliteration of the original, but simply a rendering of the sounds as they are given in singing.

I.

Sōng ganda, nay bōogyee mă,
Bēy teē mă pă bă,
Chyit dēe thōō thălōō yoh hnĭn,
Mō kăh lăy moung,
Lōng lăy oung.

As I go far in the noonday sun,
Without a cover from the heat,
My lover with a palm leaf,
Shades me round and round,
To shelter me so safe.

II.

Pwin bōo dēe hnĭt gnon,
Naylay yă pōh lō, lwon bă ēy,

[1] Yule's *Ava*, p. 15.

Thwin shnay yohpou,
Kau kwā lō, way lay tin,
Huitmā lǎy mǎ myin yā yin,
Wāygā chyit yā.

Two opening twin buds we;
Though far my love, my heart is there;
My bright idol of molten gold,
Evil fortune has placed her far.
Though I see not my little sister,[1]
From far off I will love her.

III.

Deing-deing, det doung doung,
Kyǎt kōsin, ngǎ gin tāh deě,
Sā nāy gya kyǒung,
Thee kyǒung mǎ, kyǒung bwāi gyan,
Wine yan lo pan.

Deing-deing, det doung doung,
The fish over the fire,
The cat has run off with;
This pussy so naughty,
Round, round till we catch her.

As has been said, the possession of a clear and musical intonation among the professional actors or singers is highly valued, and the Burmans may certainly be ranked as a more musical people than their more civilised Aryan neighbours the Hindus.

[1] A term of endearment. Compare 'my sister, my spouse,' in Solomon's Song, ch. iv. 9.

CHAPTER VII.

FESTIVALS AND FEASTS.

Almost every important event in a Burman's life is made an occasion for a festival and a feast. But the two principal ones, which even the poorest celebrate to the best of their ability, are the naming of a child, and the admission of a boy into the monastery.

One pleasing trait of the Burman character is the general generosity of their dispositions and the ready help they render each other. The preliminary to every ceremony is to send round to all relatives, friends, and acquaintances an invitation in the shape of a packet of pickled tea ('let-pet'), the messengers, generally three or four young girls, relatives or friends of the family, dressed out in their best silks and jewels (often borrowed for the occasion), stating when and where the ceremony is to take place. On the day named all, those invited, and indeed all the neighbours, assemble at the house, where tea, betel, pickled tea, and tobacco is provided for the guests, and sometimes there is a dinner as well. All make presents according to their means and the position of the parents, even those who cannot personally attend sending their contributions, and this friendly assistance enables the poorest to perform with certain *éclat* the usual ceremonies which it would be a disgrace to neglect. No one feels it a tax, since each in his turn experiences the same benefit. The native officials, however, often make it a means of gain: I have known a magistrate give a grand 'pway' or feast in honour of the boring of his daughter's ears, and of course every one in his jurisdiction presented some offering according to custom; he obtained 60*l*., spent 40*l*. on the affair, and pocketed the remainder. Such conduct is, however, regarded in the same light as it would be among ourselves. The conclusion of any of these festivals is generally a 'pway' or dramatic performance at night in front of the house, or in some convenient open space.

But perhaps the most important event in the life of every Burman is his assumption of the monastic robe. Every Buddhist, who has the slightest claim to be a respectable member of society, must at some time in his early life enter the monastic order, if it only be for a few days' time. A fortunate day having been found, generally in the couple of months before the beginning of the Buddhist Lent (in July), during which no ceremony or feast is lawful, the invitation notice, as described above, is sent round.

On the appointed day the young lad—or perhaps two or three of them, as relatives and friends often join together on this occasion—clad in the gayest silk he can procure, covered with all the jewellery in the form of gold chains, earrings, rings, &c., his parents possess or can borrow, sometines with a tinsel tiara or crown on his head, is mounted on a pony, a gilt umbrella of state carried over him. Two friends lead the pony, and preceded by a band of music, and surrounded by his relatives and friends, the young women dressed in their gayest, and covered with jewellery, the young lads dancing and capering round him, he proceeds through the town, calling at the houses of all his friends, and, if in a respectable rank of life, beginning at the house of the highest official, European or native. A small *douceur* is customary, which provides betel and tobacco for the musicians and followers; but presents from friends to the lad, or as assistance towards the expenses, are either taken or sent to the house. At this ceremony it is usual among well-to-do persons for the parents to settle some property, as cattle or gold, on the lad, and this gift, according to the Law of

Menoo (recognised in our Courts), has the peculiarity, that it can never be resumed by the parents, whereas all other gifts to a child can be so. This gay perambulation is a figurative representation of the youth's abandonment of the pomps and vanities of the world, and also of Gaudama's entry into the city of Kapilawot previous to his forsaking everything to become a Buddha.

After these visits the procession sets out again through the town to the monastery the lad is about to enter, bearing the presents intended for the phoongyees, as well as the yellow robe intended for the young postulant. This last is, in accordance with one of the many wise rules of the founder of this order, that each aspirant for admission into its ranks should come provided with all the necessary clothing and utensils, and before the ceremony begins should be distinctly asked whether he is so provided. On entering the monastery the lad's head is shaved, his parents or nearest relatives receiving the hair as it falls; he is then bathed and clothed in a yellow monastic robe. His father or guardian then presents him to the head phoongyee, and he is received without further ceremony among the other probationers. Here he may remain only a few days, to fulfil the obligation of his religion, or for two, three, or more years, completing his education. During their residence the 'moung shins' or 'thāmanays,' as these probationers are called, are under strict discipline, and, besides the five great precepts binding on all Buddhists, are also subject to the other five proper to the monastic order. These will be detailed in the account of the phoongyees, but we may mention them here. 1st. Not to take life; 2nd. Not to steal; 3rd. Not to indulge in unlawful passions; 4th. Not to speak falsely; 5th. Not to drink intoxicating liquors. The second five are—1st. Not to eat after midday; 2nd. Not to dance, sing, or play any musical instrument; 3rd. Not to paint or colour the face; 4th. Not to stand in elevated places; 5th. Not to touch gold or silver. At any time after his entrance that he or his friends think proper, the probationer may throw off the robe, and leave the monastery.

The religious order under the pure Buddhist system has no priestly or ministerial duties to perform; strictly speaking, they are engaged solely in working out their own salvation, and have no concern with that of others.

It is true that the phoongyees attend, when invited, at funerals and on other occasions, and recite passages of the Law—that is, the relations of the existences of Gaudama; but they are in no way the religious guides and instructors of the people. Where they appear, it is simply to receive the offerings, that are always made to them on such occasions; and it must be remembered that they owe no gratitude to the givers; on the contrary, they are conferring a favour and benefit on the donors by affording them the opportunity of acquiring merit by fulfilling the law in making alms to the rahans, or holy men.

There is nothing laid down anywhere in the Buddhist books or in the teachings of Gaudama respecting the formulas of worship; and these differ so materially in the various Buddhist countries, that they should properly be considered in connection not with the religion, but with the customs of the people. The objects of worship are the Lord, the Law, and the Assembly; the last is worshipped by the reverence paid to, and the offerings made to, its present representatives the phoongyees; the second (the Law) by reading, hearing, and obeying its precepts; and the first (the Lord) by honouring the visible representations of Gaudama, and the pagodas erected in his honour, the more celebrated of which also contain some of his relics.

The Burman months are lunar, consisting of twenty-nine and thirty days alternately, an extra month (about the time of our August), being intercalated every third year. The month is divided into two periods, the waxing and the waning of the moon;

and these again by four worship days, namely the eighth of the waxing, the full moon, the eighth of the waning, and the last day of the month. From the full moon of 'Wā-tso' (about our July) to the full moon of 'Thadingynot' (October) is the 'Wā,' or Buddhist Lent, for no other term can properly describe it, during which religious observances are strictly enjoined; no feasts, marriages, or public amusements are held, and many phoongyees retire for meditation into small huts in the forest. With the more devout a worship day commences on the previous evening, when they repair to the zayats or bungalows round the pagoda or the monastery, taking their sleeping rugs and eatables, and sleep there. Before daylight they rise and cook the food intended for the phoongyees and for themselves, and at daylight are joined by others also bringing offerings and food for the day. When all those, who usually form one party, are assembled, the food and offerings for the phoongyees are placed in the middle of the zayat, and, notice having been sent to them, the yellow-robed monks come from the monastery, and occupy a divan raised about a foot at one end of the zayat with their palm-leaf fans before their faces. After a decent pause, one of the monks recites portions of the Law, *i.e.* of the sayings and teachings of Gaudama. The oldest monk then sometimes leads a kind of litany of praises of Gaudama, glorifying his excellent attributes, the congregation joining in with a choral chant, all squatting on their knees holding up their hands joined, with generally a real or artificial flower between them. When this is ended, the phoongyees solemnly walk back in file to their monastery, to which the food and offerings are at once conveyed.

The congregation then sit down to their own breakfast, each family together, though they often interchange little delicacies, and any stranger would be at once invited to share the meal. Having finished, the remains of the food are thrown out for the dogs and birds to devour, this being a charitable and therefore meritorious act. After this early meal a really devout Buddhist eats no more for the day, and, if he or she finds the company in the zayat too noisy, will retire under a tree, or to some other shady place, to tell his beads and meditate. The general congregation, however, more often spend the time in discussing the whole local gossip of the past week, and chewing betel, some paying a visit to the monastery, and having a chat with the phoongyees. Sometimes an Elder will assemble a group round him in the zayat, and read from one of the sacred writings, one of the 'Jatakas' (the existences of Buddha). If it be a large village or town, there will be several monasteries and zayats, where the same is going on as above described. The Buddhist beads or rosary consists of 108 beads made of wood, bone, marble, seeds, &c. As each five beads in succession are slipped through the fingers the formula repeated is 'Aneitsa, Doka, Anatta, Phrá, Tará, Thinga yāydana thou ba,' *i.e.* 'Transitoriness, Misery, Unreality, the Lord, the Law, the Assembly, the three precious ones.' Old men and women constantly carry their beads with them, and may be seen at any idle moment, or going along the road, counting them and muttering the prescribed formula. There is no trace in Burma of the singular system of 'prayer wheels,' of which so much has been written in accounts of Tibetan Buddhism, unless it be in the 'prayer flags' of the Lamas, and the small streamers, on which are rudely printed the signs of the eight planetary bodies, or certain religious formulas are written, and which the Burman Buddhists stick up in front of the pagodas or images, when they pay their devotions. But there is not among the Burmans the slightest idea of offering vicarious prayers by means of these streamers as there is among the Lamas; they are merely slight votive offerings, of the same kind as some flowers would be. The famous Lama prayer or formula, 'Om mani padme haun,' is utterly unknown in Burma. Elderly persons, especially those who are looked on as leaders and Elders in the congregation, generally either wear white garments, or else cover their shoulders with a white scarf when going to worship. After a day spent as above, in the cool of the evening all return to their houses. Besides these, which we may call the regular Sabbaths, there are several local festivals pertaining to various pagodas of more or less repute, like the annual festivals of the different shrines of Catholic Europe, to which pilgrimage is made. But the only feast of universal observance is that of the New Year. Others, such as the end of Lent, and the Tawadeintha feast in November, though acknowledged by all Buddhists, are not kept up except in certain places, or at least not every year. The New Year's feast, being the greatest one in all parts of Burma, deserves a detailed mention.

The commencement of the new year is movable, depending on the astronomical calculations made at Mandelay, and is thence made known over the country, but it only varies between April 9 and 12. It is denominated Thingyan (pronounced Thegyan), and the legend is that once the Thagya Min, or chief of the Náts, and a Byamma[1] wagered their heads on some dispute; the Byamma losing the wager, his head was cut off by the Thagya Min, who, afraid to throw it on the earth or yet into the sea, placed it in charge of

[1] The beings in the next higher state above the Náts.

seven daughters of the Náts, who at the commencement of each year transfer it from one to the other. At the moment this is done, the Thagya Min descends to the earth, where he remains three days and then reascends to the Nát country. According to what he is supposed to bear in his hands when descending—as a sword, a firestick, a waterpot, &c., which is learnt by astrological calculations—the wise men foretell the destinies of t he new year.

For some days before its arrival the petty shops may be seen filled with tin syringes of all sizes from four inches to two feet long, as our village shops are with fireworks before Guy Fawkes Day, and the little urchins begin practising with these or with bamboo ones on each other.

When the calculated hour and minute has arrived as nearly as they can judge, it is often announced by the headman of the village firing off all the guns he can muster, and leave to do so is often asked even in the towns. The great feature of the festival, the 'Waterfeast,' as it is generally termed by Europeans, I prefer to describe in the quaint language of Symes:—

'On April 12, the last day of the Birman year, we were invited by the Maywoon to bear a part ourselves in a sport, that is universally practised throughout the Birman dominions on the concluding day of their annual cycle. To wash away the impurities of the past, and commence the new year free from stain, women on this day are accustomed to throw water on every man they meet, which the men have the privilege of returning. This licence gives rise to a great deal of harmless merriment, particularly among the young women, who, armed with large syringes and flagons, endeavour to wet every man, that goes along the street, and, in their turn, receive a wetting with perfect good humour. Nor is the smallest indecency ever manifested in this or in any other of their sports. Dirty water is never thrown. A man is not allowed to lay hold of a woman, but may fling as much water over her as he pleases, provided she has been the aggressor; but if a woman warns a man that she does not mean to join in the diversion, it is considered an avowal of pregnancy, and she passes without molestation.

'About an hour before sunset we went to the Maywoon's and found that his lady had provided plentifully to give us a wet reception. In the hall were placed large china jars, full of water, with bowls and ladles to fling it. Each of us on entering had a bottle of rose-water presented to him, a little of which we in turn poured into the palm of the Maywoon's hand, who sprinkled it over his own vest of fine flowered muslin. The lady then made her appearance at the door, and gave us to understand that she did not mean to join in the sport herself, but made her eldest daughter, a pretty child, in the nurse's arms, pour from a golden cup some rose water mixed with sandal wood, first over her father, and then over each of the English gentlemen. This was the signal to begin. We were prepared, being dressed in linen waistcoats. From ten to twenty women, young and middle-aged, rushed into the hall from the inner apartments, who surrounded and deluged without mercy four men ill able to maintain so unequal a contest. The Maywoon was soon driven from the field, but, Mr. Wood having got possession of one of the jars, we were enabled to preserve our ground, till the water was exhausted. It seemed to afford them great diversion, especially if we appeared at all distressed by the quantity of water flung in our faces. All parties being tired and completely drenched, we went home to change our clothes, and in the way met many damsels, who would willingly have resumed the sport.'[1]

Thus for Symes. The idea of 'washing away impurities' is a fanciful one of his own; otherwise the description is perfect, although of only a part of the ceremony, the festive and not the allegorical part.

[1] Symes's *Embassy to Ava*, A.D. 1795.

Early in the morning pots of clear cold water are taken to the monasteries and offered to the phoongyees; others are presented before the pagodas and the images of Gaudama, which are then washed with the water. They then proceed to the house of the chief official; what happens there will perhaps be more amusingly described by giving a personal experience. Knowing what to expect during the day, I am, like Colonel Symes's party, prepared, and, having on only a light white suit, am sitting smoking when a servant comes to say the 'Loogyees' or Elders are outside. Being told to enter, some ten or twelve respectable and many of them grey-headed men enter, each carrying a small pot of water in his hands, and, having placed the pots on the floor, sit down behind them. Following them come some twenty or more of the prettiest damsels in the town, got up in bright silks and snow-white jackets, with gaudy silk handkerchiefs on their shoulders, each bearing a pot of water, some rather large, holding a gallon or so, which they also place with the others on the floor, then retire and sit down behind the men.

The most considerable Elder then says that, according to Taline-Burman custom, they have come to pay their respects to me with water—literally, 'beg pardon with water;' all then make the usual obeisance, the head bent three times to the ground.

The Elder again says that, according to their custom, they wish to make a propitious beginning of the new year and the coming rainy season by pouring water over me as being the chief civil authority, if I will graciously permit it. Having given permission, he takes up one of the pots, and, as I sit, he gravely pours the contents over my head, which I as gravely receive. He and the other men then, with another bow, retire to the background. I snatch up a pot and splash the water over the young ladies, on which they rise in a body on me, and, like the Maywoon, I am soon driven from the field; but all my servants, armed with their waterpots, rush in to the rescue, and I quietly watch the fun till the water is exhausted. A few rupees given to the girls, all depart highly delighted.

The real origin of the custom is no doubt an emblematical one; but it is connected with the near approach of the rainy season, and not with any idea of moral purification.

During this season of the New Year, among all classes, a ceremony termed 'ko-daw,' literally 'beg pardon,' but which is simply paying respect, is performed by inferiors to superiors, juniors to seniors, the nobles to the king, the king and all children to their parents, wives to husbands, scholars to their teachers, servants to masters. It is merely kneeling and bowing down three times, saying, 'Kŏ daw ba,' and sometimes accompanied by a present. At the end of the third day the Thagya Min is supposed to reascend to the Nát country, and the feast ends.

One of the most striking festivals, where it is properly kept up, is the 'Tawadeintha' Feast, to explain which two legends in the life of Gaudama must as shortly as possible be related.

Just before he attained the Buddhaship, a certain damsel prepared a rich offering of milk obtained by carefully feeding 1,000 cows, and then with their milk nourishing 500 others; with the milk from these again 250 more, and so on until from the last eight a milk of the most marvellous flavour and richness was produced. This milk she poured into a large caldron, and set it to boil. Wondrous signs took place. Four chiefs of the Náts watched round, a Byamma supported a golden umbrella over the caldron, the Thagya Min brought fuel, which emitted no smoke, and the Náts infused celestial honey into the boiling milk, imparting to it the flavour of the food of the Náts. When the milk was boiled, pouring it into a golden cup, she offered it to Gaudama.

The second legend is that while Gaudama was sojourning in the country of Thwattee, the modern Fyzabad, he ascended to the 'Tawadeintha region,' one of the Nát heavens situated above Mount Myemmo (Meru). This he reached in three steps, and there he remained some time, preaching the Law to the Byammas and Náts, among whom his mother, Maia, was now a queen. In his supposed discourse on this occasion, while dwelling on the gratitude due to parents, occurs one of those beautiful sentiments, scattered, and that not sparsely, among the Buddhist writings. He says: 'So great is the love and gratitude due to the mother, who nourished you at her breast, that I, the Lord, the Buddha, though I can, by expounding the Law to her, lead my mother into the path of deliverance and salvation, even I, all-powerful as I am, can only satisfy the gratitude due to one of her breasts; what return, then, can men offer?' After having preached the Law to all the Náts—that is, the Dewas or Devas of Hindu mythology, not the Náts who are the objects of the primitive ancestral worship of the Burmans and Karens—he descended by a triple ladder of gold, silver, and precious stones near the city of Tsampa-thanago, and entered it with his disciples to receive the customary morning alms. This is a slight summary of the legends.

The feast commemorating these two events is only regularly kept up in some places, and in them with more or less splendour in different years. In some towns a lofty erection of brick with two long flights of brick steps, in others a similar one of wood, forms a permanent representation of Mount Myemmo (the legendary and typical Mount Meru), while poorer places erect the same, when required, of bamboos. The festival lasts properly three weeks, but is generally curtailed to three days, always ending on the full moon of Thadingynot (October). For days and weeks before, great preparations are made in the town and villages around, each quarter and village vying with the other. 'Pyathats,' or bamboo and paper representations of the lofty, graceful, and fantastic spires peculiar to Indo-Chinese architecture, and 'Padaytha-bins' (a fabulous tree, supposed to bear whatever is wished for, but here made of bamboo), hung with miscellaneous offerings for the phoongyees, are the principal features in the show; but, besides these, they tax their ingenuity in a variety of ways. To present, if possible, a picture of the whole, I ask the reader to come with me on the day before the full moon, about 3 P.M.

First we will look round the pagoda hill on which the festival takes place. In an open space is a lofty wooden stage or platform some fifty feet high and fifteen square, raised on teak posts, from two sides of which sloping ways lead down to two buildings at the bottom. Half-way up, on one of these slopes, stands a spire of bamboo and gilded pasteboard; the summit is crowned with a similar but larger one of nine stories, beneath which is placed an image of Gaudama, in front of which is another image representing his mother Maià in an attitude of devout attention, and at the four corners are other figures representing Náts, or Devas.

The whole is a figurative representation of the Myemmo Mountain and the legend mentioned above. The building at the bottom on this side is the monastery, in which Gaudama was sojourning when he made his celestial journey above related; the spire halfway up is the Oogandaw Mount, upon which he rested in his ascent; the high spire-crowned stage is the Nát heavens, in which his personification is represented preaching to his mother and the surrounding Náts. The sloping way on the side is the triple golden ladder by which he descended; and the building at its foot is the Níbban Monastery, in which he remained on his return.

We can ascend without offending any prejudices and observe the image of Gaudama, which is on a wheeled platform, on which it was drawn up by ropes and a windlass along the sloping way, halting for one night at the halfway spire, or Oogandaw Mountain, on the first day of the feast. Every afternoon during the feast, about three o'clock, a respected Elder mounts to the summit, and, till darkness falls, reads aloud to the kneeling people down below the law which Gaudama is supposed to have taught to the inhabitants of the heavens. This evening, however, this ceremony is omitted, as the offerings are coming, and the place is rather empty, except some old men and women, who are too feeble to take part in the procession.

Let us take up a point of vantage on the side of the road, for the music is coming nearer. First comes an indiscriminate mob of men, women, and children in parties and groups. Looking down the road we can see approaching a moving tower, a many-storied fantastic spire, covered with gilding and colours flashing in the brilliant sun, the top ending in an elastic gilt bamboo some ten feet long, crowned with a golden ball that sways about with every movement of the bearers. In front comes the usual band, the big drum or drum orchestra being carried in a cart; next ten or twenty young men of the quarter to which this spire belongs, dressed in their gayest cloths and headkerchiefs, and snow-white linen jackets, dancing with an energy that speaks well for their training, considering they have been keeping it up on the way for more than an hour. They halt for us to inspect and admire their show, and begin again their best saltatory figures for our pleasure.

Probably some of the women and girls join in; then old men, unable to restrain their excitement, caper away as lightly as any. Such a scene as this makes one understand how and why 'David danced before the Lord *with all his might.*' The lofty and singularly graceful spire having been set down on the ground by its bearers, some twenty or more stalwart men, does not show so well on a close inspection, any more than would one of Grieve or Telbin's beautiful opera scene-pieces; in fact, it is not made to be looked at close; but the taste and ingenuity displayed with such poor materials is worth noting—bamboos, mats, or pasteboard covered with coloured and tinsel paper, forming the whole. We shall see many more of these spires, some larger, some smaller, from twenty to fifty feet high, all on the same model, but differing in ornamentation and detail. Behind this comes a 'Padaytha-bin,' which forcibly reminds us of a gigantic Christmas tree fashioned with flexible strips of bamboo for the branches. It consists of a small platform on which this tree of bamboo is fixed, and on the branches hang almost every conceivable object to be found in the bazaar shops—plates, cups and saucers, teapots, candles, knives, razors, small kerosine lamps, writing-paper, palm leaves for native manuscripts, and other similar articles; while at the foot of the tree, on the platform, lie European hearthrugs, native pillows, rolls of yellow cloth, or perhaps silk for phoongyees' robes, &c. Sometimes a 'silver tree,' as it is called, is made by hundreds of small bamboo strips springing from the central stem, each having hung from the end a rupee enclosed in paper tinsel of different colours, shaking and glittering at every movement. Often 500 to 700 rupees (50*l.* to 70*l.*) hang on one of these trees. All this is an offering for the phoongyees. Behind the tree come the rest of the people belonging to this village or quarter, as gay as they can make themselves in particoloured silks and white jackets. They pass on, and more joyous groups succeed in quick succession. But now there comes from the direction of the town a noise that is indescribable, but overpowering.

Now, move a little this way, so that you can see nearly two miles down the road from the pagoda hill through the principal street of the town, which before I had purposely kept you from seeing. From our elevated position we almost look down on it, or rather on a rolling river of colour, out of which shoot up an apparently interminable array of spires, enormous white umbrellas, gold umbrellas, long bamboos like gigantic fishing-rods, but gilt and covered with tinsel, all dancing, swaying, flashing in the sun. The noise we heard is the mingled clashing of some dozen of Burmese bands, and the songs and shouts of thousands of human voices.

As they approach in long procession, each separate party halts for a few minutes before us, and the dancers figure right merrily to gain our approval, and if any one be introduced as a stranger fresh from England, they will be delighted at the honour of showing off before him. 'Pyathats' and 'Padaytha-bins,' as before described, pass along. In front of one comes a party of twenty or thirty young men, all dressed alike, and riding hobby-horses of pasteboard, with which they curvet and prance, march and counter-march, in the most admirable time. The next party has two gigantic figures nine feet high, to each of which a man concealed inside gives movement, and which execute a most comical dance. Following after comes a similarly animated turtle some six feet long, crawling along on the ground. Behind it a village party of Karens bear aloft their humble show—an enormous bamboo sixty feet high covered with red cloth, its tapering elastic top crowned with a gilt ball. After them comes a party of maidens, decked in the gayest colours, and covered with a profusion of gold ornaments, surrounding a still more richly-dressed damsel, who wears a high pinnacled cap of pasteboard and tinsel, the customary head-dress of stage princesses. She represents the damsel who made the offering of milk to Gaudama; and as, according to the legend, this maiden had been his daughter in a former existence, it is sometimes difficult to get a girl to take the part, from a fear of incurring some danger in thus representing one so near akin to Buddha. These also go through a dance, in which arms, heads, and bodies move together in perfect time. Forming a part of their group is a cart, on which stands a large pasteboard cow, emblematic of those which furnished the offering of milk to Gaudama; and behind this another cart, containing an immense pot covered with gold leaf, in which the sacred milk is to be boiled. We fear to tire the dancers overmuch, and bid them pass on. Other parties follow; some carry a gigantic white umbrella ten feet in diameter, made of paper with a deep fringe around it, cut in a pattern that at a little distance looks like a rich lace, but is only paper cut by hand, this paper-lace work being one of the commonest and prettiest ornaments in all Burmese shows. Others bear ten or twelve smaller ones on handles twelve feet long; and others, again, carry gilt umbrellas, such as are the signs of office and authority in Burma. It would take too long to describe each party, similar in general character to those preceding it, but differing in the details. A louder noise and a denser crowd now approaching herald the great show of the day; it belongs to the rich traders' quarter of the town.

Following the usual 'Pyathat' and 'Padaythabin,' comes a large platform on six wheels, drawn by oxen, which supports what, as it draws nearer, is seen to be a model of a paddle-steamer, between thirty and forty feet long. Smoke issues from the funnel, the paddles revolve, the helmsman turns the wheel, a Lascar at the side takes soundings mixed with jokes, addressed to the people round, in a jargon of Hindustani and Burmese. On the deck is the captain, got up in 'Europe clothes' and sun helmet, with a tin telescope, to which he ever and anon applies his eye and views the crowd; others on board represent in character passengers of all nationalities in Burma. See! there sits even an English *lady*, dressed in white and a straw hat, with whom the captain occasionally talks and flirts in what he thinks a correct European manner. I recognise *her* as the most mischievous young blackguard in the town, a handsome lad of seventeen or eighteen years. *She* has her face whitened to the European standard; while sitting beside her on the deck is her ayah, represented as a fat Madrassee woman, who creates roars of laughter by quarrelling with the sailors in a gibberish containing a few Hindustani words. Some hitch occurs in drawing the waggon, and the captain immediately cuffs the helmsman, as if for steering badly; and so, amidst shouts, roars, and personal jokes at the expense of the actors, the show moves on. If we examine the steamer, we shall find it is ingeniously constructed of the indispensable bamboo, painted mats, paper, and a few rough planks put together with fastenings of pliant cane.

The procession is nearly ended, and we take our stand on one of the terraces of the pagoda, so as to look down on the crowd of several thousands now assembled. It is like looking at an immense tulip-bed, or the ever-shifting colours of the pendant prism; while the forest of graceful and fantastic spires of long decorated bamboos, and of umbrellas white and gold, all glittering in the rays of the setting sun, and now arranged around the pagoda, give an unreal and fairy pantomimic character to the scene. On one side of the imaginary Myemmo Mount a bamboo stage is erected, upon which a large hearth of mud has been made; hanging over this is the gilded pot, which we saw in the procession, and men are arranging firewood beneath it to cook the sacred milk offering. Near by sits in state the damsel of the legend, but neither she nor any woman may share in preparing it; men alone must perform the whole service, except that she gives it one stir, like the children's stir of the Christmas pudding. The sides of the road to the pagoda are for a long way lined with little stalls, in which small wax tapers, scented Chinese joss-sticks, paper flags and streamers, and paper flowers, are sold to the worshippers, to be offered before the pagoda and the images; in some, but not many of these stalls, cakes and sweets of fearful and wonderful manufacture may be had; while here and there are temporary stands, with large jars of water, placed by pious souls for the general benefit, whereby to win also merit for themselves. Some even do more than offer a cup of cold water; for see here, under a shady tree, is a table at which the wife and daughters of the native magistrate, clad in silk and velvet, are dispensing sherbet to all passers-by, who will accept it, be it the European officer or the wild Karen from the hills.

A constant succession of worshippers crowds the foot of the pagoda and the buildings containing the large images of Gaudama. They place their offerings of streamers and small candles, till the shrines are at last one blaze of light from thousands of wax tapers, under which the great images, with their passionless faces, and their whole bodies covered with gold leaf to represent the yellow robe, stand out in bold relief; while the daïs on which they sit, the pillars, and often also the roof of the building, encrusted with a mosaic of various coloured glass and tinsel (a work in which Burmans excel), sparkle and shine as if set with precious stones. And as they come and go, joyful and overflowing with excitement, not a drunken man do we meet among all these thousands: no quarrelling nor rude jostling, all good-humouredly accommodating themselves to the general enjoyment. There are often rivalries, even fights, about the getting up of these pageants between the different quarters of a town, but these take place elsewhere. Here upon the sacred ground they would be ashamed to continue them.

Difficult as it is in words to give even a faint idea of these scenes, there is yet one, perhaps the prettiest, feature in the show to be mentioned. It is now dark; but we must leave the lights and fires around the pagoda and go to the brow of the hill, looking down on the road into the town. At a little distance, apparently advancing in long sinuous movements, is what seems a gigantic fiery serpent, with two glaring red eyes, now reared aloft, now sweeping near the ground, while the luminous body (100 feet long) twists and folds, unfolds and lengthens itself out again, as it slowly glides along through the air. As it comes nearer in the darkness, we see that it is—or, at least, that such is its semblance—a glittering white dragon, with enormous blood-red head and fiery eyes, and in front of it, dancing up and down to this side and to that, rolling along the ground, is a ball of light, which the monster ever pursues with wide open jaws, now slowly, now with a sudden rush as the ball shoots ahead. When we go close up to it, the illusion of course vanishes, and we see that the body of the serpent is formed of thick muslin stretched on some thirty hoops three feet apart; each hoop contains a lighted candle, and has a handle by which it is borne up; the head is made of the shiny dark-red tinsel used in theatres, fashioned most beautifully as a dragon, *more Burmano*. This also is lighted from within, and is carried on a pole by the strongest and most active man of the party. Another carries in front the ball that the dragon pursues, a paper lantern on a long handle. The movements of the thirty or more men bearing the body of the dragon aloft, give life to it, as they dance it up and down, or twist in and out to represent the folds; while the bearer of the enormous head pants and perspires with his exertions, sweeping it in every direction and following the ball in front. Thus, after perambulating the town, it makes its way through the admiring crowds near the pagoda, around the base of which it is finally deposited, the emblem of the 'Nágas,' or

'Nágs,' the dragon race, who play so great a part (but one not yet clearly understood) in Buddhist mythology.

The sights of the day are ended; but the crowd, or the best part of it, remains, listening all night long to the pooëys or plays, two or three of which are going on. To complete our observation of the festival we must come back at daylight. We shall find that during the night the car bearing the image of Gaudama has been let down from the Myemmo Mountain (the stage above), and has arrived in the building at its foot. Most of the townspeople, or at least the elder portion, have returned to their houses to prepare for this the last part of the feast; but there still remains a great crowd of villagers. All the phoongyees, the novices, and scholars, are assembling from the various kyoungs; and when the 'Gine-Ōke,' or Bishop, appears, the car with the image, surmounted by a canopy, is drawn from the simulated monastery, and the long file of yellow-robed monks, some 200 or more, the Bishop at their head, range themselves behind it. Then the principal elders and supporters of the pagoda and of the monasteries bring forward the milk offering, which has been cooked during the night: they pour it out on the platform before Gaudama. No monk nor man may presume to taste of it. This done, the procession in the same order moves slowly into the town, the oldest, the highest, the richest, deeming it an honour to put a hand to the ropes, which draw the representation of the Lord, as he proceeds with his disciples into their town to receive the morning alms, as he did over 2,000 years ago into the city of Tsampa-thanago.

In the centre of all the streets along which the procession is intended to pass, a narrow lane is marked out by a double 'radza-mat' or royal trellis, made of thin interwoven bamboo, on each side of which the people stand before the houses with their offerings of food. As the phoongyees move down the narrow passage prepared for them, each opens his 'thabeik,' or begging-pot, held in front of him, and receives the rice poured in by the people on each side; when it becomes full he empties it out to one side on the path, and begins again. Thus they move through the town, then so back to their respective monasteries. The feast is ended.

As a contrast to the glare, noise, and gaudy show of the 'Tawadeintha' feast, let me describe another festival observed at the end of the rains. It is that of Shin Oopaga. The legend says, that in a former state of existence he once (as a jest) hid the clothes of some person bathing, and thus put him to shame, as a penalty for which he himself now, clothes-less, abides in the water till the arrival of the next Buddha, when will he become a great Rahanda (a Holy Being).

To witness this festival, let us go, not to the dust and bustle of the roads, but to the river's bank in the cool gloaming of the evening. As soon as it is dark, the villagers proceed in boats to the centre of the stream, provided with a quantity of small earthen saucers about two inches in diameter, and slices of the stalk of the plantain or banana tree, which is formed of series of concentric rings, something like a section of an onion, and is perfectly buoyant when green, being one mass of air-vessels. Some offer only fifty saucers, others a thousand, some even ten thousand. The little saucers being filled with oil, and a wick laid on the edge, are placed on the pieces of plantain stalk, each lighted, and separately consigned to the stream. In half an hour, looking from a high bank down a long reach of the river, the whole centre of the stream is dotted with thousands of twinkling points of light, which in the far distance blend gradually into an apparent sheet of phosphoric flame. I remember once going up the Irrawaddy on the day after this feast, and some miles below a large town our steamer passed through a regular 'bank' of hundreds of thousands of these tiny floats, their oil burnt out, their lights extinguished, and nothing left of them but the clay vessels which had held the vital flame, drifting on together, out into the limitless ocean.

Besides the general feasts observed everywhere there are others annually recurring pertaining to certain pagodas, and answering to the yearly pilgrimages to sacred shrines in Christian Europe. The word 'pagoda' seems to be a corruption of the Sanscrit 'dhátugarbha' or 'dhagoba,' meaning a 'relic-shrine.' The Burmans know no such word; they style the pagodas 'bhoo-ra' (pronounced 'pŏ-yah' or 'pŏ-rāh'), the primary meaning of which is 'Lord.' The pagodas, properly so called, are edifices enshrining some relic of Buddha, generally one or more hairs of his head. There are other smaller erections in a similar style, but containing no relics, erected as pious memorials, or to commemorate some event, which are properly styled 'dzédees.' In Upper Burma, at the old city of Págau, there are magnificent ruins of buildings of another style of architecture, which may be correctly termed temples,[1] and which were confessedly borrowed from those in the ancient Mōn mother city of Thatone, the

[1] See the elaborate description and illustrations in Col. Yule's *Embassy to the Court of Ava*, chap. ii.

originals being completely destroyed by the Burman conqueror Anawrahata, circa A.D. 1057. But the pagodas in British Burma are all solid edifices of masonry, consisting of a pyramidal cone placed on a more or less elevated platform, the whole being surmounted by a 'htee' or umbrella spire of iron tracery gilded. There are many varieties in detail and ornamentation, some of the largest having arched wings on each face of the lower platform, forming, as it were, side chapels, and containing an image of Gaudama.

The great 'Shwé Dăgōng Pŏyăh' or 'Golden Dagōng Pagoda' of Rangoon, is the largest, most celebrated, and most sacred in Burma, indeed in Indo-China. To it pilgrims resort from all parts of Burma, from Yu-nan, from Siam, from Cambodia. Placed on the last spur of the Pegu Yōma, or range, it dominates the whole vast seaboard plain, and its bright golden pinnacle is visible for miles, glittering in the sun. The date of its erection, according to Burmese history, is 585 B.C., but the site had been sacred in the unknown ages of Buddhas pre-existent to Gaudama. The legend is as follows: Two brothers, said in the native books to have been Mōns or Taleins, having made an offering to Gaudama, begged in return some relic of himself, on which he stroked his head and gave them eight hairs that came out. These he desired them to deposit in a pagoda in a spot, where had already been buried certain relics of his three great predecessors. They accordingly started with them for 'Suvarna-bhumi,' the Sanscrit name of Pegu, but on the way lost six of the hairs. However, they were recovered in a miraculous manner, and the holy site pointed out to them by the Náts. Here, on digging, the relics of the former Buddhas, viz. a water scoop of Kaukathan, a robe of Gau-na-gong, and a staff of Kathaba, were found, and these, together with the eight hairs of Gaudama, were deposited in a hole on the top of the hill on which 'Shwé Dagong' now stands, and a solid pagoda of stones 66 feet high was erected. This pagoda is thus especially sacred to all Buddhists, as the only one known to them as now existing, which is supposed to contain the relics not only of Gaudama, but also of all the Buddhas of this present world. At the time of its erection, and for centuries afterwards, no town existed on the site of Rangoon, and the pagoda stood, like many others at the present day, in the midst of the wild forest. The history of the pagoda, which is rather a long one, contains detailed particulars of the various improvements, repairs, and enlargements made to it by various kings. The edifice has been cased several times (as was also the custom with the Ceylon dagobas) with a fresh outer surrounding of bricks several feet thick, thus each time increasing its height and size. Thus in A.D. 1447 the King of Pegu encased it afresh, and made its height 301½ feet. In 1462 the reigning King of Pegu cast, it is said, a colossal bell 168 feet high, 12 feet in diameter, and 36 feet in circumference, also several other smaller bells, and paved the platform or terrace of the pagoda with 50,000 flat stones. This wonderful bell, it is perhaps unnecessary to say, is not (now at least) in existence.

In 1564 Tsin-byoo-mya-shin repaired the pagoda, raising it to its present height of 372 feet, and a circumference of 600 feet. (St. Paul's Cathedral is 370 feet in height.) About 1769 the King of Ava, who then possessed the whole country, placed a new 'htee' or umbrella on the pagoda, a sign of sovereignty, and covered the whole with gold leaf. In 1840 King Tharrawaddee visited Rangoon with great pomp, and cast the present great bell which stands on the pagoda platform, and is 14 feet in height, 7½ feet diameter across the mouth, 22½ feet in circumference, 15 inches in thickness, and 94,682 lbs. in weight. It is, of course, very roughly cast, and in the interior may be seen half amalgamated lumps of gold and silver, from the ornaments cast in by the pious, while the metal was being run. The Burmese are not a little proud of its history, as it stands in its present position, for after our conquest of Rangoon in 1852 it was removed to be sent to Calcutta as a trophy, but was accidentally sunk in the river. One or two attempts were made by our Engineers and sailors to raise it, but without success. After a few years the Burmans petitioned that it might be restored to them if they could recover it, and, their prayer having been accorded, they set to work, raised it from the bottom of the river, and triumphantly carried it back to its old place on the pagoda terrace, where it remains, a monument of Burmese ingenuity and perseverance. The last great event in the history of the pagoda was the replacing the old 'htee' or umbrella with a new one. This was made by the present King of Burma, and for a couple of years he and his Ministers perseveringly attempted to obtain permission to place it on the pagoda at his own cost and by his own men. This, however, our political officers as steadily and firmly refused; whatever might be the King's own idea, it was well known that such an act on his part would be regarded by our own Burman subjects as a sign of suzerainty, and therefore must be guarded against. At last the King gave in, and sent the golden 'htee' down with great pomp in one of his steamers to Rangoon, where it was handed over to our native officials and a committee of Buddhist Elders, by whom it was finally placed on the summit of the pagoda, as the King's offering, but the actual placing it was defrayed by public subscriptions and offerings.

The 'htee' is a series of constantly diminishing bands of hoop iron scroll-work, strongly and rudely put together, ending in a rod and small vane. The iron-work is covered with thin plates of gold, and the uppermost band and vane set with precious stones. On each band are hung gold and silver bells, which tinkle musically in the air. The cost of the 'htee' in gold and jewels, as supplied by the King, was 27,000*l.*, and the value of voluntary labour supplied, subscriptions towards the expenses, and offerings of new gold and silver bells made by the people of Rangoon and British Burma generally, perhaps amounted to 20,000*l.* more. I know one man and his wife who presented a small gold bell set with emeralds, of the value of 70*l.*

There are several other celebrated pagodas in British Burma, at Pegu, Prome, Maulmain, Arracan, and other towns; almost every conspicuous hill peak is crowned with a pagoda large or small, and some of these, especially in the Pegu province, have a great reputation for sanctity, and are associated with marvellous legends.

Of one of these last, and of the scene presented

at the annual pilgrimage to it, I will endeavour to give a description.

About half-way between the Sittoung and Beeling rivers is the town of Kyeik-hto, and 14 miles north-east of this lies a conspicuous peak 3,600 feet high, on which there is a small but remarkable and celebrated pagoda generally called 'Kyeik-tee-yoh,' which is a corruption of the old Mōn name of 'Kyeik-ethee-yŭh,' signifying 'the god carried on the head of the hermit.'

Leaving the town of Kyeik-hto on a day in March during the week of the annual festival of this pagoda, we ride along towards the mountain. The road is thronged with pilgrims, some from a distance in carts, the greater number on foot—whole families, from the grey-headed grandmother to the infant at the breast. Each person carries a bundle or a small basket, 'pah,' made of woven palmyra leaves, the cover completely fitting over the bottom part. These contain a change of clothes and other little matters; and, in addition, each carries over the shoulder, or wrapped like a shawl round the body, a couple of sleeping rugs. They come not only from the country round, but from distant places; some are from Upper Burma making a round of pilgrimages to the most sacred pagodas. As we pass any group more striking than the rest, and address a few words of inquiry or salutation to them, we are smilingly responded to, and counter inquiries made as to who we are, and where we are going; and we leave them pleased at the notice of the English officers, sure of a cordial and respectful salute, if we chance to meet again. At length we arrive at the foot of the mountain, where one of the small rest-houses has been prepared for our accommodation, and there we spend the night, together with several hundreds of pilgrims, waiting to ascend the hill in the cool of the morning.

Next morning we start on our upward march, and, as we near the summit, we are struck by the singular spectacle presented by the many huge granite boulders, scattered about on the sides of the mountain, several apparently just arrested in the midst of their fall by some magic power, with nothing visible to restrain them from crashing down the steep slopes. Most of the larger ones are crowned with small brick pagodas, three to six feet in height. There are two peaks, and in the depression between them are several 'zayats' or rest-houses; and now during the festival every available space is occupied by huts or booths made of bamboos and grass, erected by enterprising speculators from the villages lying round the mountain, for the temporary accommodation of the visitors. Several of these booths are occupied as shops, in which eatables of all sorts are displayed, for many of the pilgrims do not take the trouble to bring provisions with them: in some years there is a scarcity of water from the small stream on the hill, and then a thriving trade is driven by the Karens in bringing water from below, and a grand opportunity is afforded the pious and benevolent pilgrim to obtain a great store of merit, by providing large earthen jars full of water for general use. In other booths small paper streamers and rosettes, wax tapers and Chinese 'joss-sticks,' for offerings, are to be obtained. But most important, placed near the native magistrate's hut and that occupied by the police guard, so as to be under their protection, are the huts of two or three men, who have for years had the monopoly of selling gold leaf to the worshippers. I much regret not having ascertained the value of gold leaf sold during the festival; it must be something considerable. The quantity of gold expended by the Burmans on their sacred edifices attracted the notice of the early travellers. Cæsar Frederick, writing in 1569, says: 'In that countrie they spend many of these sugar-canes [1] in making of houses and tents for their idols, which they call Pagodas. The said houses within are full of earth, and walled round about with brickes and dirt instead of lime, and from the top to the foot they make a covering for them with sugar-canes,

[1] He means bamboos.

and plaster it with lime all over. Also they overlay all the tops of these houses[1] with gold, and some of them are covered with gold from the top to the foot; so that with this vanitie they spend great abundance of gold.' The greater part of this gold leaf, it must be remembered, is pure gold; it is sold in small packets (like gold leaf at home), worth five to six shillings each. A couple of these packets at least is expended by every family, except the very poorest, present at the festival; many, of course, spend much more.

Leaving the encampment of huts, we reach the higher peak on which is situated the sacred pagoda. But first let us survey the scene before us. Looking directly on the down below, we can discern nothing but a mass of foliage covering the lower hills that stretch away like an undulating sea till they sink into the plain. Beyond them, far as the eye can reach, extends the great Pegu plain; through its centre a shining sinuous streak marks the course of the Sittoung River, and we can plainly see the gigantic S curve that it takes after passing the town of Sittoung, and then rapidly widens out till it is lost in the shallow waters of the Martaban Gulf. That dark spot on this side of the river almost in the centre is the hill and pagoda of Sittoung, while the

[1] The pagodas.

glittering speck that the eye sometimes catches, is the gilded summit of the Phwé Maw-dau pagoda of Pegu, some 45 miles away. On the extreme verge of the horizon to the right is the Pegu Yōma, or range. But after all, except from the names of localities, it is impossible by mère word-painting to make the description of one great plain seen from a lofty height differ from that of any other similar view. Let us then turn to the wonder of the mountain. At the summit of the peak on one side, detached by a chasm several feet wide from the mountain itself, stands out like a buttress a flat, sloping crag, which overhangs the precipitous side of the mountain sheer down into a valley hundreds of feet below. On this flat rock is perched a huge granite boulder, more than half hanging over the perpendicular face of the cliff, and, as you look at it, you hold your breath waiting for it to take its final plunge into the depths below. Nothing tangible keeps it back, the laws of gravitation are outraged by its position, and yet there it stands, and has stood for centuries, one of Nature's miracles. As one of the few European visitors to the spot has aptly described it: 'There it hangs, as it has hung, and I suppose, will hang yet,—one might indeed almost say, there it *slides* and *will slide* for many an age.' How came it there and what force arrested its sudden descent, and what holds it back from now slipping off its smooth sloping pedestal, are the questions forced on us. No wonder the Burmans, in their ignorance of the wonders of nature, and with their old ancestral fetishism, regard this phenomenon as truly miraculous, and even more wonderful than it is. They firmly believe, that the boulder does not touch or rest on the table rock at all; that in the pristine and purer ages of the Buddhist faith it hung suspended above, 'so that a hen could sit beneath,' but that in these degenerate days it is only possible to pass a hair between the two. All the Burmese drawings of the spot—and it is a favourite subject—represent a space of some inches between the two rocks. The boulder is about 30 feet high and the pagoda on the summit 15 feet. Across the chasm separating the table rock from the mountain is a wooden bridge, and a bamboo ladder allows the more daring worshippers to reach the pagoda and affix their offerings of gold leaf upon it. The pagoda itself is completely gilt, and after a festival nearly the whole inner face of the boulder is covered with gold leaf; but this is almost all washed off during the rains, and indeed some of it is picked off at the conclusion of the feast by natives of India, who are in waiting. The intervening chasm or cleft in the rock narrows as it goes down to an unknown depth: down this are every year thrown offerings such as gold leaf, gold rings, earrings, and other articles of jewellery to a considerable amount; and it is said that some of these also are recovered by the Kolāhs (natives of India) by means of long bamboos provided at the end with a ball of cloth dipped in some sticky substance. If it be asked, to what end this absurd waste? I answer, the Burman looks on it in the same light, as doubtless the Jews did on the consumption uselessly of *burnt* offerings; the motive is not any external good the act can effect, but the sacrifice of something we hold valuable to the honour of a superior power.

This pagoda is peculiarly sacred, not only on account of the impressive singularity of its natural surroundings, but also as being one of those containa 'Tsan-dau,' or hair relic of Gaudama. Thus saith the legend: A certain hermit, having received one of the hairs of the Lord, wandered about searching for a suitable spot where to enshrine it; in the meanwhile he reverently carried the sacred relic on his head. After some time he arrived on the summit of this mountain, and deposited the holy hair in the cleft of the rock, and erected the pagoda on the great boulder. From this legend is derived the name 'Kyeik-ethee-yŭh,' meaning 'the object of worship borne on the head of the hermit.'

Among the sights are two of the large bells

that are hung near pagodas in Burma. These bells have no clappers, but are struck with a deer's horn, sometimes with a piece of wood. They are not rung for the purpose of calling the worshippers together, but each person, on the completion of his devotions, before he leaves the pagoda precincts, strikes the bell three times, some muttering a formula as they do so. The meaning is to give notice to the Náts and to the four worlds of what they have been doing.

The two tall flagstaffs and streamers are also usual accompaniments of every pagoda and monastery. The one on the extreme right is a wooden one, surmounted by a figure of the 'heuza,' or sacred goose, the other in the foreground is a simple bamboo. The streamers are made of muslin, either flat and kept extended by small cross pieces of bamboo, or round, stretched on small bamboo hoops. They are merely votive offerings, and I believe similar objects are found in Tibet and China.

The large jar on the right has the word ရေး, 'yay,' meaning 'water,' written on it, and is one of those placed by charitable individuals for the public benefit.

Among these thousands assembled on the top of this wild mountain there is perfect order, good-nature, and happiness, and on the morrow after the full moon the hill side will be deserted and without the sound of human voice until the same time next year. These pilgrimages take place generally after the harvest, when the agricultural community is at leisure, and all the roads open for traffic.

Strange as it may sound to European readers, one of the greatest festivals among the Burmans is the funeral of an old and respected phoongyee. Indeed, the extraordinary scene of apparent mirth and levity, that seems associated with all funeral rites among the Burman Buddhists, is to a stranger one of the most incomprehensible things in the country. Yet it is evident that this custom is not the effect of any natural heartlessness, but has come to them with their religion, for we find in their sacred books, derived from the Pali, that the same or similar ceremonies were observed at the funeral of Gaudama himself. In the 'Malla lingara Wăttoo,' or 'Life of Gaudama,' it is related that, 'having arrived at the place, where the remains of Buddha were lying, the princes began to make offerings of flowers and perfumes with the greatest profusion, in the midst of dancings, rejoicings, and the continued sounds of all kinds of musical instruments.' If any one will take the trouble to compare the account of Buddhist funeral ceremonies as exhibited in Burma with those of the Brahministic Hindus, it will, I think, be seen that the marked difference is owing to the deep antagonism between the two religions, and is but the outcome of the teachings of Gaudama himself, who, when his favourite disciple was weeping for the death of one of his companions, said to him: 'Anandah, I have on former occasions endeavoured by my teaching to shelter your soul from the impressions caused by such emotions. Can it be possible that any occurrence, how painful soever, can warrant wailing and lamenting?'

In the following account of the obsequies of a Buddhist monk of standing and reputation in the order, it must be remembered that it applies wholly only to such as the popular consent deems worthy of peculiar distinction; the ordinary village monk is disposed of in much quieter fashion.

The ceremony is styled 'Phoongyee pyau,'[1] or 'the Phoongyee's return;' for, according to Burman etiquette, a phoongyee does not *die*; he *returns*, that is, to the Nát heavens.

As soon as a phoongyee has expired, the body is reverently washed by the Elders, who were his supporters. The body is then opened, the viscera extracted, and buried anywhere without ceremony. The cavity of the abdomen is filled with hot ashes and various preservative substances. Long swathes of white cotton cloth are wrapped as tightly as possible

[1] Pronounced 'byau.'

round the corpse from head to foot, over which are placed the yellow robes of the order. Another coarser wrapping of cotton cloth is tightly wound over this, and then thickly covered with black varnish, on which gold leaf is applied, so that the whole is gilt. A coffin is prepared from a single log hollowed out, which many old phoongyees keep in their monasteries ready for their demise. The body, having been placed in this, is left for some weeks to dry up, for most of such venerable and aged recluses are little more than a framework of bones covered with a withered skin. The cover is at length nailed on; the coffin is thickly covered with a resinous varnish, and gilt over. It is temporarily laid in state in the monastery, on a high daïs ornamented with tinsel, gilding, and paper lace, surmounted by a white umbrella or canopy of muslin, and is constantly visited by pilgrims from the surrounding country, who make their obeisances, and present offerings of flowers, &c., to it. This ends the first act.

The monks of all the subordinate or friendly monasteries, together with the native officials and Elders of the community, assemble in solemn conclave, and it is then decided about what expense shall be incurred in the funeral ceremonies, and how long the departed phoongyee shall lie in state, which depends a good deal on the time considered necessary to collect the funds, and may be three or four years. The whole country is then placed under self-imposed taxation; the phoongyees visit every place where they have any influence to obtain contributions; every person of any consequence, in however distant a town, who from connection with the deceased either by blood or spiritually as a former disciple, is appealed to for assistance. Some give money, some give necessary materials; one presents a dozen logs of teak, another a single large post of ironwood. As soon as sufficient funds have been collected, a building called 'Níbban Kyoung,' the 'Monastery of the Dead,' is erected for the reception of the body. With obscure and inferior monks this is only made of bamboos and thatch; but with a distinguished and venerated recluse such as we are now supposing, it is a substantial edifice, with large, handsome posts or pillars of ironwood or teak, roofed with shingles. This is open all round, or is only surrounded by a railing to keep out animals. In the centre, within a high sarcophagus, richly but rudely adorned with gilding, glass, mosaic work, and painting, is enshrined the coffin, to await, perhaps for four years, the final funeral rites. So closes the second act.

At length the preparations are complete; a fortunate day has been fixed on, and for weeks previous the town where the ceremony is to take place, and all the surrounding country, has been astir with the arrangements for and expectation of the great event. A wide open plain on the outskirts of the town having been completely cleared of any brushwood or long grass, towards one end of it is erected the funeral pile. This is one of those elegantly designed and proportioned, and from a distance tasteful looking, constructions of bamboos, mats, pasteboard, and tinsel that have been so often described in these pages, only this is on a much larger scale. It is between 30 and 40 feet square at the base, and rises in a series of constantly diminishing estrades up to about 20 feet. On the top of this platform is constructed a kind of cenotaph of boards covered with glass mosaic work and the usual gilding and tinsel decoration. This is intended for the reception of the body. At each corner of the cenotaph are often placed carved and painted figures of 'kinnaras,' fairies with a human face and bird's body, as guardian spirits. Above this towers a richly gilded and coloured many-turreted canopy, making the whole edifice 60 or 70 feet high. The lower basement is adorned at each of the four corners with smaller pinnacles, and the centre of each face has a miniature representation of the series of rising roofs that cover the steps leading up to large pagodas. The faces of the basement and of the successive estrades are decorated with rude paintings of all manner of subjects, sometimes with good taste appropriately pourtraying scenes in the various existences of Gaudama; at other times, with that strange perversity and levity so often cropping out in the Burman character, these paintings represent the most absurd and incongruous, and even, but this *rarely*, indecent subjects. At one end of the maidan (plain) are a number of huts for the accommodation of the phoongyees, of whom great numbers assemble in honour of their departed brother.

Every village, or quarter of the town, in some cases one or two private individuals in partnership, have been preparing each its contribution in the shape of 'Pyathats' and 'Padaytha-bins,' and drilling the maidens and youths in the posture dances that have been before described. The festival lasts for from three days to a week.

On the first day, generally in the afternoon, the procession is formed from the monastery where the body is lying, and, passing through the town, makes its way towards the open plain. The coffin is placed on a gigantic car, solidly constructed, and with four heavy solid wooden wheels, surmounted with a canopy similar in form and construction to that crowning the funeral pile. This lofty turret is drawn along by hundreds of men, and placed in the centre of the plain; the smaller spires or 'Pyathats' are disposed on the ground round the funeral pile, and the 'Padaytha-bins' with their offerings are presented to the phoongyees. The next day the *fun* begins. Two enormous ropes of twisted canes, or coir, if they can be got, are fastened to the funeral car in front and behind, long enough for a hundred people or so to hold on to each. At first a few lads and idlers begin pulling at either side, without much effect on the heavy mass. Each side call some more of their friends, then perhaps a headman of a village to which some of the lads belong joins in, the numbers on each side gradually increase and the car begins to oscillate, and the attention of the crowd is drawn towards it, the villagers of A and B villages coming up join their friends on either side. Suddenly a headman of B village sees the headman of A pulling away and inciting his men: he gives a yell, shouts for all his people, and rushes to the ropes, which are now well manned. The car, strongly made as it is, shakes and quivers with the strain, while the lofty canopy of elastic bamboo rocks violently backwards and forwards. I have seen the struggle last for an hour or more without either party stirring the car more than a few feet. The crowd, as usual, get violently excited; every man that has a friend or acquaintance in either village joins in; I have seen policemen on duty frantically waving their staves to encourage the contending heroes, or rush at some shirker and bring him back to the lists—it was no use taking notice of the want of discipline. Now perhaps one side gain the advantage, and with deafening shouts drag the car some paces; but lo! in rush fresh forces. Led by some excited old lady, all the women and girls of the losing village fly to the rescue, and mingle with their husbands, brothers, and lovers at the ropes. Now then—if you are men—'yoūkyā bā thā'—pull for very shame, till you snap the cables. Hurrah! 'lā byēe!' lā byēe!' it comes! it comes! and with a ringing cheer away we go triumphant some hundred yards or so.

What is the meaning of all this? Well, the chief meaning is, that it is supposed that the conquering village will get the better of their losing rivals in all sports, contests, or other matters during the year.

The afternoon of each succeeding day is spent in a similar manner; but, of course, there exists also the undefined pleasure of being one of a gay and happy crowd, all decked in their best, sunning themselves like peacocks. Then such a gathering brings together relatives and friends from distant villages, and affords opportunity for hospitality and kindness.

On the night before the last day of the festival

the coffin is removed from the car and placed in the cenotaph of the funeral pyre on an iron grating under which is a quantity of wood, made more inflammable by means of oil, resin, &c., mixed with which is generally more or less of fragrant woods and other odoriferous substances. Early on the day decided for the cremation, from the different villages parties begin to arrive with the appurtenances for the great event. These consist of rude rockets of every size, from a foot long and an inch calibre to monsters nine to twelve feet in length and a bore of six to nine inches diameter. All are crammed to the muzzles with gunpowder, the tubes being hollowed logs of wood strongly bound with cane. The larger ones are placed on rude cars with four wheels, while the smallest are hung on long guiding lines of cane or rope fastened at one end to a strong post, and at the other to some point of the funeral pyre. The object is to strike the pyre with the rocket, and fire the combustibles placed inside. Happy will be the village which owns the fortunate rocket, and great their prosperity during the ensuing year. But as rockets, even scientifically handled, are dangerous things, and there is nothing to prevent these monsters on wheels from turning round on the uneven ground, after having been ignited and started, and charging down breathing volumes of fire and smoke on the paralysed thousands of spectators, it behoves the authorities here to interfere, and see that every precaution, and above all order, is observed, so that no rocket shall be fired without permission or out of its turn.

Accordingly, the ground having been cleared, and the spectators kept at a safe distance, the larger rockets are placed in line about four or five hundred yards from the pyre. Each rocket is surmounted by some fanciful figure, such as a tiger or a man. All being ready, men of each village are allowed to go up in rotation and discharge their weapon. The smoke, the flame, the roar is tremendous, to the intense delight of the shouting crowd. But most of these large fire-monsters come to an ignominious end; tripped up by the inequalities of the ground, they tumble over, and lie uselessly spouting forth volumes of smoke. Others, after having been ignited, obstinately refuse to move, and stand vomiting out their fiery contents backwards amidst the derisive cheers of the spectators. These being all finished, the smaller aerial rockets are next attempted. Most of these also fail of the desired end: some burst; the guiding lines of others break; some stick half-way; others reach the funeral pyre indeed, but their life is exhausted and they fall harmless. One at length strikes as it seems with full power: a pause, a little smoke, then a little flame issues from one corner of the pyre, and a shout from thousands of throats proclaims the auspicious event. The crowd rushes forward, fire is carefully applied to the mass of combustibles under and around the coffin, and soon the whole is in a blaze. The people watch round, giving a cheer as each small pinnacle falls in, and wait anxiously looking for the lofty canopy itself to topple over into the flames. This event is greeted with a tremendous shout, and then all disperse homewards, happy and merry. A few Elders remain to watch the burning pyre till all is consumed, and the next day the monks of the monastery collect the fragments of half-burnt bones, and the ashes of the deceased, and reverently inter them in some fitting place, and perhaps a small pagoda is erected over them as a monument.

CHAPTER VIII.

SUPERSTITIONS, FOLK-LORE, ETC.

ALTHOUGH the Buddhist religion admits of no God, no Providence, to whom prayer for help or blessing can be addressed—nay, perhaps for that very reason—the Burman finds refuge in what might justly be called a second religion, for it is in truth the survival of his ancestral one. 'They believed that every animate and inanimate object had its soul or spirit; that the spirits of the dead could still make use of weapons, ornaments, or utensils, which they had used in life.' This to the present day is the creed of the Karens and other still uncivilised Hill tribes, who hem in their Buddhist cognates, the Burman and Mōn nations.

In spite of their long conversion, their sincere belief in, and their pure form of, Buddhism, which expressly repudiates and forbids such worship, the Burmans and Taleins (or Mōns) have in a great measure kept their ancient spirit or demon worship. With the Taleins this is more especially the case.

Indeed, with the country population of Pegu the worship, or it should rather be said the propitiation, of the 'Náts' or spirits, enters into every act of their ordinary life, and Buddha's doctrine seems kept for sacred days and their visits to the kyoung (monastery) or to the pagoda. In some of the least mixed Talein villages a reverence for the snake still exists. How far this is a relic of the old serpent worship it is hard to determine, as they do not like being questioned on the matter, and are rather ashamed of it. Almost every Talein village has a small 'Nát-sin,' or 'Náts' shed' placed, if possible, under a large tree just outside the village, in which are put fruit, flowers, rice, and other offerings for the 'Náts.'

These spirits of nature—'Nát' in Burmese, 'Nah' in Karen—must not be confounded with the Dewas or Devas of Hindoo mythology, to whom the Burmans apply the same word. These last answer to the Geni and Peris of Eastern story. Nor do the 'Náts' seem to represent quite the same idea, though more resembling the graceful Dryads and Oreades of Greek fable. They appear to be essentially Turanian, and to be the embodiment, if we may apply the term to spirits, of the soul or nature of every object in creation.

This system, which is almost mystical, in its fullest

development among the Karens, whose sole religion it is, becomes among the Burmans only a superstitious propitation for a temporary purpose of some unknown beings, who have power to injure them. Thus fishermen make a small shed termed a 'Nát-sin' near their fishery, in which every morning offerings of fruit, leaves, rice, or some such tribute is placed; if this were not done, they say the Nát would destroy the fish. A man going a journey through a forest, comes to a large and conspicuous tree; he halts, plucks a few leaves near, or perhaps takes a little boiled rice out of his bag, and places them as an offering to the Nát of the tree. In a boat-race, a preliminary row over the course is always taken, a man in the prow holding in his extended arms a tray or basin containing a cocoa-nut, bunch of plantains, betel leaves, &c., as an oblation to the Náts of the stream to ensure their causing no accident to the boat in the race. Among the agricultural class of the Taleins, hardly a day passes, that they do not thus in some way propitiate the unseen spirits of nature.

It naturally follows that this people have great faith in omens.

To meet a funeral, or a person crying when starting on a journey, is unlucky, and the journey should be postponed.

A snake crossing the road shows that the journey will be long.

To meet with mushrooms foretells a prosperous journey.

Any unusual wild animal or bird entering a house is a sign of great honour for the owner.

The earth-heaps thrown up by the white ants, if under a house, will bring wealth to the occupier.

The itching of the palms of the hand is a sign that some money will soon come into them.

Here is a little anecdote told to the writer in perfect good faith by the relatives of the heroine. In the time of Kong-boung Mien, the father of the present King of Burma, there were two officials of two neighbouring towns now in our territory, who were intimate friends, and had each a daughter Mā Mya Tsine and Mā Mya Galay, the latter's father being the lower and poorer of the two. One day, while Mā Mya Galay was quite a child, her little dress, being spread out to dry, was carried off by a kite. Her father, hailing the omen as one of future greatness for his daughter, from that day forth stinted himself to bring her up in luxury, and in a manner suitable to her hoped-for rank. In time, when she had arrived at maturity, Mā Mya Tsine being some years younger, the King passed down to Rangoon, and according to custom the chief official of the place, who was the latter's father, was called on to provide a damsel for the King's harem. He presented his daughter, hoping she would find favour in the monarch's eyes, but, as she was still a child, sent his friend's daughter Mā Mya Galay as her companion. As fate had decided and foretold, so it happened; the King conceived so great an affection for the latter, that he elected her one of his four queens or legitimate wives. The end of poor Mā Mya Galay was tragic. She was put to death by her husband's son and successor, the Pagán Men, on a charge of conspiracy, about A.D. 1846.

Like most half-civilised races, or rather like uneducated human nature generally, the Burmans have implicit faith in astrology, alchemy, and witchcraft.

In almost every bazaar, and at all large gatherings of people, will be found one or two old men sitting with a slate or a Burman writing-board before them, inviting the passers-by to have their horoscopes cast, and the best educated and most enlightened native officials will in any difficulty or trouble send for one of these diviners to consult the fates. One or two lucky hits will of course raise any special prophet's reputation throughout the country.

I knew a case, in which an old woman who had lost a suit in my own Court, consulted a soothsayer who advised her to appeal. She did so, but the judgment of the lower Court was confirmed: he told her to appeal to the Court above, and she again lost. On reproaching him with his false promises, he said all he had promised was, as the stars foretold, that she would gain the case, and there was still another Court, the highest in the province. The old lady took heart of grace, appealed a third time to the Chief Commissioner, won her suit, and joyfully told me the story herself.

Their system of astrology, like their astronomy, is founded on, if not identical with, that of the Hindus, from which it is derived. At the Court of Mandelay some eight or ten Brahmins are always maintained for the purpose of assisting and advising the King with their astrological calculations. The art of divination is expressly forbidden by the Buddhist creed. So strictly is this interpreted by the most bigoted phoongyees, that they do not teach in their monastery schools even the simple rules of arithmetic, as being the door to this forbidden art. The legend runs that, after the preaching of Gaudama, the people collected all the fish-traps, nets, and other implements for taking the life of animals, together with the four books of 'Bédin,' the 'Vedas' of Brahminism (but which were supposed to contain unlawful knowledge), and made a holocaust of them. But

'Mahn-Nát,' (the Dewadat of the Pali books, the Evil Spirit of Western theology) came and pulled some of the writings out of the fire and saved them. Thus the art is less perfect than it formerly was; at the same time it became associated with the great enemy and opposer of Gaudama and his religion.

There are among the Burmans and also the Shans many fervent believers and adepts in the alchemical art. As in Europe during the middle ages, there may now be found in Burma men of better education than their fellows, wasting time, health, and fortune in these visionary but absorbing pursuits. They may be laughed at by their neighbours for their individual want of success, but there is no Burman who does not firmly believe in the possibility of obtaining the grand secret of the philosopher's stone; though, indeed, he only believes what Sir Humphrey Davy himself said was *possible.* Of course this credulous spirit is constantly taken advantage of by clever rogues, and the Courts afford frequent instances of the most surprising simplicity. To give one:—

Two Burmans arrived in a Karen village, and, pretending that one of them was sick, obtained leave to stay for a few days in the small 'Kyoung,' or monastery, near the village. Here, when the simple villagers were paying their respects to the phoongyees or assembled to gossip, they gradually introduced the subject of making gold and silver, and after some time admitted that one of them was a master of the art. They then proceeded in presence of all to transmute some lead, and produced two lumps of silver about the size of a crown piece as the result, and presented a lump each to the phoongyee and the headman of the village. The cupidity of the latter was roused, and he begged them to operate on his behalf. He and his relatives produced 400 rupees (40*l.*) worth of coin and silver ornaments, which they handed over to the Burmans, who promised a three-fold out-turn. The usual juggling followed, and the silver, lead, &c., apparently deposited in three large pots, and placed in a room of the headman's house with strict injunctions that the room was not to be entered for four days. The next day the adepts had disappeared, but the simple Karens religiously waited for four days before they opened the covered pots to find a quantity of lead. When the case was tried, and the dupe reproached with his folly, he indignantly repudiated the imputation against his common sense, triumphantly pointing to the lump of silver in the magistrate's hands as ocular demonstration, that the prisoners were able if they chose to transmute the base metal, although in this case they had preferred to cheat him and reap the advantage themselves.

With so superstitious a race it may be supposed the belief in witchcraft is very strong. Reputed witches are very common, and whole families are sometimes credited with possessing this power. Any person afflicted with epilepsy, or with any unusual ailment, is at once set down as bewitched. A witch doctor, 'Hman Tsaya,' is sent for, and, after certain prayers and ceremonies, he calls on the witch within the possessed person to declare who he or she is, and to depart. This not being successful, he proceeds to beat the unfortunate possessed with a heavy stick, and the more the wretch howls the more his friends encourage the 'doctor' to 'lay it on;' for, say they, it is the witch that is really suffering the beating, and is howling *through* the possessed person, who himself feels nothing; but if the witch can be traced, she would be found bruised and groaning from the castigation.

In what follows it may be thought that a colouring has been given to perfect the singular resemblance with European ideas; but I have simply stated the common belief of the Burmans. When a person is supposed to be afflicted by a witch, the friends take about a handful of rice from the pot before any one has eaten of it, and cook a curry without pepper or other hot condiment in it. The rice is then placed in a sieve, and the curry poured on it. About dusk the sieve is placed on the ground at the front or back of the house, the person doing so striking the sieve seven times with the bamboo spatula used in cooking, calling out at the same time, 'Come, oh daughter of the village (a polite term for the witch), come and eat! here is no poison, nothing hot, nothing hurtful; we feed you from friendship.' The whole is then left, water having been poured on the ground round it, till morning, and the omens drawn as follows: If the witch is pacifically inclined, but wants a further offering, she leaves a small part of the rice, and the ceremony is repeated. If a blade or two of grass or thatch is found in the sieve, it is a sign the witch has no malice, and the afflicted person will soon be relieved. But if a piece of bamboo, earth, or, worst of all, charcoal be found, it shows deadly enmity, and small hope for the victim. Should a watch be kept after the food has been deposited, the witch will be seen to come and devour it in the form of some animal, as a dog, for instance. If the watcher then has courage to throw a knife or stick so as to wound or break the leg of the animal, which runs yelping away, next morning the witch, if she can be discovered, would be found with a similar injury to that received by the dog. The

Karens have a similar belief, adding that the witch can also take the form of another living person ; and relate how a man, being beaten at night by some one resembling his own nephew, the next night, by the advice of the young man, with one blow of his sword cut off the intruder's head. The next morning, hearing that a man had died in the village during the night, they quietly went to look at the body, and found that it was headless. Then they knew this was the nocturnal visitor. I need not point out the connection between these fancies and the German 'Wehrwolf.'

The old Burman custom for the trial of witches is the same as in England in former times: the thumbs and toes being tied together, the suspected person was thrown into the water, and sinking was a proof of innocence, floating of guilt.

The belief in the 'Evil Eye' is quite as common as it is in Italy or Spain. I have constantly seen, in villages where the people were not well accustomed to the sight of Europeans, a mother cover her child's eyes, if I looked in that direction, or even one little urchin would put its hands over a younger companion's eyes as I passed.

Are not these striking coincidences between the East and the West—relics of that primæval Shamanism which pervaded all the races of the Central High

Asian home from whence Aryan and Turanian both spread outwards in different directions?

The efficacy of philtres of all kinds is firmly believed in. I have two or three times found in my sugar or salt a curious little lump of dirt, as it seemed, composed of what I could not make out, but doubtless placed there by one of my attendants, in the hope I would unwittingly swallow it in my tea or soup, and my favour towards him would be ensured.

If a man has been rejected by a girl, he goes to the 'Hman Tsaya,' and engages him to make a small image of her containing inside a piece of her clothes, or of something which she has been in the habit of using. Certain magical charms or medicines also enter into the composition of the doll, which is then hung up or thrown into the water. Soon after this ceremony the girl is supposed to become mad.

The date and day of birth should never be mentioned before inferiors, or those likely to be ill-disposed towards the person, as they may be used in bewitching him: a knowledge of these facts being deemed a great help to the witch in her enchantments.

Peculiar diseases, especially epidemics, are popularly supposed to be the work of spirits, evil-disposed 'Náts.' If cholera or small-pox be in the neighbourhood, the roads into each village are guarded by magical formulæ, written on a board or piece of paper, and stuck up at the entrances to keep out the evil spirits. Should they unfortunately enter, and a death or two occur, other means must be resorted to. Suddenly, about sunset, on a preconcerted signal, the ears of a stranger would be greeted with a most bewildering and deafening din, caused by every one, man, woman, and child, in every house, beating the house walls, the floors, tin pans, anything to make a horrible noise, which certainly it would take a deaf spirit to withstand. This, repeated three nights, is considered very effectual in evicting the unpleasant visitors. Absurd as it may seem, I have been obliged, while living within a village, to suffer this to be done in my own house, otherwise my Burman servants would have been persuaded the spirits had found refuge there. Its practical effect was to drive me out, while it was going on.

In any cases in which the mind is affected as it were unnaturally, in delirious fever, or hypochondriasis and similar disorders, it is ascribed to a possession by the 'Náts' ('Nát pan tsā thee), and the assistance, not of the physician, but of 'Hman Tsaya,' is called in, and the demon sought to be expelled by incantations and exorcism.

These professors of magical arts are not looked on as reputable by the legitimate disciples of Esculapius, of whom there are two schools in Burma—the 'beindaw tsayas,' who administer drugs; and the 'dāt tsayas,' who give no medicine, but nourish the various 'elements' (dāt') of the body, of which there are sixty, by prescribing various sorts of food. As a learned man of *each* school is sometimes called in to attend a sufferer, and each acts independently of the other, the result to the patient may be imagined. Thus a fever case may just have been treated with some febrifuge by the one, when his learned brother will arrive, and decide that some element requires to be nourished by a dish of fowl's flesh cooked with chillies and assafœtida, and the recipes will be religiously followed.

The Burman doctors have no knowledge of surgery: here and there a very good 'bone-setter' may be met with, but operations, even simple blood-letting, they never attempt. They possess a certain empirical knowledge of the virtues of sundry herbs and drugs, but are always ready to fancy some latent quality in any new substance, or curious-looking stone or root, they may chance to get hold of. Yet they have many useful and powerful remédies in such diseases as fevers, bowel complaints, and the like. I have also known very old and obstinate sores, that resisted European treatment, yield to the native simples.

I should be ungrateful did I omit to mention the professional shampooers, who are always old women. Many a time have I obtained relief from rheumatic pains and indigestive flatulency by half an hour's shampooing; and, though anatomy is an unknown science in Burma, the knowledge these women have of the various muscles, tendons, and viscera in the human frame is wonderful. Although the operator was pressing very lightly, the firm and searching manner in which she followed up the ramifications of the cramped muscles, has often made me bite my lips with pain; and then the delicious sensation of relief, when a tangled knot of muscles seemed to come undone under her fingers.

The Burmans are subject to a disease, which has never, I think, attracted the notice of European medical men, or been described, except by Father Sangermano, and, as he had a good knowledge of medicine, I quote his account of it. 'There is a complaint found in this country only, to which all people are subject at a certain age. It is called "tet," a word signifying to mount, and takes its name from its commencing in the feet and ascending upwards through all the members of the body. It presents the appearance of a stupor or numbness, by which the patient is at last deprived of all feeling and even of speech. The Burmese attribute it to the wind; but its true cause seems to be the congealing and torpor of the humours, particularly of the nervous fluid, from the want of exercise, as also from the intemperate use of viscous and acid meats. . . . Its only cure seems to be a violent friction of all parts of the body with the hands to excite pain, and in this two or three persons are employed. Sometimes, where the hands produce no effect, they have recourse to their feet, and tread upon the sufferer with more or less violence, as the circumstances require, till animation is restored.' A servant of my own died in my verandah in this way, in an hour. He was in the prime of life, had not been ailing in any way, but suddenly complained to his companion of torpor in the lower part of the body, and asked him to shampoo him, and then to tread on him. He mentioned, as the torpor mounted higher, where he felt it, till it reached his chest, soon after which he expired suddenly, the whole happening while I was out for a ride.

As is generally known, the Burmans and Taleins of Pegu tattoo the body. This is done from below the navel to just below the knee. The tattooing instrument is a single split needle, set in a heavy brass socket, with which the operator pricks the pattern into the skin, the needle pen being filled with a preparation of indigo, and the marking is indelible. The patterns are generally the figures of lions, tigers, 'beloos' or devils, and dragons, the interstices filled in with dots. In old age the pattern gets blurred and lost, though the marking remains. It is considered unmanly not to be properly tattooed; boys begin to have a figure or two done on each thigh at about seven or eight years old, and when they reach twelve or thirteen they are generally fully tattooed, one thigh being completed at a time, with an interval of a few days between to lessen the iritation and fever. A dose of opium is often, or almost always, administered, and some sad cases of inadvertent poisoning by an overdose occasionally come before the Criminal Courts.

Some young fellows, who affect the character of 'fast men,' and others as fighting men, robbers, &c., who desire to charm themselves against dangers, have various figures of tigers, devils, and squares containing cabalistic signs or words, tattooed in red on their breasts, backs, and arms. This red tattooing is coloured with vermilion and fades after a time. The 'professors' (for it is considered a profession) delight to get hold of the white skin of a European to operate on, and our soldiers and even officers afford them many opportunities.

I knew a soldier of H.M.'s —th Regiment, who

got himself tattooed from his neck to his feet. On asking him the reason, his answer was: 'Well, sir! me and my comrade Jem is going to get our discharge home, and Jem he was in the show-line before he 'listed; so, when we gets home, he is going to show me as the man what was captured by the cannibals and tattooed, and I have learnt a little of this 'ere Burmese language to talk to the people.' Have any of my readers ever met or heard of this precious pair since?

The Shans, who belong to the same race as the Siamese, tattoo in a similar way from the navel down to the ankles; and the Karen-nees, an independent tribe on our north-east frontier, have in addition a device consisting of radiating lines resembling a rising sun tattooed on their backs, which is a clan badge, or distinctive mark of their tribe, assumed by every youth before he can claim to rank as a man.

The earliest European traveller in Burma, Nicolo Conti, in A.D. 1425, mentions this custom. 'All, both men and women, paynte or embroider their skinnes with iron pennes, putting indelible tinctures there unto.' It is either a mistake of Conti's, that the *women* were tattooed—for the travellers who succeeded him do not mention it when speaking of the subject, nor is it now practised—or else the custom died out as regards them very soon after his visit; but it is most probably an error.

What relation there is between this custom as it exists among the Indo-Chinese and the Polynesian races, would be an interesting subject for speculation; but it is worthy of remark that it is unknown among the Chinese, and also among the cognate Tibetan family. Absurd stories of its origin and reason have been printed, founded on the fables of the old travellers, which the wide extent of the practice would be sufficient evidence to confute after a little consideration.

One of the most weird and extraordinary superstitions among the Burmans is connected with tattooing, and is called 'Bandee-tha.' Certain among the professional tattooers, who, in addition to their legitimate business, claim far more mysterious knowledge, search eagerly for the flesh of a man who has been hung, or who died on a Saturday; most precious of all would be the body of a man, born, hung, and buried on a Saturday. Certain parts of the body, the nose, fingers, and ears especially, having been dried and carefully compounded with various magical drugs, the mixture is preserved. An instance has been known, where the relatives of a criminal who had been hung sold his body to these 'doctors,' as they are called, after it had been handed over to them for burial by the authorities. The writer once had a case in which, after, in the performance of his duty, having superintended the execution of a murderer, finding no relatives come forward to claim the body, caused it to be decently interred; but, in consequence of information received, on opening the grave a couple of days afterwards, the body was found mutilated as above described. When some credulous Burman wishes to become a great warrior, or, more probably, a great thief and robber, he applies to one of these 'doctors,' who directs him to procure a piece of flesh about six inches long from a human corpse. After sundry ceremonies, the figure either of a cat or a demon, 'beloo,' is tattooed on the patient's breast with the medicine prepared as before described, he all the while biting and chewing the piece of raw human flesh. The supposed effect of this wonderful and disgusting operation is to enable the man to leap like a cat prodigious heights and lengths—a hundred feet would be nothing; or else to endow him with the strength, ferocity, and power of a demon. It does not always, however, succeed in the way intended, as the patient sometimes goes mad instead, and frequents (it is said) the burial-grounds, tearing up and trying to devour the corpses; becomes, in fact, a 'ghoul.' I have not personally known such a case; but it is quite probable, considering the superstitious, excitable temperament of the Burmans.

'Kyats' (pronounced Jats) are elfs or goblins, who live in the earth mounds found in the forest. In the night they issue out, and their haunt would appear, to any mortal chancing on it, to be a large village, with men, women, and children going about, others cooking and weaving in the houses, and all the usual sights and sounds of village life. All this disappears at daybreak.

A certain damsel had a lover, who used to come and see her at night, and gave her presents of money and jewellery, which all turned into broken pieces of potsherd. The girl was induced to go with her lover at night into the forest, and came to a large village, where she saw all the people going about their usual avocations. In the morning all had disappeared, and there was nothing but the jungle and some ant mounds. Her parents then knew that her lover was a 'Jat,' but still could not conquer the girl's infatuation. She had some children by the elfish husband, and then she pined away. One day a witch doctor came to the house, and seeing the children running about, suddenly pointed to one of them and said, 'That is not a human child;' and then, looking at the girl's husband, said, 'That is a "Jat," not a man.' He then covered up the girl, the husband, and their children with a blanket, sprinkled it with some magical essence, and on withdrawing the cloth the 'Jat' and his elfish brood had vanished, and only the girl remained, wasted away to the bones.

A great witch doctor in the town of Thayetmyo, who had immense power over all the children of darkness, was one night called on by a stranger, mounted and leading a spare pony, to come and attend a sick person at some distance. His wife, fearing this was a device of the evil spirits, entreated him not to go, but he laughed at her fears, and set out with the messenger. On arriving at a large village quite unknown to him, as soon as they dismounted the steeds turned into palmyra leaves. Then he knew that he had been entrapped by the 'Jats.' His companion tried hard to induce him to lay aside his shoulder-bag, which contained a powerful charm and protection; namely, a piece of a phoongyee's broken begging-pot; but, knowing that, as long as he had that about him, he was safe, the poor man held fast to the bag. The goblin then swelled out to gigantic proportions, and threatened the doctor in all manner of horrible shapes. So the contest went on for a long time, until the adept, feeling his strength becoming exhausted, called on the 'Myin-byoo-shin' Nát (or Lord of the White Horse), the guardian Nát of the town of Thayetmyo, for help. Immediately the Nát appeared on his white steed, told the frightened man to cling fast to his pony, and escorted him through the goblin village and the forest to his home, on reaching which he fell utterly exhausted, and long remained in a dangerous state.

If a 'Hman Tsaya,' or magician, desires to terrify any one from spite, or to obtain presents, he goes at night to the cemetery and collects a handful of coals from several old funeral pyres. He then summons the ghosts of those who have been burnt on those spots, and, bidding them remember he is their master, orders them for seven nights to throw stones on the roof of such a one. The coals the magician deposits secretly in some corner of this person's house, and for seven nights the inmates are disturbed and terrified by the stone-throwing of the ghostly visitants.

A small monastery standing in a solitary position was one night burnt down. I ordered an inquiry by the native magistrate, who officially reported that there was no conceivable origin for the fire, which had begun on the very summit of the roof, and the only explanation he could offer was that '*ghosts had thrown a firebrand on it.*'

The Fatal Promise.

Once upon a time, a youth and maiden who deeply loved each other, made mutual vows of constancy, and swore that, whether they could marry or not, neither would take any other spouse. Thus they lived happily, till the youth had to go on some business to a distant town. When taking leave of his beloved they renewed their pledges of fidelity, and added, that if either should die when absent from the other, the dead body should not be buried until the survivor arrived.

The youth departed on his journey, and soon afterwards the maid fell sick and died. Then was beheld a wonder: when they attempted to remove the coffin, the efforts of the whole village were ineffectual to do so; the coffin remained as if rooted to the earth. Terrified at this prodigy, the villagers abandoned the place, leaving the corpse and the coffin as they were.

A few months afterwards the young man returned from his journey, and, as he neared his native village, he saw his beloved sitting on the river bank, dressed in her gayest finery. She called to him to know if he was well, and then said his mother was not there, but had gone to live at a village a little way up the river. He therefore went on to see his mother. On his arrival she began lamenting the death of his betrothed; on which he angrily chided her for such jesting, saying he had seen the girl only an hour or so before. His mother then told him all the circumstances; but he would not believe her, and after a little while went down the river in his canoe to the village of his betrothed.

He found her waiting for him, and she led him to her house, which seemed all perfect and in good order. They sat down and talked, the youth telling her how his mother had pretended that his beloved was dead.

'No,' said the girl; 'I don't look as if I were dead.'

Thus they sat talking till dusk, when suddenly the head, and then the body, of the damsel began to swell out to an unearthly and gigantic size before the astonished youth.

'Oh! my mother said true,' thought he, terrified at the sight.

'Oh! my mother said true,' echoed the spectre in a terrible voice.

'Oh, dreadful! why did I come?' thought the poor boy, as the eyes rolled in the horrible head.

'Why did I come?' again echoed the frightful form.

Mastering his terror in some degree, the youth pretended to play on his flute which he had brought, and in doing so intentionally let it fall through the bamboo floor. He tried to leave the house as if to pick it up; but the spectre stopped him, saying she would get it for him, and lolled out a long red tongue from the distorted jaws, which lengthened till it picked up the flute from under the house.

'Ah mai! ah mai!' whispered the mortal.

'Ah mai! ah mai!' echoed the voice.

'Oh! if I could get away!' he *thought*.

'If I could get away!' responded the spectre, in mocking irony.

With the hope of contriving some way of escape, the youth asked his terrible hostess to make a bed for him, as he was sleepy. She agreed, and went into the inner room, where, hearing a great noise, he peeped in, and saw her banging and tearing to pieces her coffin and bier, to get boards and mats to spread for his bed-place. When she invited him to repose, he made an excuse to go outside first and wash his feet. She consented, but tied a cotton thread to his foot as a security. As soon as the youth got outside he fastened the thread to a post, and took to flight. After a few minutes' pulling the thread (which broke short), the angry spectre knew that her prey had fled. Snatching up her coffin under her arm, she started in pursuit. Fear lent wings to the terrified lover, and he had just gained his home and was going up the house-ladder, when the pursuing spectre came up, and, with a 'Hey! cat,' threw her coffin at him and killed him on the spot.

When the neighbours discovered him, they went back to the old village, where they found the corpse of the damsel lying in her coffin, and had now no difficulty in removing it. They brought it away and burned it, with that of her lover, on the same funeral pyre.

CHAPTER IX.

WILD TRIBES OF BRITISH BURMA.

THE various tribes and clans in British Burma who fall under the designation of 'wild tribes' may be divided into two classes—those belonging to the Tibeto-Burman family, and the Karens. The former are to be found on the slopes of the Arracan Yōma (or range), chiefly on the western side, whilst the Karens are much more widely diffused all over the rest of the province.

The territory occupied by the tribes allied to the Burman race lies between Chittagong, a district of Eastern Bengal, and Independent Burma, Arracan, and the Lushai country. It is a wild, intricate congeries of mountain ranges, drained by two large rivers, the Koladan and Laymroo, and their affluents, covered by vast forests, only here and there broken by patches of elephant grass, or the insignificant clearings of the Hill men.

The tribes inhabiting these hills are the Chyins, or Chins; the Kumis, or Khwaymis; the Kyoungtha, or Rakhain; the Mroos, the Khoungtsos, the Chaws, and, northernmost of all, the Shindoos, or Shandoos. These last, though nominally within our frontier—at least their foremost clans, which are pushing further south from their own country every year—can hardly be said to be subject to British authority, and little is known of them except by name.

The Chyins are by far the most widespread and civilised of the tribes; they are found all over the Arracan range on both sides, southwards to Cape Negrais, and northwards into Burma Proper. They are being gradually pressed down into the plains by the wilder tribes behind, and in some places have settled as agricultural communities.

The next most powerful tribe are the Kumis, or Khwaymies, who occupy the upper courses of the Koladan River; the others are more insignificant, the Chaws now consisting of only a few families. All the tribes are subdivided into separate clans, often at deadly feud with each other.

It would take up too much space, besides which it pertains more to the domain of scientific discussion, to adduce the proofs of the affinity of these Hill tribes with the Tibeto-Burman race. A close examination and comparison will leave little doubt that these, together with the Kukis, Abors, and various Nága clans extending northwards and eastwards over the valley of the Brahmapútra, are only branches of the great Tibeto-Burman family, which they represent in its primitive state, making allowance for the deterioration caused by ages of isolation and barbarism. The differences in speech among these remaining fragments of our original stock are not, when we consider the circumstances of the case, nearly so surprising as their affinities.

Max Müller says: 'We hear the same observations everywhere where the rank growth of dialects has been watched by intelligent observers. If we turn our eyes to Burma we find that the Burmese language has produced a considerable literature, and is the recognised medium of communication, not only in Burma, but likewise in Pegu and Arracan.[1] But the intricate mountain ranges of the peninsula of the Irrawaddy afford a safe refuge to many independent tribes speaking their own independent dialects; and in the neighbourhood of Munipúra alone Captain Gordon collected no less than twelve dialects. Some of them, he says, are spoken by no more than thirty or forty families, yet so different from the rest as to be unintelligible to the nearest neighbourhood. The Rev. N. Brown, who has spent

[1] The Professor seems to forget that the Arracanese and Burmese are the same race, and that the former in speaking Burmese only use their mother tongue.

his whole life in preaching the Gospel in that part of the world, tells us that some tribes who left their native village to settle in another valley *became unintelligible to their forefathers in two or three generations.'*

The principle of the dialectic growth of language under similar circumstances, among the various broken units of an uncivilised tribe, has been exemplified in other parts of the world; but perhaps it is nowhere more striking than in these regions. Among the Nága tribes on the borders of Assam sixteen different dialects, mutually unintelligible, exist in a circle of twenty miles.

The affinity of the Arracan Hill tribes with the Burman race has been recognised by actual observers like Sir A. Phayre, and by most modern ethnologists; and we may, I think, go further, and embrace also in the same family most, if not all, of the many tribes in the valley of the Brahmapútra.

The similarity in language and configuration between these various tribes extends in a great measure to their manners and customs. They have, with few exceptions, preserved the primitive spirit worship of their Turanian progenitors, of which the reverence paid to the 'Náts' among their Burman brethren, although Buddhists, is a survival. It is doubtful if they have any idea of a Supreme benevolent Creator; all worship is directed to the spirits of the rivers, woods, mountains, and rocks, who alone have power to avert evil or bestow good. Almost every object in nature is supposed to have its presiding or indwelling spirit. Their oaths are generally taken by drinking the water out of a jar in which a musket, spear, sword, a tiger's and a crocodile's tooth, and a stone hatchet or 'celt' (which they deem a thunderbolt), have been immersed, calling on the spirit of each of these means of death to punish the committal of perjury. They have sundry devices by which they think they may 'dodge' the spirits. The Chyins all point to Upper Burma, near the Khyen-dwin River, as their original seat; and all endeavour, if possible, to transfer thither at certain intervals the bones of their dead, to find their last resting-place in the ancestral burying-ground. They believe in the existence of a future state, in which the good remain in perpetual happiness—that is to say, in a state of unlimited feasting and drinking. The soul of a wicked man after death, they hold, goes to a dark cave, where there is a great heap of the entrails of every kind of animal. The disembodied soul puts forth its hand and blindly draws one of these entrails from the heap, and in its next state of existence it becomes an animal of the species to which that entrail belonged. Very wicked men have not this chance given them; they become, strange to say, butterflies. Among some other tribes, the bones of the dead, together with food, arms, and various domestic implements, are placed in a miniature house in the jungle outside the village, and in some cases an ox, goat, or some animal is tied down to a picket near to die unless it can free itself. This is but a survival of the Turanian customs, brought with them from the regions of High Asia. A death, especially that of a man of influence, is the occasion of a great expenditure in the way of feasting; numbers of buffaloes, oxen, and gayals (mountain cattle) are slaughtered, both as a propitiation of the spirits and to provide material for the feast, and hundreds of pots of 'khoung,' or rice-beer, are brewed. The skulls of all slaughtered cattle are carefully preserved and form a kind of wealth, the importance of a chief being shown by the number of skulls arranged round his house. The slaughter of animals is a necessary accompaniment of every important event, whether it be the preparation for a raid, or the conclusion of a treaty of alliance or peace.

The Chyin account of the genesis of the human race is as follows: After the earth, sun, moon, and stars had appeared—though to what cause these owed their origin is not clear—the earth of its own productive and generative power gave birth to a woman, who was named Hlee-neu. She produced a hundred eggs, from which were born the different races of men. One egg, which failed to hatch with the others, she threw away; but a certain bird found it and sat on and hatched it, when it produced two beings, a boy and a girl. These two were separated before they grew up; and the boy, having no mate, took a bitch to wife, and lived in the valley of the River Khyen-dwin, or Chyin-dwin, in Upper Burma. After some time the girl and he met again, and he wished to make her his wife; but, as they were brother and sister, they went and consulted their great mother, Hlee-neu. She ordered that the bitch which the man had married should be killed, and then they should marry, and that among their descendants in all time brothers' sons should intermarry with brothers' daughters. This they give as the origin of two of their peculiar customs—the sacrificing of dogs to the spirits (and eating them afterwards), and the right a man has to claim his cousin on the father's side as his wife. The great mother, Hlee-neu (query, Nature personified), is supposed to be the author of all their laws and customs.

Among these tribes polygamy is the rule, and the chastity of unmarried girls is not much regarded;

indeed, a man thinks it rather a matter of rejoicing to marry, and for his wife to have a child a week afterwards, even though he knows it is not his. On the death of a Chyin chief his eldest son is bound to take all his father's wives, except his own mother, and any posthumous children of his father's are *his* children. The object of this law is to keep property in the chief's family. Another fixed rule is that the eldest son must marry the youngest daughter of his father's eldest sister.

The greatest peculiarity of the Chyin tribe is the practice of tattooing the faces of their women while young. This is not a slight line or spot here and there, to serve as a beauty mark; but the whole face down to the lower bend of the jaw is completely covered, as with a black mask, with a tattooing of close transverse lines, in marked contrast with their natural yellow skin; and a more hideous disguise cannot be conceived. They can afford no satisfactory reason for this custom: one which is offered is that the Burmans in former times were accustomed to carry off their maidens for the king's use; another is that the custom was imposed by the men to ensure the fidelity of their wives; but neither of these reasons would seem to account sufficiently for the origin of so strange a disfigurement. It has also been ascribed to the desire to be able readily to identify their women if carried off by other tribes in their continual wars; but in such a case we should expect them to put some mark for the same object on the male children also, who are deemed of far more importance than the female in all fighting savage tribes.

The Khwaymi women, on the contrary, are rather good-looking when young, though possessing the sturdy, squarely-built forms of all Hill people, which are fully set off by their dress, consisting simply of a short dark-blue kilt reaching to the knee, fastened round the waist with a belt ornamented with beads, and open at the side; while across the breast is worn a sash or narrow strip of cloth. The Chyin women wear a kind of short gaberdine on the body, like the Karens.

The state in which all these tribes have for ages lived is that of a constant warfare and raiding, tribe against tribe, and even villages of the same tribe against each other. The most trivial cause is sufficient to establish a vendetta, which then goes on increasing in intensity as more and more victims are added. Two or three years ago one of our officers brought to a close a feud that had subsisted between two villages for over, it was said, a hundred years, and had cost many lives. The origin of it was that a man of one village had lost his pipe in the other, and suspected it to have been stolen. Finally the feud was compromised by a payment to the value of Rs. 300 (30*l.*).

Not only is *raiding* a sacred duty when undertaken against hereditary foes, but it constitutes the greatest excitement and delight of these wild races; no disasters, no dangers, can extinguish the desire for it. One of the chiefs had, when a young man, been the head of a flourishing clan numbering eighty to one hundred houses. By constant reverses the tribe became reduced to a miserable remnant of ten hearths. He collected his remaining warriors, made a final raid on his enemy, slaughtered some ten or twelve men and women, and then moved with all his belongings into safety across the British boundary, and settled there as our subject, content to give up his dearly loved independence for the satisfaction of having gained the last successful throw in the game of vengeance.

In the year 1841 Sir Arthur (then Lieutenant) Phayre writes: 'The Hill tribes within British territory may, as regards their relation with the Government, be divided into two classes: first, those near the plains; second, those residing at a greater distance, and whose country is inaccessible for ordinary purposes. Among the second class no inquiries are made regarding the number of cultivators, but the chief of the clan pays a fixed sum yearly as a token of his fealty. The tribes of this class are not interfered with in their internal arrangements; but of course they are bound to abstain from all attacks on tribes within the British frontier, and indeed beyond it. Too frequently, it is to be feared, they join in the former, or furnish information which leads to them.'[1]

The true meaning of this is that the tribes were necessarily left to do pretty much as they liked, any extraordinary aggression on their part being condoned on the slightest sign of submission, by which the wily savages, who lost nothing by a few penitent words and promises, secured the substance for the shadow. A few cases in which their contumacy led to an attempt at punishment did not end very successfully. Within the last few years, however, the tribes have learnt to respect the British authority, the police outposts have been pushed far up the country, and our officers have succeeded in gaining the confidence and esteem of the people so far that even some of these wild, lawless chieftains beyond our nominal boundary have lately submitted their differences to our arbitration. 'Raiding' has become less common; and there is no doubt that opening up of the country, and the introduction of some of the products, and thereby of the wants, of civili-

[1] *Journ. As. Soc. Beng.* vol. x. p. 701.

sation among them will gradually develop peace and order. Salt is the greatest luxury and want they have, and among the remoter tribes raids are often made simply for the purpose of obtaining stores of salt from the villages nearer the plains. This places a powerful means of enforcing submission in our hands, as by laying an embargo on the obtaining of salt by any recusant villages, they are soon brought to reason. Within the last year or two men of distant clans, whose fathers had never been more than a few miles outside their own villages, have been met with, staring open-mouthed at even the trifling signs of civilisation to be seen in a frontier police station.

One of our officers gave me an account of the first interview of one of these wild men with a European. The officer was lying on his bed in a little room inside the stockaded police post, which had a narrow gate with an armed sentry on guard; the Hill man, with the minimum of clothing, was introduced by a smart sergeant, who coaxed him to approach. He cautiously and distrustfully, and with great persuasion, advanced stooping to the bed; when close to it he gave one long, steady look at the white man, suddenly with a yell threw himself up straight, turned round, dashed out of the room through the gate, upsetting the armed sentry, rushed across a little stream at the bottom of the stockade, and, clambering like a monkey sheer up the side of the opposite mountain, never stopped till he was lost to sight in the forest.

There is not much to be gained from a closer study of these tribes, even in a scientific point of view. Once the fact established of their mutual relationship and their connection with the Tibeto-Burman family, the minor differences in language and customs are not worth noting; for man in his savage state is not a pleasing object, and his observation is only useful to us when it affords data to science.

Dr. Logan justly remarks: 'Perpetual aggressions and frequent contests, extirpation of villages, and migrations mark the modern history of nearly all these Tibeto-Burman tribes, and of the different clans of the same tribe. Their normal conditions and relations, while extremely favourable to the maintenance of a minute division of communities and dialects, are opposed to any long preservation of their peculiarities. We find the same tribe separating into clans and villages, permanently at war with each other, Kuki fleeing from Kuki, Singpho from Singpho, Abor from Abor. We can thus understand how in such a country, and before the Aryans filled the plains, the lapse of a few centuries would transform a colony from a barbarous Sifan clan, descending the Himalaya by a single pass, into a dozen scattered tribes, speaking as many dialects, and no longer recognising their common descent.'[1]

The system of agriculture pursued and most of the important matters of domestic economy are similar among the tribes of which we have been speaking, and the far more important tribes of the Karen race. To avoid repetition, these will be considered in reference to the latter people; but it will be seen that the customs of both on the above points are due to a similarity in physical and local surroundings, and not to any connection between the races. Outwardly the ordinary observer would see little distinction between the wilder specimens of the Karens and the same class of Chyins; but we shall find that their traditions, their religion, and social customs all point to a diversity of origin.

The Karen tribes are scattered over the mountain ranges east of the Irrawaddy River, though a great number of the most civilised and important tribe, the 'Sgans,' have now settled down in the plains as regular agriculturists. Among none of these tribes is the word 'Karen' recognised by themselves as a national appellation. Karen is a term which we have adopted from the Burmans, and the meaning of which is not very clear. Most of the tribes, like

[1] *Journ. Ind. Arch.* vol. ii. p. 82.

many other savage races, adopt as their national name the word 'man' in their language—that is, they are 'men' *par excellence*: thus the Sgans call themselves 'Pgha-ka-nyo,' 'men,' and the Red Karens, 'Kă-yá,' 'men;' but they have no comprehensive appellation for the whole race or nation.

They have attracted more attention than any of the rude races of these regions, owing to the readiness with which they at first accepted the teachings of the Christian missionaries, and the singular and quasi-biblical traditions found amongst them. The American Baptist missionaries, men of learning like Drs. Wade, Mason, and Cross, have carefully studied their language, their character, and traditions; and if they were at first a little too eager in building theories out of the strange facts they observed, it is an excusable fault common to most discoverers, and does not vitiate the plain statements made by them. The peculiar feature that stands out prominently distinguishing the Karens as a race from all the peoples around them is their universal and vivid tradition of their former possession of a purer religion than their present worship of the spirits of nature, and the embodiment of that religion in writings now lost, even to the very trace of letters amongst them. Within the last forty years the missionaries have reduced their language to writing, adopting a modification of the Burmese alphabet to express it, and they now possess, for a semi-savage race, a very fair literature. Their European teachers have so identified themselves with the people that in all things connected with their language, religion, and traditions, we can only fall back on what the missionaries have written as affording the best information.

The Karen language is different, both in construction and vocabulary, from the Burman. It resembles Chinese in possessing six tones besides the simple root, each tone forming a separate word with a different meaning. That is, for example, the combination of letters 'me,' may be pronounced with six different tones or inflexions of the voice, according to which its meaning is 'fire,' or 'sand,' or 'ripe,' &c.

Dr. Mason says: 'Their traditions point unequivocally to an ancient connection with China, for Ti or Tien is spoken of as a god inferior to Jehovah, and offering to the manes of their ancestors is as common among the Karens as it is among the Chinese.' 'Among the Kay or Ká tribe (of Karens) when a chief or any other slaveholder dies, one of his slaves is said to be buried alive with the corpse to wait on him in the next world—a custom that formerly existed in China. It must not, however, be forgotten that both these are not purely Chinese, but primitive Turanian, customs.

Dr. Logan writes: 'The highly monosyllabic, vocalic, and tonic character of Karen appears to have been caused by long and intimate connection with the Chinese. That it came directly and deeply under the influence of that language, and did not receive its Chinese element through the Burman, is further shown by the Chinese vocables it has acquired.'

The Karen traditions on the point have been mentioned, and their physical characteristics support the theory. That the Chinese at an early period in their history possessed a purer faith than their now popular one, is shown by their earliest books. 'The deep impression of religious faith on the national mind continues to be apparent throughout the history of the Shu King, terminating B.C. 650. It was during the time also that the Shi King, the invaluable collection of old national poetry, was written; and here the same reverence for the Supreme Ruler, and faith in his providential government of the world, are abundantly manifest. Monotheistic faith only became weakened on the arrival of an age of speculation, in the latter part of the Cheu dynasty.'[1]

[1] Edkins's *China's Place in Philology*, p. 28.

This faith the Chinese probably brought with them from the cradle of the human race in the plains of Mesopotamia, from which they were among the earliest immigrants. However that may be, they were the only race that we know of having held such a faith in the regions eastward of Iran, and there is little if any objection to the idea that the Karens drew their inspiration thence.

It is to be regretted that the missionaries have been induced, by a preconceived notion of a Mosaical or Jewish origin, to give the highest colouring to traditions and words that are sufficiently singular and striking if left in their simple form. The Karens have, no doubt, a wonderful conception or tradition of a Supreme Being, whom they name 'Y'wah.' The meaning of this word is 'to flow,' as a river or stream; and it is always coupled with 'Htoo,' which means 'perpetual.' In their carefully preserved oral traditions it is said: 'Y'wah (God) is immutable, eternal, and existed at the beginning. He was from the beginning of the world. He existed in the beginning of time. The life of God is endless. God is perfect; he is good. God is omnipotent, but we have not obeyed him. God created man anciently. He has a perfect knowledge of all things to the present time. The earth is the footstool of God. His seat is in the heavens. He sees all things, and we are not hid from him. He is not far from us. He is in our midst.'

All this is very sublime; and, although there is too great a disposition to use the *exact words* of our English Bible, I believe it conveys very fairly the meaning and feeling of the original. But, unfortunately, this same 'Y'wah' is made the subject of the most absurd and puerile myths and stories. We find an equally grand conception of the one God among the Mexicans (also a Mongoloid race) united with the basest and most bloody rites of heathenism.

The most singular portion of the Karen tradition is that referring to the creation and the early history of mankind, and to their own former possession of written books. They say: 'Y'wah created man. Of what did he create him? He created man at first from the earth, and finished the work of creation. He took a rib from the man and created the woman. He created the soul (spirit). How did he create spirit? The Father God said, "I love these my son and daughter; I will bestow my life upon them." He took a particle of his life and breathed into their nostrils, and they came to life and were man. Thus God created man. God made food and drink, rice, fire, and water, cattle, elephants, and birds.'

The name of the first man and woman were 'Tha-nai' and 'E-u.' The Karens have preserved these early traditions in the form of poetic couplets; one of their characteristics being a natural love of melody and of music, which develops itself as soon as they have the opportunity, as among the Christian converts. The following lines give the tradition of the 'Fall:'—

Y'wah in the beginning commanded,
But Nauk'plau[1] came to destroy.
Y'wah at first gave command,
Nauk'plau maliciously deceived unto death.
The woman E-u, and the man Tha-nai,
The malicious fiend enviously looked upon them.
Both the woman E-u, and the man Tha-nai,
The Serpent regarded with hatred.
The great Serpent deceived the woman E-u,
And what was it that he said to her?
The great Serpent deceived them unto death,
And what was it that he did?
The great Serpent took the yellow fruit of the tree,
And gave it to Y'wah's holy daughter;
The great Serpent took the white fruit of the tree,
And gave it to Y'wah's son and daughter to eat.
They kept not every word of Y'wah—
Nauk'plau deceived them. They died!
They kept not each one the word of Y'wah,
And he deceived and beguiled them unto death.
They transgressed the words of Y'wah.
Y'wah turned his back and forsook them;
After they had broken the command of Y'wah,
Y'wah turned from them and forsook them.

The prose version of the legend, containing the conversation between the Tempter and E-u, her

[1] The name of the Evil Being.

persuasion of the man, and their punishment by the Lord God, so closely resemble the Mosaic account that it is really almost impossible to repress grave doubts of the spontaneity of its origin among the Karens; and yet whence derived? However much they have Europeanised and embellished their native myths after their intercourse with the missionaries, there is not the slightest doubt that these existed amongst them prior to their earliest intercourse with Europeans. It was their very belief in these legends, as having been contained in those books long lost to their nation, that induced them to listen so readily to the teachers who suddenly appeared among them with *a Book*, out of which they taught words so strangely agreeing with their own traditions. Moreover, these ideas are not found merely among the tribes that have received the Gospel, but everywhere among the heathen Karens, though in different degrees of completeness.

With regard to the great Evil Being, the Tempter, they say:—

> Nauk'plau at the beginning was just,
> But afterwards transgressed the word of God.
> Nauk'plau at the first was divine,
> But afterwards broke the word of God.
> God drove him out and lashed from his place,
> He tempted the holy daughter of God.
> God lashed him with whips from his presence,
> He deceived God's son and daughter.

Their tradition respecting their lost books is, that formerly God gave them books written on skins containing his law; but these books the Karens carelessly lost, and then the knowledge of God and how to worship him departed from them, except as a misty tradition of their ancient wise men, and they had nothing left to protect them from the powers of evil but to propitiate them as they now do. The description of these lost books is most curious, and is given according to the version of Dr. Mason.

> The palm leaf book that is written in circles,[1]
> The letters of the palm leaf books
> Teach ancient wonders:
> The pages of the palm leaf books
> Show wonders of antiquity.
> God sent us the book of *skin*,
> It is at the feet of the King of Hades;
> The book of *one-sided* letters, the letters ten,
> The book of one-sided letters, of letters many,
> All men could not read.

Allowing for the attempt to render poetically in English the language of the original poetic couplets, there is in the above a noteworthy point—namely, the contrast drawn between the palm leaf books with round or circular letters, such as their neighbours, the Burmans, Mōns, and Shans possess, and these sacred books on skin written with one-sided (probably angular) characters. It may also be observed

[1] *i.e.* in circular characters like the Burmese, &c.

that parchment for writing is quite unknown to all these nations, and even to the Hindus.

If the traditions above referred to are singular from their coincidence, as far as they go, with the Mosaic story, perhaps it is equally singular that they go no farther than the 'Fall' of man, and contain no allusion, at least none at all clear, to the great Cataclysm of the 'Deluge,' the tradition of which has been found so generally diffused among the early myths of other savage races. This fact is in itself almost sufficient to dispel the idea that the Karens derived the traditions they have preserved to the present time from any early intercourse with Semitic nations, or at a later period with Europeans, for had such been the case they would have infallibly possessed some traces of the legends of the Flood and the Dispersion. Dr. Mason thought he had discovered such; but, with every wish to find them, he was constrained to admit that they were very faint, and can hardly be taken into account. It must not be supposed from the above that the Karens are a simple Monotheistic race, preserving in some wonderful manner the primæval form of a natural religion. The pure and often sublime conceptions that have been mentioned are but a kernel enveloped in a coarse husk of the most childish and fantastic legends; and, moreover, they do not any longer profess to worship their Father God and Creator, Y'wah. He has departed from them; they know nothing of how to serve him; and so, as the whole world is filled with demons and various spiritual beings more or less malevolent and powerful, they must perforce devote themselves to the never-ending task of propitiating these spirits. They have no images, nor, properly speaking, any visible object of worship; the invisible and spiritual beings pervading all nature do not, as they believe, *deserve* any reverence; but, God having forsaken them and left them at the mercy of these beings, they are forced for self-preservation to appease their enmity or gain their good-will by prayers and offerings.

The demon worship obtaining among the Karen tribes is similar to that of the Tibeto-Burman Hill tribes to the westward. The word 'demon' is here to be taken in its old Greek sense, 'dæmon sed non diabolus,' as signifying a spirit, but by no means necessarily an evil one. The labours of the Christian missionaries among the Karens have, however, rendered our knowledge of their religion much clearer than any we possess of that of the Arracan tribes, though there is reason to believe that among the Chyins, Kumis, and their kindred, the religious sentiment is merely a blind dread of the invisible and unknown, of which they could give no reasonable account to themselves or to others. It must not be inferred, from the slight and condensed sketch that follows of their psychology, that such are the ideas of every wild Karen to be met with, or that even the best informed among them could so express his own rude conceptions; but to render intelligible the thoughts and ideas gleaned here and there among them by various observers, we must clothe them in a European dress. We must also remember that there are great differences among these tribes intellectually as well as physically. The belief in the immortality of the soul and a future state, which is common to most of them, is entirely rejected by others, who hold that the life of man, as of animals, ends with death. It is, therefore, an account of the various beliefs existing among them, rather than a succinct description of a defined religious system, that is offered.

The most important point is that which teaches the existence of a soul or spirit in every object, animate and inanimate, in the most insignificant and the mightiest in nature. This they call 'Lá,' or 'Ka-lá.' The word itself means 'pure,' 'transparent.' We may perhaps express it as 'essence,' but it is very difficult actually to define it. We may here, however, trace another connecting link with the Chinese, with whom 'Lé' is 'spirit or mind,' and also 'fate.'

Not only animals, trees, plants, have their separate and individual 'ka-lás,' but spears, knives, arrows, stones, &c. 'It would seem to be simple self or individuality, or the general idea of the object,'[1] the Ego of the metaphysicians. When the 'ka-lá' is absent the objects dies, or is destroyed, or does not come into existence. To illustrate the last idea may be given the prayer after the planting of the rice: 'Oh! come rice ka-lá! Come to the field, come to the rice, come with fructifying power of both genders. Escape from the rat, the elephant, the horse. Oh! rice ka-lá! come to the rice!' The idea is that the 'ka-lá' of the rice sown may not be in it, but must be called from some other place, and may be caught and devoured on the way by some bird or beast; for the strangest point is that this 'ka-lá' does not always remain in the object, but wanders forth, and any accident preventing its return causes death in a short time. This is the case with plants and animals.

The human 'ka-lá' exists, before the man is born, in some mysterious region, whence it is sent forth by God; 'it comes into the world with him, it remains with him until death, lives after death, and, for aught that appears to the contrary, is immortal. Yet no moral qualities are predicated of it. It is

[1] Dr. Cross.

neither good nor bad, but is merely that which gives life to mortality.'[1] There is a great distinction made between it and the 'thah,' the human heart or soul. As it was expressed by a native: 'When we commit sin, it is the "thah" which sins. Again, when we perform any good action, it is the "thah." Praiseworthiness or blameworthiness is alone attributed to the "thah."' The 'ka-lá' is not the soul, and hence has no moral responsibility.[2] It is remarkable that this doctrine of the *tripartite* nature of man—body, soul, and spirit—should be found so plainly and elaborately developed among these simple savages. The 'ka-lá' is constantly in the habit of wandering forth from its body, and its continued absence would cause death. This idea gives rise to further weird beliefs in the 'Therets,' or spirits, who lie in wait to seize and devour these errant 'ka-lás,' and in the 'wees,' or sorcerers, who have the power of summoning back the wanderers even from the land of shadows.

In these days of spiritualism the account of the following experiment may be interesting, for the belief in which by the Karens, though not for its truth, the writer can vouch. Dr. Cross says: 'One method of ascertaining whether the "ka-lá" has actually been destroyed or not may illustrate a fact of electric or animal magnetism. The rude coffin

[1] Dr. Mason. [2] Dr. Cross.

containing the corpse is placed in the middle of the floor. A slender rod of a peculiar kind of bamboo is thrust through a hole in the lid, so as to be in contact with the body. An attenuated thread is tied to the upper end of this rod, and small tufts of raw cotton, alternating with lumps of charcoal, are tied along the thread till they nearly reach the lower end, on which is fastened a silver or copper ring. Under the ring is placed a cup with a hard-boiled egg in it, which nearly comes in contact with the ring, which hangs over it. The ring soon begins to draw down towards the egg, it is said, and to sway back and forth. The force is sometimes so great that the thread is broken. This is the best consummation of the omen. If the thread breaks, the ring is picked up and put in the coffin; for it is inferred that the "ka-lá," though not permitted to destroy life, is nevertheless present, and is not divorced or irrecoverably lost. The experiment sometimes fails; there is no acting of the ring. In this case the omen is bad. The "ka-lá" is destroyed, and there is no hope for the happiness of the departed.'

This extravagant superstition seems in some way connected with the old form of dactyliomancy, or divination by a ring, except that in this latter process the ring was held in suspension by a *living* person.

Without the 'ka-lá' the man can no more exist

in the future state than he can in this. Mason says: 'The Lás (ka-lás) of some go to Hell, where they suffer punishment; while others go to the Deva Heavens, where they enjoy happiness.' 'Although in this state, the "lá" and the man himself, the Ego, are said to be distinct, yet in nearly all the descriptions of the Future State the man seems to be absorbed in the "la;" and, inconsistent as it is with previous representations, it then appears equivalent with the Soul.'

A simple, uneducated race like the Karens, possessing so singularly complicated a psychological system, derived from and handed down by tradition, cannot be expected to reason logically on all points; and it need not excite wonder that there are contradictions in some details, which, moreover, may be only apparent and caused by the want of union between Eastern and Western modes of thought and expression.

Besides his 'ka-la,' every man has another principle or spirit attendant on him, called 'tso,' which is interpreted 'power,' 'influence.' This may perhaps be defined as 'Reason,' guiding and controlling every man. In addition to heaven and hell, the abodes of bliss and punishment, the Karens have a third region, 'Plu,' which may be designated Hades, whence in due time the departed may be transferred to one of the two other states, according to the judgment of 'Koo-tay, the King of "Plu," or King of the Dead.'

It would take too long to enter on all the beliefs respecting ghosts and various classes of spiritual beings, some fiercely malevolent. It is sufficient to say that the Karen lives his daily life in an atmosphere of most intense spiritualism—the air, the water, the woods around him teem with invisible, intangible, and often malicious beings, rivalling in grotesqueness and number the wildest fancies.

If what has gone before has been clearly followed by the reader, it will be understood that the worship paid to the 'Náts,' or Spirits of Nature, is not one of love or even veneration, but simply of fear and propitiation. It is only to entreat the spirits not to afflict him with sickness or other bodily calamity, or to remove those afflictions which he believes have come from them, that the Karen addresses these spirits with prayers and offerings.

One of the most important parts of this worship is that paid to the spirits of their ancestors. After cremation the remains of the bones are carefully preserved by the nearest relatives, and every year a grand festival is held, during which the bones of all of the clan or family who have died during the year are solemnly carried to the tribal common burial-place, which is most religiously kept secret from all of a different race, and is generally situated on some most distant and inaccessible mountain, the whereabouts of which is unknown to all save themselves, and is called 'Ayo-toung,' or 'Hill of Bones.' There, although it is very difficult to learn the facts from the Karens, it is believed they are finally deposited, with the best of the clothes, arms, and valuables of the deceased. This is another point of connection with the Chinese; for we know that the tissue-paper figures of animals, clothes, money, &c., buried at a Chinese funeral are but a survival of an older practice, when the actual objects now represented were sacrificed on the tomb.

Both these customs of a particular tribal burying-place, and the offering the most valued possessions of the deceased for his use in the land of spirits, are found among many widely separated savage races; they almost seem instinctive ideas of human nature, but are, perhaps, most strikingly developed by the Mongolian nations.

The problem offered by the singular religious traditions of the Karens may afford matter for speculation and theory, but there seems little probability of arriving at any satisfactory conclusion. At the same time, in these days science has advanced too far to attribute such phenomena to a fortuitous accident.

Their national traditions point, as has been said in a former chapter, to a comparatively late date, as that of their arrival in their present localities, which may be fixed as between A.D. 500–600. Their route was from the north, or rather the north-west, across the southern corner of the Great Desert of Gobi, described in their oldest traditions as 'the River of Running Sand, where the sands rolled before the winds like the waves of the sea.' Taking their own and Chinese traditions as in some degree lights to guide us in the dark, we may conjecture that their more powerful brethren, the Chinese, having established themselves in Kansu and Shensi, the Karens followed the southward course of the great Yuengleng range into the mountainous province of Yu-ñan, where for some centuries they settled themselves. Driven out thence by the establishment of a Shan kingdom about the seventh century, they migrated southwards, following the watershed east and west of the Salween River, spreading themselves over all the uninhabited mountain ranges.

Both Panthier and Marsden, in their editions of Marco Polo, entertained the idea that the province of Karaian or Yu-nan was inhabited in Polo's time by the Karainers, whom they believed to be the same race as that now known in Burma as the Karens. This has, however, been clearly shown by Yule, in his edition of the great traveller, to have been an error. The races then inhabiting Yu-nan, or Cara-jan, as Polo really calls it (the Kárájáng of the Mongols), were evidently, in his time, the same as those now found there, the Shans and their congeners being predominant.

The Karens have remained very much as they were described by Father Sangermano in A.D. 1785: 'We must not omit here the Carian, a good and peaceable people, who live dispersed through the forests of Pegù, in small villages consisting of four or five houses. These villages, upon the death of any inhabitant, are thrown down and destroyed in a moment by the survivors, who suppose the Devil to have taken possession of the place. It is worthy of observation that, although residing amidst the Burmans and Peguans, they not only retain their own language, but even in their dress, houses, and everything else are distinguished from them. And, what is more remarkable, they have a different religion. This, indeed, only consists in adoring, or rather fearing, an evil genius whom they suppose to inhabit their forests, and to whom they offer rice and other food when they are sick or apprehend any misfortune. They are totally dependent on the despotic government of the Burmese.' [1]

At present the Karens of British Burma must be

[1] Sangermano.

divided into two classes—those who have permanently settled in the plains and betaken themselves to a regular system of agriculture, and those who still remain in all their primitive freedom on the hills. Although the former still to a great extent retain their peculiar dress and language, they have become greatly influenced by their more civilised neighbours both in manners and in religion, most of them professing Buddhism, though it is doubtful if their Buddhism consists of much more than considering Gaudama as a great Nát, to be added to their own ancestral objects of worship. Thus, although much of what follows is therefore equally applicable to them, I shall speak chiefly of their brethren, the wilder denizens of the forests.

The great peculiarity of the Karens, which they possess in common with *all the Hill races*, not only of Burma and Assam, but of the whole of India, is their unsettled and ever-changing mode of life, which entitles them to the designation of 'nomadic cultivators.' To raise their scanty crops, the virgin forests on the steep slopes of the hills must be cleared and burnt; but the excessive rainfall washes the friable soil off the surface, so that only one crop can be raised on the same spot until it has again become overgrown with jungle, and a fresh deposit of earth has formed. This system of agriculture naturally requires a large extent of country. It is not every hill side that is favourable for cultivation; consequently in two or three years all the culturable patches near a large village become exhausted, and the whole community must move off to new localities, perhaps thirty or forty miles away, since they may not trespass on what is regarded as the range of another village. Hard and bitter indeed is the struggle for life of these Hill men. Every year the dense forest must be attacked, and with infinite labour large trees, six feet in girth and 100 to 150 feet or more in height, felled, cut up, and then burnt with the smaller undergrowth, to clear the ground. In some cases fences have to be made to keep out wild animals. About April the 'toungyas,' 'hill gardens,' as these clearings are called, are set on fire, and the whole country in the neighbourhood of the hills is filled with smoke and ashes, while at night the mountain sides, covered with long irregular lines of glowing light, present from the plains a singular and beautiful spectacle. After the first rains in May have softened the ground and infiltrated the lye of the ashes, the crop is sown in the simplest way: a hole is made with a pointed stick, and two or three seeds are dropped in—a rude form of drill sowing. The usual crop is hill-paddy, or rice, maize, esculent roots of different kinds, betel vines, and various pot herbs, with perhaps a small patch of cotton to supply the housewife's loom. Having planted his crop, the Karen has to guard it against depredators in the shape of elephants, deer of different kinds, wild hogs, and the whole tribe of birds. But there is one enemy against which all his precautions are useless when it appears in any number—the 'hill rat.' Fortunately the visitations of this pest occur only at long intervals of forty or fifty years; but they generally settle down on a tract of country for two or three years in succession, till, like a swarm of locusts, they have reduced it to a desert. The rats are rather larger than the common house rat; they swarm by myriads, crossing the streams in shoals, so that the water is black with them. Of course the natives have most wonderful stories about them—that they have a king snow-white and as large as an elephant, who has his court in the bowels of the earth; that some of them are so large that three of them nearly pulled down and killed a man in fair fight; and so on. However, the Karens have some consolation in the *lex talionis*; if the rats eat their crops, they salt the rats by thousands and eat them. From 1870 to 1874 the hill country east of the Siltoung River was devastated by one of these irruptions, and 10,000*l.* was expended by Government in relieving the Karen tribes.

Unlike the Burman rice cultivator, who idly waits

between the sowing and the reaping of his crop, the Karen has to occupy himself continually in weeding as well as watching it. The hill rice crop is reaped in October, about two months earlier than that grown in the plains. After their harvest the Karens begin to come in from the hills to the villages and small towns in the low lands; long single files of men, women, and children, carrying on their backs long conical bamboo baskets, supported by a strap across the forehead, containing the surplus produce of their gardens, to sell or exchange for salt, ngapee, gaudy silk handkerchiefs, or other luxuries. In all mechanical and industrial arts the Karens are far behind the Burmans; but with the rudest appliances they manage, except some of the wildest tribes, to weave excellent cotton cloths for their own wear, often in handsome patterns of bright colours. Their rugs or mauds are so thickly and closely woven as to be almost waterproof. The principal tribes, which perhaps were the original stirpes of all, are distinguished by the stripes or embroideries at the bottom of the sleeveless *white* tunic which forms the national dress. Thus the Sgan has a few red horizontal parallel stripes; the Bghai has the same kind of lines, but a few inches long, arranged perpendicularly; the Paku has no stripes, but a variegated embroidery at the bottom of the tunic. Different patterns in the embroidery, again, serve to mark different villages or clans of the same tribe. This white sleeveless tunic, reaching half way down the leg below the knee, and embroidered round the bottom with the tribal mark, forms the sole dress of the men. In working it is generally dropped from the right shoulder, so as to leave the arm free. The women wear a petticoat from the waist to below the knee, and above that a tunic like the men's in shape, only shorter, and black instead of white.

Both men and women have their ears bored, and wear large cylinders of black wood an inch in diameter, though some of the richer ones have silver. The women wear enormous silver bracelets, sometimes nearly an inch thick, hollow, and filled with resin. The men also, in some of the wilder villages, adorn their wrists with smaller bracelets.

Both sexes keep their hair long, and dress it in a knot like the Burmans, and the maidens are very fond of decorating their hair with orchids and the other gay flowers of the forest. The unfailing equipment of the Karen, if he stirs a few yards outside his village, is his 'dha,' or bill, and his shoulder-bag. These bags, which are their only pockets, are woven by the women in bright and handsome patterns, and often prettily ornamented with the 'Job's tears' seeds (*Coix lacrima*).

In person the Karens are much lower and more squarely built than the Burmans; in general they are fairer, and the obliquity of the eyes and the cast of countenance more nearly approach the Chinese. Among some of the Hill maidens in the higher parts of the mountains rosy cheeks may be met with that would not disgrace an English girl.

Among these tribes, though there is said to be a great deal of licence allowed to the unmarried of both sexes, the marriage tie is held in much greater reverence than among the Burmans. Children are generally betrothed by their parents in infancy, and heavy damages are exacted for the nonfulfilment of this obligation. A jilted damsel is entitled to a 'kyee-zee' for her head, another for her body, and a 'gong' to hide the shame of her face. A 'kyee-zee' may be described as an enormous metal drum with only one head. It is the standard of wealth among the Karens, as herds and flocks are among pastoral nations. As they vary in value from three up to one hundred pounds, a Karen damsel has a wide limit within which to lay her damages.

According to their laws a Karen is allowed only one wife, and the easy and mutual system of divorces common among the Burmans is not in force. Divorce is only permitted in cases of adultery; and, *after payment* of the fine settled by the Elders, the offending party is at liberty to marry again. 'But,' pathetically said an old Karen, in giving his evidence in Court on this matter, 'the young people now do not listen to the words of the Elders, or keep the ancient Karen customs, but do as they please.'

The villages are generally built in the midst of the jungle, and remote from any frequented track. The houses are of the poorest description, entirely made of bamboos, which form the posts, the floors, the sides, and the rafters, which are covered with a thatch woven of grass. Some of the smaller villages consist of but a single house sixty or seventy feet long, and divided into compartments, each forming a separate hearth for a distinct family. Underneath are pens for the pigs and poultry. Of course all the inhabitants in a village form really one large family, being all connected by blood or marriage. No stranger can settle among them. Here, in almost inaccessible positions, they live unmolested and almost independent. Many large villages have never seen a white man within them. Some few even manage to keep the tax-gatherer outside by sending their revenue to him, he gladly avoiding the trouble of the journey. This life of freedom and independence is dearer to them than all the luxuries of the plains.

The Karens are much more of sportsmen than

the Burmans. For small game they use a powerful crossbow and arrows. They are much wider in their range of diet than their lowland neighbours. They eat certain kinds of snakes and lizards, one species of monkey, field rats, and every kind of larger game. They are not bound to temperance by their religion, as Buddhists are, and the highest pleasure a Karen can conceive is to get drunk. They brew a kind of rice-beer, called 'koung,' which is an indispensable accompaniment of all feasts and ceremonies. Perhaps the recipe may amuse the reader.

Cook thoroughly by steaming half a bushel of 'kouk ngyin' rice (a peculiar kind), then spread out to cool. Mix the rice with a wort prepared from certain roots, and place in a basket for about two days to ferment. Place half the above fermented mixture, well pressed, into a large glazed earthen jar holding from 70 lbs. to 85 lbs. Mix the remaining half with paddy husk, and press it down over the other. On the top of this press in tightly as much plain paddy husk as the jar can hold. The jar is then buried in a cool place for a month or two. When produced for use, cold spring water is poured in and allowed to soak through till the jar can hold no more. A number of slender reeds are then stuck into the mass, some pointing inwards to the house, others outwards to the door, and through these the mixture is imbibed like a gigantic sherry cobbler; but strict etiquette must be observed that no visitor use the inside reeds, which are reserved for the family use. Among the wilder tribes a breach of this rule would be sufficient to establish a feud.

The Karens can by no means be called a hospitable people; but perhaps this is to be attributed to the state of constant suspicion and dread in which they have for centuries lived—their hand against every man, and every man's hand against them—rather than to any innate churlishness of their dispositions. In the remoter hills, where our authority is still almost nominal, no Karen would dare to enter a stranger village unless introduced by one of the villagers, who thus makes himself his sponsor; when admitted, a certain place is pointed out for the stranger to occupy, and he would certainly be speared if found wandering about the village. When he wishes to leave, he must first obtain permission of the headman, for, if he departed without it he would be followed and killed. In villages that are nearer the plains, and more under our control, they reverse the process; and on the appearance of a European or a Burman who looks like an official, the village is instantly abandoned by its inhabitants. I have often, on suddenly riding unexpected into a small hamlet, been greeted by shrieks and yells, as women and children tumbled down ladders, and rushed into the jungle, upsetting each other in their haste. But this was only, in great part, pretence, or the influence of early custom on the older women, who set the example; for their own husbands and brothers with me would stand laughing and calling to them to come back, which after a short time they would do, laughing heartily themselves. Even the most civilised villages retain many of their exclusive and suspicious habits; especially in times of a prevalent epidemic all the paths leading to a village are stopped by a branch of a tree cut and thrown across, and none would venture to trespass over the barrier. In cases where it was necessary for me to enter such a village on duty, the Karens of other villages accompanying me would never pass within the bounds marked, but, shouting till some of the villagers came, would leave me to enter alone. Had they entered and any sickness afterwards happened in that village, the blame would have rested on them.

There exists a singular institution of brotherhood among them, and to a certain extent among the Burmans, although I believe the latter have borrowed it from their wilder neighbours. When two Karens wish to become brothers, one kills a fowl, cutting off its beak, and rubs the blood on the front of the other's legs, sticking on them some of the feathers.

The augury of the fowl's bones is then consulted, and, if favourable, the same ceremony is repeated by the other party; if the omens are still auspicious, they say, 'We will be brothers ("dōhs"), we will grow old together, we will visit each other.'

After this pledge they are bound together for life, for good and for bad, obliged to help each other in adversity, and even to protect each other against their own kin and clansmen. They never call or address each other by name, but always as 'my dōh,' or 'dōh,' the Karen name of this relationship. They are said to be very faithful to these engagements, which are, moreover, not confined to their own people, as I know a European subordinate officer of police who has been thus adopted as a brother by Karens. It is another instance, like the rite of 'taboo' among the Polynesians, of the necessity even the wildest and most savage tribes find for establishing some means of social intercourse and alliance between natural enemies, under cover of a sacred or religious bond.

Among Burmans the ceremony is generally performed by mixing a few drops of blood from the arms of the contracting parties with some water, which both drink; hence they are called 'thway-thouks,' 'blood drinkers.'

Even among those who have been most completely under our rule and influence from the time of the English occupation, and who sometimes resort to our Courts in disputes with their neighbours the Burmans, their own unwritten law and the decision of the Elders still in a great measure retains its force. The price of blood is still demanded; and although, if refused, cannot, from fear of the foreign ruler, be peremptorily enforced as of yore, public sentiment has yet a powerful influence. Two anecdotes of cases coming under the writer's own observation may serve to illustrate their customs in this respect.

A Karen, whom we shall call Nga Poo, came to the village of a friend to cut bamboos in the neighbouring jungle. The friend being too busy to go himself, sent his little son, about eight years old, to show the stranger a suitable spot. Towards evening, as they were returning to the village, a tiger (whose head is now in my possession) sprang out on the child. The man at once attacked the brute with his long chopping-knife, and forced it to retire. He then took the child up, dead as it seemed, on his back, holding it by the hands round his neck, and thus went on. Twice the tiger came out again from the jungle, and twice he faced round and drove it off, and, nearing the village, his shouts brought assistance. The father of the dead child then demanded 100 rupees as blood money; but the Elders of both villages met, and decided that the man having done all he could, and saved the body of the child from the tiger, thus enabling the father to perform the funeral rites, he should only pay thirty rupees (3*l.*), which was done. As a Karen remarked to me, had he not brought in the body as proof, the father might, according to old custom, have claimed his life.

Again: In a certain circle inhabited solely by Karens, the 'thoogyee,' or revenue official, was much more than a mere tax-collector, his family having long been hereditary headmen, and his father, under the Burman Government, a rather influential chief. One day I was surprised by his resigning his appointment, and refusing, in spite of coaxing, and even of bullying, to continue to hold it. He would give no reason except that he did not like it. It was only after hints obtained elsewhere, that on again sending for him I elicited the true cause. Some time before, coming into the headquarter station with revenue, or on some other public business, he had brought, according to custom, two or three young men of his village as a guard on the way. In the town, unfortunately, one of them, a young married man, caught small-pox and died. A meeting of the Elders decided that the thoogyee, having called him, was responsible for his death, and assessed the price of blood at 300 rupees (30*l.*). This, the poor man said, had almost ruined him, and he could not risk similar accidents in future. 'But,' I urged, 'why did you not come to me? You called him on Government business, therefore, as it were, by my order; let them come on me for his price.' The man looked at me with a smile of almost contempt: 'I know, sir, you would have ordered me not to pay it, and even now, if you choose, can get it back from them; but what good would it be to me, if I could not live amongst my own people, as would be the case if I did not abide by the decision of the Elders.' And so the matter had to rest, and I learnt a lesson of the powerlessness of law and of authority against the moral force of social feeling and tribal custom.

It need hardly be said that the belief in witches, necromancers, ghosts, omens, and superstitions of every kind is rife among these people. They offer animal sacrifices, to the spirits and demons, of pigs, dogs, and fowls. The most solemn sacrifice is that of a fowl, from the bones of which omens in all important matters are derived. 'The thigh bones of a chicken are taken out, and, after prayer and making a condition that the bones may exactly correspond, or they may differ in some particular; that the indentations for the tendons may be like or unlike; that the bones may be even or uneven—the two bones are held up abreast of each other between the thumb and finger and carefully examined. It requires a practised eye to read the result accurately; and there are many nice distinctions known only to the Elders, who do not always agree in their readings.' All their sacrifices are accompanied by plentiful supplies of ardent spirits, which, after having been dedicated to the spirits, and a libation poured out, are consumed by all present.

All the Karens, but especially the wilder Bghai tribes, hold certain stones in great reverence as possessing superhuman powers. I do not know exactly what spirits are supposed to dwell in them, but rather fancy they are regarded more as amulets or magic stones than as gods. Yet sacrifices of hogs and fowls are offered, and the blood poured on the stones. These stones have the wonderful property of always returning to the owner if lost or taken away. They are generally private property, though in some villages there are stones so sacred and powerful that none but certain of the wisest Elders dare look on them. These stones are generally pieces of rock crystal, or curiously stratified rock; anything that strikes the poor, ignorant Karen as uncommon is regarded as neccssarily possessing occult powers.

The strange mixture of blind ignorance and puerile superstition, with an inner and often dimly perceived consciousness of something better and purer, which characterises this wild and primitive race, must have struck the reader. We shall only give one more instance from the account by Dr. Mason of the ceremony of the greatest and most important of their sacrifices—namely, that to the 'Lord of the Earth'—the Earth Spirit, as it were.

After the hogs and fowls killed in sacrifice have been cooked, the flesh, together with ardent spirits, are placed in a booth especially erected, and all laid out for eating in order.

'The next morning all repair to the place, when the Elders commence eating the food and drinking the spirits that have been prepared and placed in the booth. All are allowed to partake that choose; but the food is considered holy, and none but holy, clean, and upright persons are considered as proper persons to partake of it. The question of fitness is, however, left for every one to decide for himself. If a man feels persuaded in his own mind that he is guilty of no transgression, but is upright and holy, he goes forward and partakes of the food; but if his conscience reproves him for some wrong deed or word, he joins the throng outside the booth, and occupies the time with others in dancing.'

The customs, traditions, and beliefs that have been mentioned are not found universally among all the tribes in the same degree. If, according to the traditions of the *most* civilised amongst them, they have retrograded from a still more advanced state, there are some of their clans who seem to have almost reached the extreme of barbarous debasement. In one corner of our province between the Sittoung River and the Red Karen territory (Karennee) lies a mass of precipitous mountains, where British authority has hardly, if at all, penetrated. Here the Karens may be found in their wildest and most degraded state. Knowing no arts, not even how to weave their own garments, too lazy or proud to cultivate more than absolute necessity compels, they present, within a few miles of an English military station, a perfect picture of all that ethnologists and travellers have written about man in his most savage state.

In 1860 Dr. Mason wrote: 'When the English took possession of Tonghoo the villages were engaged in constant feuds among themselves, robbing and killing, and kidnapping and carrying into slavery whenever opportunity offered. As no village would help another, they became an easy prey to the Red Karens, who made constant inroads on them. Such was life in the hills long after the British flag stood waving over the city in sight on the plains below.' And such it remains to the present day in the more distant hills, although the Government has within the last year begun to take measures for introducing order, and ameliorating the condition of these poor savages.

CHAPTER X.

BURMAN BUDDHISM.

To gain a complete and exhaustive knowledge of Buddhism in all its multifarious phases and philosophical intricacies, as developed in a literature that exceeds that of any other religious system, except perhaps Christianity, is a task that would demand the whole energies of the greatest and most industrious scholar. But the many learned inquirers into its many forms, as exhibited in Tibet, in China, and Ceylon, have made it comparatively easy to obtain a general knowledge of its more salient points.

What we may term the European literature of Buddhism consists either of translations from, or comments on, the Buddhistic writings of the early ages from Pali, Chinese, and Tibetan sources. Books of travels have given accounts of popular Buddhism as it exists at the present day in Ceylon, China, and Tibet. As regards the latter country, many amusing and popular works have made the public acquainted with the many and monstrous idols, the extraordinary system of 'prayer wheels,' and other strange devices in religious worship found there, and most readers have formed their idea of Buddhism from such accounts. But the Lamaism of Tibet, the mixtures of Confucianism in China, and Hinduism in Ceylon, with the ancient Buddhism which form the ordinary religious faith of those countries, have little in common with the creed of Gaudama Buddha as we may suppose it was held and practised by his immediate followers. To find the nearest approach to this we must search in the Indo-Chinese countries, and more particularly in the Burman Peninsula, which received the Buddhist faith and scriptures about A.D. 409, and has preserved them almost uncorrupted to the present day.

I think there is no exaggeration in saying that the general idea in England concerning Buddhism is that it is one of the many strange religions of the East, whose votaries worship a god called Gaudama, and who believe in annihilation after death. It will perhaps be best, before we advance any farther, to state broadly and clearly that *the Buddhists of Burma do not worship Gaudama or his image as a deity, nor are the multitude of images seen near pagodas and monasteries gods. So far is the Burman from having a multiplicity of deities that, in our sense of the word, he believes in* NO GOD AT ALL.

I shall endeavour, then, to give a sketch of Buddhism as it presents itself to the mind of an ordinarily educated Burman, as taught to him in the monastic schools, which are the sole means of education, both secular and religious, to the mass of the people. But to obtain a correct idea of the doctrines held by Buddhists, it is absolutely necessary to learn first something of their cosmogony, which forms an intimate part of their religious system. Complicated and absurd as it may appear, it is only by carefully considering what follows that a real conception of the religion—nay, of the very character—of the people can be arrived at.

Matter is eternal, but the present world or universe is *not*. The mundane systems succeed each other in perpetual renewals and destructions, influenced not by any creative wisdom or power, but by fixed and immutable laws, which are independent and self-existing. 'Necessity,' said the old Greeks, 'ruled the gods;' it was the *fons et origo* of all existence; and this is very nearly the Buddhist doctrine.

'Nobody, not even Gaudama himself, ever knew which was the first world and which will be the last; and hence the Burmese doctors deduce that the series of successive dissolutions and reproductions never had a beginning, and will have no end; and they compare the system to a large wheel to whose circumference it is impossible to assign any beginning or end.'[1]

In order, then, to understand the origin of the present world, we must commence with the destruction of the previous one.

A world—or rather the duration of one revolution of Nature involving the formation, existence, and final destruction of a world—is divided into four great periods.[2] In the fourth period man appears as an inhabitant of the earth. This period, again, is divided into sixty-four 'antara-kats' (Sanscrit, 'anta-kalpas'), during each of which the life of man increases, through the influence of the law of merit, from a short space of ten years to an almost inconceivable number, represented by a unit and 140 cyphers; and then, through the force of demerits, returns again to its former short duration.

Of the *causes* of demerits there are three great principles—Lust, Anger, and Ignorance. According as each of these principles is predominant in an existing world will be the effects. Should *lust* reign supreme in the hearts of men, as they reapproach the minimum of their existence, 'then will they, worn away by hunger, thirst, and misery to so many moving corpses, almost all perish. Should *anger* be

[1] Sangermano, p. 7.

[2] 'Athingyays': Sanscrit, 'assankya.'

the reigning vice, then men will turn their weapons against each other, and in furious combats labour for their mutual destruction. If in fine, as is generally the case, *ignorance* prevails over the world, then will a horrible consumption waste mankind away to mere skeletons, and thus will they die. After this almost universal mortality, a heavy rain will fall, which, carrying off all the impurities of the earth, together with the unburied corpses, will discharge them into the rivers; and this will be succeeded by a shower of sandal, flowers, and garments of every kind. Then shall the few men who have escaped the extermination just described come forth from the caves into which they have retired; then shall they begin to do penance for their sins, and thus deserve prolongation of their life beyond the period of ten years.'[1]

Sixty-four of these successive diminutions and augmentations of the span of human life take place during the duration of a world, and in the last period the principle of demerit that is predominant sets in action its peculiar agency of destruction. Thus Lust has for its destroying agent fire, Anger has water, and Ignorance wind. Each of these has a different ratio of effect on the entire system of what we may term the Universe. Thus the destroying element of fire only reaches the five lowest seats of the Byam-

[1] Father Sangermano.

mas, while the destructive violence of the wind reaches even as far as the ninth seat. But here it is necessary to explain shortly the other parts of the system besides the one which is the habitation of man. There are five great divisions, comprising the seats or abodes of all sentient beings, of which there are again thirty-one subdivisions, as follows: Below our earth are the four states or seats of punishment—hell. Then comes the earth. Above the earth, reaching to incalculable heights, are the six seats of the Náts (or angels)—the lowest heavens. Above these, again, are the sixteen seats of the Byammas, or Brahmas, called 'Rupa' ('visible form or matter'), the inhabitants of which are beings still retaining some slight stains of matter—the second heavens. High above all, in the immeasurable infinite, are the four seats called 'Arupa' ('immateriality, spirit'), the abodes of the immaterial, passionless, perfected, spiritual essences that only await the advent of a Buddh to sink into Nirvána, or non-existence. These last have entirely freed themselves from the influence of all passions. They have broken even the slightest ties that would attach them to matter, or the material universe. They have reached the summit of perfection; one step farther and they enter into Níbban (Nirvána), the consummation of all perfection.

The destruction of the world, which existed previous to the present one, was effected, say the Burman teachers, by the agency of fire, which involved in ruin everything, including the lowest hell below the earth down to the fifth seat of the Brahmas. Nevertheless, by whatever agency the destruction of a world is effected, *water* is the sole cause, the *primum mobile* of its reproduction. That this is doctrine derived from the Hindu schools is plain, but whence did Thales and the school of Miletus draw a similar theory? The earliest philosophy of Greece and that of modern Burma meet on the same platform.

After incalculable eras, during which water or rain pours down on the destroyed world, mighty winds blowing from every direction lash and beat the waters, as it were, into yeast, and on the surface appears a greasy scum. In proportion as the waters dry up under the unceasing action of the winds, this scum or crust increases in thickness, and thence is formed the earth and all the regions above and below it that had formerly been destroyed. All this is told in minute detail, with still more extravagant and childish ideas; and I would ask pardon for inflicting thus much on the reader, but that it is absolutely necessary for understanding thoroughly the Buddhist creed, to see how completely and immutably this *self-existing* law of change, of destruction, and reproduction governs all things, and how utterly devoid the system is of the slightest shadow of an idea of an independent Creative Power.

Suffice it to say that the same laws, that brought about the formation and existence of the present world, in like manner governed those of the infinite number of worlds that have already existed, and that hereafter exist in the infinite future.

But even after the formation and reproduction of a world, ages upon ages pass away, and it is not till in the last of the four great periods of the duration of a mundane system, as has been already observed, that *man* appears.

The Burman account of the genesis of mankind is worth noting, in order that it may be compared with similar legends in other Buddhist countries, especially as such a scholar, as Brian Hodgson, states his belief that in Nepál almost the same story was stolen from the Mosaic history as taught by the Christian missionaries.[1] I give it as taken down from the lips of an old Talein, or Mōn phoongyee, over eighty years of age, as contained in the oldest Mōn scriptures:—

'After the burning of the former world, ninety-nine Byammas, or Brahmas,[2] descended, and some of

[1] *Languages, Literature, &c. of Nepál and Tibet*, p. 55.

[2] Not in any way connected with Brahm, the Supreme Deity of

them ate of the new sweet-tasted earth; ninety returned to the Brahma heavens, but nine could not return, their wings failed them, weighed down with the earthly element they had absorbed. These sustained themselves for a time by eating the savoury earth. When that had lost its delicious flavour they fed on the 'patala' (a sweet creeper); and, when that became scarce, strife and anger arose among them. Then they chose one of their number, and said, "Be thou chief over us, and of all the food that we obtain we will give thee one-tenth part." Thus they covenanted; and afterwards the 'thalay' rice appeared, of which they ate. Then amongst four of them the male parts, and amongst four the female parts, developed themselves, and thus the earth was peopled.'

After man has thus appeared on the earth, the continued flux and reflux of the duration of human life from countless years to the short span of ten, goes on, as before explained; and after succeeding generations and sixty-four vast cycles of time have occurred, one revolution of Nature is complete, the law of destruction begins to operate, and the existing world yields in its turn to the agency of one of the

Hinduism, but beings belonging to the second rank in the Buddhist celestial hierarchy.

three destroying elements to make way for a new one.

A world is fortunate and happy according as it is honoured by the appearance of many or few Buddhs. Some worlds are produced, exist, and perish without the advent of a Buddh at all. The present existing world has been favoured above all former ones by the advent of four great Buddhs, or Buddhas, of whom Gaudama was the last; and the fifth, Areematéyah, is still to come, after the religion of Gaudama shall have existed 5,000 years, of which 2,519 have already passed.

What, then, is Buddha, the God, as he is sometimes so incorrectly termed, of the Buddhists? Buddha—the 'wise'—is but a mere man, like all mortal beings; but through countless ages and endless transmigrations he has diligently sought, learnt, and fulfilled the law, which, when perfected, he preached to the world. 'What I have preached,' said Gaudama, 'has no reference to what is within me or without me. I am now very old; my years number eighty. I am like an old cart, the irons, wheels, and wood of which are kept together by constant repairs. I feel truly happy whenever I consider the state of "Arahat," which is the deliverance from all the miseries of this world, whilst at the same time it sets a being free and disentangled from all visible and material objects.'[1] This is not the language of one claiming divinity.

A Buddha, then, is only a rare and illustrious being, who, after having thus gone through myriads of successive existences, through the practice of every virtue, particularly self-denial and the total abnegation of all things, at last reaches to such a height of intellectual attainments that his mind becomes gifted with a perfect and universal intelligence, or knowledge of all things. He is thus enabled to see and fathom the misery and wants of all mortal beings; and, his benevolence being equal to his intelligence, he devises means for relieving and removing the same. The law that he preaches is the wholesome balm designed to cure all moral disorders. He preaches it with unremitting zeal during a certain number of years, and commissions his disciples to carry on the same benevolent and useful undertaking. Having thus established his religion, he arrives at the state of Níbban (Nirvána).

A Buddh, then, is a mere man, superior to all other beings, not in his nature, but in his transcendent science and perfection. Gaudama, the last of these mighty teachers, laid no claim whatever to any kind of superiority in his nature. He exhibits

[1] From the *Malla lingara Wattoo*, or *History of the Excellent Flower*: The Life of Gaudama in Burmese.

himself to the eyes of his disciples as one of the children of men, who has been born and is doomed to die. All his superiority is owing to his complete knowledge and fulfilment of the law. 'Oh! Thoubat,' he says, 'from the age of twenty-nine years up to this moment I have striven to obtain the supreme and perfect science, and I have spent to that end fifty-one years following the way that leads to Níbban.'[1]

If Gaudama be not God, what is the worship or veneration bestowed on him?

To European minds atheism is so popularly associated with irreligion, and even with an absence of all moral ties, that the idea of an atheist deeply impressed with religious and moral feelings involves to most minds an almost impossible paradox.

Yet the Burman Buddhist, believing in *no* God—that is, in no eternal, self-existent, omnipotent, all-creating Being—is still full of the most lively feelings of gratitude, devotion, and affection for the Great Teacher, who, by preaching the law, has been to men a saviour, in showing the way open for escape from the endless miseries of ever-changing existence.

He eulogises in the most glowing terms and reverences this, the first and greatest of all beings, on account of his infinite benevolence and compassion,

[1] *Malla lingara Wättoo.*

which induced him to labour so much for the enlightenment of all beings by showing to them the way that leads to deliverance. But as affects his followers, to them Gaudama is no more. His interference with the affairs of this world or of his religion has absolutely ceased with his existence. He sees no one, he hears no prayer, he can afford no help, either here on earth or in any other state of existence. He has Níbban. *He has ceased to be.*

The worship or reverence due to him is equally due, and in a similar degree, to two other objects—the law, and the 'Thenga,'[1] or 'religious body'—the clergy, to use a popular but incorrect expression. 'I take refuge in Buddha, the law, and the assembly,' is the pious ejaculation of the Buddhist devotee. 'The three precious things,' they are termed. This gave rise to old Nicolo Conti's curious story that the Burmese, 'when they rise in the mornings from their beds, turn towards the East, and with their hands joined together pray, "God in Trinitie and his Law defend us."'[2]

Gaudama, then, is not God, cannot be God; but a *religion* without a god or gods is so repugnant to Western ideas, that we may still inquire, Is there not in the law that he preached at least some trace

[1] Sanscrit, 'Dharma and Sangha.'

[2] Conti's *Travels*, A.D. 1425; Purchas, vol. ii.

of an Eternal Cause? The answer is, *None.* To the Buddhist there is no Providence, and therefore no prayer; there is none that can help him. The weeping mother, watching the sufferings of the beloved child, can call on no being with the will and power to assuage them. No prayer from fond parents for the safety and welfare of their loved absent ones can be uttered. The miserable and heart-broken can cry to no one for pity and comfort; there is none to hear him.

'Aneitsa—Doka—Anatta'—'all is transitory—all is misery—all is unreality;' vanity of vanities, all is vanity. Such is the despairing cry of the Buddhist in his afflictions. Yet out of this very cry of despair arises his only source of hope and relief. All is transitory, all is unreal; but it is not eternal; for out of this whirlpool of misery in which he has moved, to be again and again engulphed, for he knows not how many past existences, Buddha has pointed out the way of escape, and that way is the law.

The 'law' is the doctrine that 'the Buddhas' have preached; not Gaudama alone, but all the Buddhas before him; for the law is eternal, without a beginning or an author.

Neither Gaudama nor, according to his teaching, *any* Buddha ever considered himself, or has ever been looked on by others, as the inventor and originator of the law. He, who becomes a Buddh, is gifted with a boundless science, that enables him to come to a perfect knowledge of all that constitutes the law. He is the fortunate discoverer of what is already existing, but placed far beyond the reach of human mind. Having arrived at this knowledge, his infinite benevolence, which is one of the chief characteristics of a *perfect* Buddh, induces him to make it known to all beings. The law itself is eternal; but between each appearance of the Buddhas becomes obliterated from the minds of men, until a new Buddha appears, who by his omniscience is enabled to find it again.

The 'law,' then, is the doctrine which Gaudama expounded; its object is 'to dispel the clouds of ignorance, which, like a thick mist, encompass all sentient beings, and shed bright rays of pure light which enlighten the understanding.' Man is thus enabled to perceive distinctly the wretchedness of his position, and to discern the means whereby he may extricate himself from the trammels of passions, and finally arrive at the state of Níbban—which is the release from all the miseries attending *existence*—a ceasing to be.[1]

[1] There is no occasion to enter here into the controversy of what Níbban or Nirvána really means. The Buddhist commentators differ about it amongst themselves, and European scholars who are generally best acquainted with the *later* modes of thought have

The great body of doctrine as laid down by Gaudama is contained in the sacred books, which consist of three great divisions: the 'Thootan,' or rules and moral instructions preached by himself. These are chiefly in the form of narratives of former existences of himself or of his chief disciples, each one conveying some moral lesson, the old Eastern form of apologue. The 'Weenee,' or rules of discipline, regulate the whole conduct of the religious order, even in the minutest particulars. Lastly, the 'Abeedama,' in which the metaphysical doctrines of Buddhism are set forth with all the refined subtlety and abstruse reasoning which is characteristic of the Indian schools of philosophy. Certainly such a system could never have originated among a half civilised Mongolian race; and it is, perhaps, not too

followed the expositors of the same. For all practical purposes, it does not matter what Nibban *is*. It is unattainable by *any* under the present Buddhist dispensation; for it is only during the *life* of a Buddha, and after hearing his preaching, that men, or even the perfected beings inhabiting the highest heavens, can attain that blissful state. That is, no being can reach Nirvána now, until the advent of the next Buddh, Areematéya. Still, as it may be asked what do the Burmese Buddhists consider Nirvána to be? I answer in the words above—*ceasing to be*. 'Annihilation' conveys to our minds something *active*, the influence of some superior power. This is exactly what the Buddhist doctrine does *not* mean. 'Nibban' is the ceasing of all action, of all influence; there is no more change, there is no more being, existence (the Das Seyn of the Germans), and no more sensations, no volition, no consciousness. What is this but, not to be; annihilation truly, if we can only divest our thoughts of the belief in any superior *active* agency.

much to say that not a Burman of the present day really comprehends fully even a small portion of the higher and spiritual meaning which many can glibly quote, using abstruse Pali terms to them practically unintelligible.

'The 'Weenee' and 'Maitheelayins,' the monks and nuns, or professed religious, to use European terms. The 'Abeedama' is in itself beyond the comprehension of the mass of the people, and it is in the 'Thootan' that the essence of the popular religion is to be found. But the whole three united form the law, the second great object of worship.

'What is the origin of the law?' is asked in one of the Burmese books. The answer is: 'All that exists is divided into distinct parts: the things which are liable to change, and obey the principle of mutability, such as matter and its modifications, and all beings; second, those which are eternal and immutable—that is to say, the precepts of the law and Níbban. These have neither author nor cause; they are self-existing, eternal, and placed far beyond the reach of the influence that causes mutability.'

The five great precepts binding on all beings, and the foundation of the practice of all virtues, are—

1st. Not to destroy life.

2nd. Not to steal.

3rd. Not to commit adultery.

4th. Not to speak falsely.

5th. Not to drink intoxicating liquors.

Gandama himself has thus described the meaning of these: 'He who kills as much as a louse or bug; he who takes as much as a thread that belongs to another; he who with a wish of desire looks at another man's wife; he who makes a jest of what concerns the advantage of another; he who puts on his tongue as much as the drop that would hang on the point of a blade of grass of anything bearing the sign of intoxicating liquor—has broken these commandments.' This is not a paraphrase to suit European modes of thought, but a literal rendering of the original.

But, besides these five great precepts, there are others, the observance of which is enjoined on those who desire to increase their store of merits, and to gradually gain that freedom from the influence of the passions and external objects, which is the only way to the state of perfection that leads to Níbban. Among the chief of these is almsgiving. Yet Gaudama guarded against too much stress being laid on this, for he said: 'No one can accomplish the commands of the law by such a vain and outward homage. The observance of the law alone entitles to the right of belonging to my religion.'

It is not possible here to do more than thus give

an idea of the principles of the law, or code of morals, which form the sum and essence of the teachings of Buddha.

There still remains the third object of worship or veneration. This is the 'Thenga,' or whole body of the religious, generally known in Burma as the 'Phoongyees,' a word meaning 'great glory.' There are several divisions and grades among these, not only in an outward, but also in a spiritual, sense; for, in proportion to a 'Rahan's' (a religious) perfection in the law, and his deliverance from the influence of the passions, is his rank in the scale of existences. But as none but a Buddha can know the *spiritual* rank and condition of any individual, of course in these days such must remain unknown, and the reverence is paid to the whole body of those who have abandoned the world, and devoted themselves to the constant practice of the law, and to the 'following the paths leading to perfection.'

The phoongyee is always addressed as 'Phra,' Lord. When a Burman enters a 'kyoung,' or monastery, he first of all, in a kneeling posture, before the images of Gaudama, always placed at one end, bends his head three times to the ground, saying: 'I make these three obeisances in honour of the three precious things—Phra, Tará, Thenga'—*i.e.* the Lord, the law, and the assembly.

We see, then, that the religion of Buddha has no object of worship but these three—the Buddh, the law he preached, and the whole body of the faithful who are endeavouring to follow his example. All three are equal in honour, and above them is —*nothing*.

There can be no doubt, therefore, that, so far from being idolatry or Polytheism, the popular religion of Burma is a bare system of morality and atheism. It is true that good and learned men like Bishop Bigaudet,[1] the best living authority on all concerning Burman Buddhism, shocked at such an idea, have put forth the theory of an unacknowledged but inwardly felt secret belief in a Supreme Cause. The Bishop says: 'The Burmese in general under difficult circumstances, unforeseen difficulties, and sudden calamities, use always the cry "Phra-kai-ba!" "God assist me!" Whence that involuntary cry for assistance, but from the innate consciousness that above man there is one ruling over his destinies? An atheistical system may be elaborated in a school of metaphysics, and forced on ignorant and unreflecting masses, but practice will belie theory. Man, in spite of his errors and follies, is naturally a believing being.' How far the latter part of this

[1] Bishop of Ramátha (in part. infid.), Vicar Apostolic of Ava and Pegu.

sentence may be true as an analysis of the human heart in its profoundest depths, I will not venture to discuss; but I have practically proved, in many years of familiar intercourse with all classes of Burmans, that, whatever may be concealed in the inner consciousness of their souls, their ordinary every-day understanding does not admit the conception of a supreme, eternal, self-existing Cause, which we call God. It is true that exclamations such as the Bishop mentions are constantly in the mouths of Burmans; an old woman walking along the road, and suddenly startled, will cry out 'Phra-Phra!' 'Lord! Lord!' but this can no more be considered a *real* cry for help to the Deity, than the similar exclamation 'Lawk-a-mercy-me!' of an old English dame.

The Burmans, but more especially the Mōns or Taleins, *have* a belief in beings who can *injure* them unless propitiated, called 'Náts;' but these are not deities, and have no connection with Buddhism. They are the relics of their old Turanian worship of the Spirits of Nature, and the honour paid to them may be paralleled by the similar faith in fairies which is so strong in many parts of Europe as almost to amount to a second religion, and which is also, without doubt, the lingering remains of a primæval Nature-worship now overshadowed by Christianity.

It is also true that a metaphysical school exists, or has existed, in other Buddhist countries, which acknowledges an 'Adi-Buddha,' or First Buddha, a Creator, and that traces of such a belief are to be found even in Burma; but the religion of the mass of the population is such as we have seen it—shall we call it atheism? I prefer to term it the worship and practice of the moral and good, but without a God.[1]

Such, then, are the main points of the religious belief of the people of Burma. It may be asked, How are they practically affected by it, and especially by that, to most inquirers, singular and incredible doctrine of successive existences, or, as it is generally termed, 'transmigration'? This to the Burman is a matter of unhesitating belief. Just before the drop fell with a wretched murderer, the writer heard him mutter his last words: 'May my next existence be a man's, and a long one!' An equally striking, but not so dismal, example, is the case of an old woman who, having lost her grown-up son, while passing along one day heard her neighbour's calf

[1] Atheism though simply meaning the 'want of a God,' or the 'no God,' has through the 'odium theologicum' come to mean an active and wicked *denial* of a God. Buddhism does not *deny*, it simply ignores, such a conception. Whether the difference between this and the popular idea of atheism will be generally acknowledged by my readers, I know not; but I feel that a difference exists.

bleat, and, believing she recognised the voice of her lost son, threw her arms round it, and at once proceeded to the owner, and, having purchased the animal, carefully nourished it as the present embodiment of her son. Her neighbours laughed at this *practical* exemplification of belief, and yet they themselves firmly held the same in theory. Similar instances are not uncommon of persons now living supposed to be the reincarnation of others who have passed away; but it may be said that, except in the matter of taking life, the doctrine of metempsychosis has little effect on the minds and manners of the people. Their treatment of dumb animals is not more than ordinarily humane; and, although their domestic animals are better cared for than amongst the Hindus, who profess the same belief, it is more from the innate good nature and easiness of their dispositions than from any effect over them of this peculiar doctrine. As a general rule his religion, if it can be called such, has apparently little influence on the Burman's mode of thought and life, until the warning hand of time begins to remind him that he is approaching another change of existence. Then he begins to lay up a store of merits, either to add to those of his former existences, or to counterbalance his demerits. This he does by abundant almsgiving to the religious order; by meritorious works, such as the erection of pagodas, monasteries, rest-houses, bridges, or other objects of religious or public utility; by constant attendance at the monasteries and pagodas on the appointed 'worship days,' to hear the law recited and meditate on its doctrines, and by a more careful observance of its various precepts. Still there are some who, even in the prime of manhood, attend to these things and prove their sincerity. Such a man I knew, a Court clerk, who, when offered a revenue appointment of four times the emolument he was receiving, respectfully declined without apparent reason; but it afterwards transpired that he dreaded the being obliged to procure fowls and bullocks for slaughter, to supply the requisitions of Government for troops or officers, who often passed that way on the march. Others, again, abandon the world and join the religious order for their lives when young and strong.

The Buddhist is, of all men, perhaps the most tolerant in religious matters towards those who differ from him. Indifference, rather than toleration, would most correctly define his feeling. He fully believes that Buddha's law is the only means of salvation; but, as in the circle of existences no man can choose what he shall become, it matters, therefore, as little that one of these existences should be in the state of a Christian (for instance) as that it should be in the state of an ox. The present Christian, if he is a good man, just and benevolent, carries the benefit of his virtuous life and actions to his credit in future existences, and will reap the reward by being born at some time as a Buddhist, and thus have the opportunity of fulfilling the 'law.' Missionaries and converts to Christianity have certainly been often persecuted under Burman rule; but political reasons were in such cases the principal cause, together with the feeling, in some more bigoted minds, that though the *present* various forms of belief mattered not in others, yet it was a kind of treason to his country for a Buddhist by birth to abandon the true 'law' for the creeds of foreigners.

CHAPTER XI.

THE BURMAN PHOONGYEES, OR MONKS.

An account of Buddhism in Burma would be very incomplete without a notice of the Phoongyees, or Religious Order, which is the complement and exemplification of the religious system. In other religions it is not necessary, in order to a complete fulfilment of their tenets, for any to separate themselves from the main body of believers. The state of the priesthood or of a monastic life may be more meritorious and worthy of adoption; but the layman can as such, equally with the priest, carry out the law of his faith, and share in its highest rewards. Not so with the Buddhist. He can only completely fulfil the law, and hope to find the path to deliverance, through the abandonment of the world, and under the yellow robe of the recluse. The entry of every Burman youth into the monastic brotherhood and assumption of its peculiar habit, for in some cases only a few days, is a symbol of this fact. The entire renunciation of the world may not take place in this present existence; but not until it does, can he hope to accomplish his salvation from the misery of ever-recurring existences.

It is well first to correct an error into which Europeans generally fall, namely, that of speaking of the 'yellow-robed priests of Buddha.' If the system of Buddhism has been fully understood, it will be seen that it does not admit of a priesthood. If Western terms must be employed, 'monks' would be the most appropriate designation of the Buddhist religious segregates. Their presence is not in any way necessary for the performance of any religious rites or ceremonies; and though they are sometimes present, and expound the law, it is only to acquire more merit for themselves by so doing, and not as a part of any duty enforced by their profession.

The constitution and influence of the order has greatly suffered under British rule. Our Government, of course, declines all interference in religious matters; sects and cliques have sprung up, and the order is without a head in British Burma. In a political point of view this, perhaps, has been a mistake, although doubtless there were considerable difficulties in the way of our official recognition of Buddhism. But all the orthodox Buddhists are now still forced to regard Mandelay, the capital of Independent Burma, and its spiritual functionaries, as the central point of their religion; and this intimate connection reacts politically. Had it been possible, on our first occupation of the country, to have recognised some one of the existing spiritual dignitaries as the head of the religion and of the order within our province, it is probable ready acquiescence would have been given by all concerned; now it is too late, even if it were possible.

Under their native rule there was and is a regular hierarchy at the head of which is the 'Thathanapine Tsayah-daw-gyee,' or 'Great Teacher, controlling matters pertaining to religion.' This great personage has generally been the King's preceptor in his youth, and is in some measure greater than the King himself; since, when he visits his Majesty, the 'Lord of many white Elephants, and Great Chief of Righteousness' descends from his elevated seat, places the teacher on his own carpet, and himself sits below him.

Under this supreme head are several subordinates, each having a number of monasteries in his jurisdiction, who are termed 'Gine-ōks,' heads of assemblies. Every monastery contains a superior phoongyee, who rules the other inmates in the manner of an abbot, whilst the lowest class in the order are the 'Oopatzins,' the ordinary recluses.

The monasteries are generally on the outskirts of the town or village, or were so, when originally erected. They are large, well-built edifices of teak wood, with a considerable amount of ornament in the way of rough but florid carving. The sites are often selected with great regard to picturesqueness, and the buildings are surrounded by handsome umbrageous fruit and flower bearing trees. All around is kept carefully clean and free from weeds; and it is really refreshing to turn in from the glare and dirt or at least disorder outside, into the cool, trim precincts of one of these old monasteries. They are erected by pious individuals, who often devote the best part of the savings of a lifetime to this object, and, strange to say, without causing any feeling of dissatisfaction to their heirs. A man in the class of a petty shopkeeper will often expend 700*l.* to 800*l.*, sometimes much more, in building a kyoung, or monastery. When finished, it is with great feasting and ceremony dedicated and offered to the phoongyee whom the founder has selected as his teacher and spiritual master. The builder acquires the honourable title of 'Kyoung-taga,' 'Supporter of a Monastery,' by which he is always henceforth addressed, and which he prefixes to his signature. Until a phoongyee is thus provided by some admirer with a separate 'kyoung,' he is not considered to have attained full rank in the order, but remains an inmate of some monastery.

Our phoongyee, though now provided with a dwelling, is still dependent on charity for his daily food. By the strict rules of his order he must beg this daily from house to house; and though, except occasionally to preserve the letter of the law, the older monks are excused from this, every morning, about half-past 7 or 8 o'clock, bands of the younger brethren and the scholars from each monastery may be seen in single file perambulating the streets of every village and town in Burma. They generally have regular supporters, in front of whose houses they halt, and with downcast eyes await motionless the approach of one of the inmates with a cupful of rice or curry, when the pot each carries is opened by the one nearest, the offering is poured in, and without word, look, or sign of acknowledgment they pass on. The obligation is on the side of the giver, who has been afforded an opportunity to acquire merit by his offering. As a general rule the elder members of the order have certain especial devotees, chiefly old ladies, who take care to provide the holy men with choicer delicacies than those obtained in these eleemosynary rounds, which supply food for the younger recluses and the scholars of the monastery. Everything that a phoongyee possesses is the result of charity; and the 'kyoungs' of some of the more respected ones are filled with offerings in the shape of images of Gaudama in marble, bronze, or silver—clocks, lamps, candlesticks, and other European articles—while the libraries contain numerous copies of the sacred writings on palm leaf, and of the 'Kamatan,' or book of devotions (breviary), on copper or ivory.

These monasteries were the schools of the people till within the last few years, the sole means of both religious and secular education. But the education given in them was without system, and in most cases very superficial. There were, of course, some well educated and even learned phoongyees as far as their opportunities allowed; but the greater number knew little beyond reading and writing, together with long passages from the sacred books interspersed with Pali, of which they barely, if at all, understood the meaning. These, in order to cloak their own ignorance, pretended to despise all secular knowledge and teaching, and to hold that the only use of learning was to read and copy the sacred writings. But such are gradually beginning to wake up to the fact that, unless they change their plan, their influence, perhaps their very daily bread, will fail them. The Government system of education, happily inaugurated and energetically carried out, has obtained the approval and co-operation of the best and most influential phoongyees as well as of their supporters. This system consists in taking advantage of these widely diffused monastic schools, and making them the basis of the elementary education of the people. To do this, it was, of course, necessary to bring them to a certain extent under Government supervision and control: and that this has been quietly and widely effected with the consent of the monks, chiefly through the influence of the European district officers, speaks well, I venture to think, for the feeling existing between the people and their rulers. Doubtless some ignorant and bigoted recluses, especially in parts removed from the large towns, will hold out to the last against any change, but they will gradually give place to a more enlightened school.

In addition to the five great commands enjoined by Gaudama on all his disciples, there are other five obligatory on all recluses, even on the young probationers and scholars as long as they remain in the monastery wearing the monastic dress. These are—

'1. Not to eat after mid-day.

'2. Not to dance, sing, or play any musical instrument.

'3. Not to use cosmetics.

'4. Not to stand in unsuitable elevated places.

'5. Not to touch gold or silver.'

But the full rule of the order, to be observed by all professed phoongyees, contains 227 precepts on every conceivable subject, from the prohibition to expose the mysteries of the higher spiritual grades to laymen, to the disposal of their old robes. A few of these may amuse the reader.

'Not to remain with women in any place where others cannot see and hear.

'No woman, unless a relation, may wash or clean his old robe.

'Unless some wise and discreet person is present, never to speak above five or six words to a woman.

'Not to eat food cooked by a woman, if he has food cooked by a man.

'Not to go to any place where troops are parading or practising.

'Not to make any one under twenty years of age an Oopatzin (or monk).

'If a woman offers rice in her hand, take, but do not eat it.

'When staying in a village, to speak in a low voice.

'When walking in a village, not to swing the arms.

'If a phoongyee has any deformity of body, not to enter a village (so as not to excite ridicule).

'Not to look into another phoongyee's begging-pot, in order to jeer at him.

'Not to eat very hot spiced things.

'Not to scrape the dish to the bottom.

'Not to preach the law to one wearing shoes, unless sick.

'Not to preach the law to one lying down, unless sick.

'Not to enter a village laughing.'

These have been taken at hazard from the rules, the great end of which is to ensure, as far as careful disciplinary precautions can do so, the virtues of humility, self-denial, and chastity.

The phoongyee must eat, wear, and use nothing that is not given to him in charity. His dress must consist of pieces of yellow rag picked up in the streets and sewn together. In these sad, degenerate days, these holy men observe more the letter than the spirit of their founder's strict rules. They only use what is presented to them, it is true; but they have no hesitation in asking their supporters for what they want; and when a gorgeous new silk or satin robe is presented to them, they fulfil the rules by tearing a small piece in one corner and patching it up again. The rules respecting chastity are the only ones that are seldom broken, and, if a breach is discovered, it is never condoned; the offender must quit his kyoung. and become a layman. On no point are the rules so carefully framed as in guarding against the temptations from the fair sex. A phoongyee may not touch a female, whether of man or animal. So far is this carried, that one of the casuistic questions given is, Can a phoongyee, seeing his own mother in a ditch, pull her out to save life? and it is decided that he may give her a stick or rope to hold, and pull her out with his back turned, thinking at the same time that he is pulling a log of wood.

Their dress, the colour of which is yellow, consists of three pieces: the first a kind of petticoat girt at the waist with a leathern belt, and falling down to the feet; over this a large rectangular piece worn like a cloak covering the shoulder, breast, and right arm, reaching down to the knee, leaving the left arm bare, something in the maner of a toga; the third piece is folded and carried over the shoulder to be used as a cloak or a covering for the head when travelling. The head is always shaved, or at least the hair cut close, whence the proverb, 'A phoongyee and a comb are far apart,' for two things that have no connection. When women are present, or when passing through the streets, the phoongyee should always carry a fan to keep before his face: this is made from the leaf of the Tala-pat palm, the handle being shaped like an S. From this, in some writers, the Buddhist monks have been denominated Talapoins.

One of the great points of etiquette is that a phoongyee must never enter any place, such as a two-storied dwelling, where there is a chance of a man, but more especially a woman, walking over his head. But even this, some of the more lax among them will not heed in European houses. An old phoongyee who belonged to one of the best families, but had taken the yellow robe, as every one said, on account of a hideous hare-lip which cut off all chance of his gaining a partner in life, was so noted for his laxity, that he was a sort of privileged ecclesiastical buffoon, on whom the lads made songs; but the jolly old fellow only laughed at them. Having added a two-storied wing to my house, he came eager to see the improvements. I was out; and my Burman boys, who did not want him there, mischievously told him there was sure to be the nurse overhead. 'Oh!' said he, peering and peeping in, and making as if to enter. 'How can you come in, sir,' the boys urged, 'with a woman overhead?' 'Get out of that, and go to your work; I don't see any woman there: you are a parcel of young scamps,' said the old man as he bolted in, and ensconced himself in an easy chair till my return.

Although great laxity has thus crept into the order of late years in minor details, yet the chief and distinctive rules are strictly observed; indeed, if a phoongyee were known to transgress these, the supporters of his monastery would abandon him, and he would simply starve. Any recluse, therefore, who finds his vows too weighty a burden for him to bear, feels it safer and better to throw off the monastic rope than to sin under it. He incurs no censure or loss of character by this course. But if he ever wishes to re-enter the order, he must again go through the usual ceremonies, which are not unlike the profession of a monk in Christian orders.

There are some very strict and austere members, who devote themselves to carrying out the rules of their order in the fullest manner, and to that contemplative mysticism so characteristic of all Eastern religious philosophy. The veneration for these men is great among their countrymen. But the generality of the Burman phoongyees strive to make their lives as happy as those of recluses can be. True they are bound to say a certain number of prayers and to repeat the 'Kamatan' (Ritual) so many times a day; they cannot eat any food after noon; but they may use certain cooling beverages, as cocoa-nut water, sugar-cane juice, and the like, after that hour, and they manage to get through the weary hours in chewing betel, gossiping, and sleeping by turns. The kyoung is never without some visitors who bring with them all the news of the day; and it is very often the village council chamber, especially if the phoongyee is respected and intelligent, where all the little local affairs are discussed for the benefit of his advice. Under Burman rule the monasteries were often the refuge of malcontents, and the nurseries of conspiracies against the reigning sovereign by ambitious members of his family; but in the English jurisdiction the phoongyees take littleinterest in political matters.

In connection with the Rahans, or phoongyees, should be mentioned another branch of the institution—the Rahanesses, Maitheela-yins, or Nuns. These female recluses, often facetiously termed by Europeans, 'phoonygees' wives,' and believed by some to be so, are not now a very numerous body. They are mostly women far advanced in life, who from piety, or from poverty, have adopted the religious life. Sometimes they take young orphans or the daughters of very poor parents to bring up in the same manner. They are all bound to chastity while wearing the religious dress, which resembles the phoongyee's, except in being white instead of yellow, and follow generally the principal rules of the monastic order. They live in one of the zayats or bungalows near a pagoda, which they employ themselves in keeping clean and free from weeds. They beg their food; and, indeed, with many it is merely for the benefit of this privilege of begging that they have adopted the dress, and they are consequently not much thought of. At the same time, I have known two or three of good family and fairly educated, who were most highly esteemed and respected, who could read the sacred writings to the women assembled on worship days, and devoted themselves to teaching female children.

CHAPTER XII.

LANGUAGE AND LITERATURE OF BURMA.

In the chapter on 'The Races of the Burman Peninsula,' it was mentioned that the language of the Mōn or Talein people and that of the Burmans were distinct; that the former was allied to the Annamitic, and the latter to the Tibetan families of speech. It would be out of place here to give a long philological discussion, but a slight description of languages so different to our own may be interesting. As Burmese is the general and official language of the country, I confine my remarks to it.

Burmese is a monosyllabic language; which does not mean, of course, that every word is of only one syllable, but that every word can be reduced into monosyllable roots. It has derived, however, an immense number of words, almost all such as relate to religion, science, or abstract ideas, from the Pali of India. This is not quite the same as the statement put forth in a book lately published, that 'the language of the Burmese is an *offshoot of the Pali*, intermixed with Tartar and some Chinese;'[1] which is very like saying, 'English is an offshoot of Latin, mixed with some Saxon and Norse.' The chief peculiarities of the language are the absence of all grammatical inflexions, and the complete reversal of the order of words in a sentence. In plain words there are no conjugations, no declensions, no genders except that of masculine and feminine of living creatures. The construction of the sentence reverses our form: thus we say, for instance, 'I shall go to the town to-morrow;' but the Burman says, 'To-morrow the town to I go shall.'

One difficulty which the language possesses in common with all the Indo-Chinese tongues, is in the number of homonyms with entirely different meanings, only distinguished by an intonation, and in writing by diacritical marks. The Burmese has three of these tones, but the Karén, Chinese, and other dialects have six. Thus in Burmese 'tso' may mean 'to speak,' 'to be wicked,' or 'to stop,' according to the intonation given to it.

The literature of the Burman Peninsula is more extensive than is generally supposed by those who have not made themselves in some degree acquainted with the subject. There are two great divisions, the Talein and the Burmese; the Karén and the

[1] Dr. Gordon's *Our Trip to Burma.*

wilder tribes never having reduced their language to writing. It cannot compare in extent or variety with the Buddhistic literature of Tibet and Nepál, nor probably with that of China or Japan; but it is nevertheless most important, as containing some of the earliest and probably most authentic recensions of the teachings of Gaudama Buddha. It is not corrupted by the imported Hinduism in the Sanscrit Buddhist books of Tibet, whence also the Chinese seem to have drawn great part of their version of the Buddhist scriptures. In Burma these were obtained from the holy isle of Ceylon, whilst its ancient faith was still triumphant, and before the persecutions of Brahministic kings had destroyed the greater part of the sacred books.

Except a few modern printed works, all the Burmese books are manuscripts on palm leaves. The leaves are those of the Talipat palm (*Corypha umbraculifera*), which are cut in strips, two and a half inches broad, and in different lengths of from one to two feet. These are written on with an iron stylus along the length, leaving margins of about two inches. When the work is completed, the leaves are placed one over the other, and a piece of thin wood or ivory forms a cover at top and bottom. To bind the whole together, a hole is made three or four inches from each end, through covers and leaves, and wooden pegs inserted; but with small works often used, instead of the pegs, strings are put loosely through the holes and knotted at each end, so that the leaves strung on them can be easily turned over. There are generally eight or nine lines on each face of a leaf, or page, and of course the number of leaves depends on the length of the work. The whole forms a kind of block, the sides of which are often gilt; and the covers also gilt, sometimes in patterns on a vermilion ground. In order to render the writing visible, and also to preserve the books from insects and damp, the leaves are well rubbed with petroleum. The 'Kammatán,' or 'Office of the Phoongyees,' is often written on gilt sheets of copper, or on ivory, in square instead of round letters, with a thick resin which raises the writing above the ground of the page. Some of these, with carved ivory covers, are very handsome and valuable.

Every monastery of any pretensions has its library, and some of the phoongyees are very proud of their collections. The subject-matter of the greatest part of these books is connected with the Buddhist religion, and with the native history; although there are several treatises on medicine, grammar, astrology, &c. The famous Pali grammar of Kachchayano, supposed to date from 500 B.C. and to be the oldest grammar in India, after being long sought in Ceylon and supposed to be lost, was discovered in Burma by Dr. Mason in 1853. Other copies have since been found in Ceylon.

The earliest known form of the Pali character is preserved in the Inscriptions of Asoka, 241 B.C., and is the origin of the Burmese, Mōn, and the other Indo-Chinese alphabets.

Comparing the Mōn and the Burmese with the earliest Pali forms, we have internal evidence, that the Mōn alphabet was formed at an earlier date than the Burmese. The detailed proof of this cannot be given here, but it is consistent with historical facts.

The mother city of Thatone, near Martaban, was a flourishing seaport under the rule of Hindu colonists or their descendants, in the third century of the Christian era; and in A.D. 408 Buddaghosa, the great Buddhist apostle of the Indo-Chinese countries, brought copies in Pali of the sacred books from Ceylon to Thatone. He is said to have been a Brahman of Central India, and his fame as a teacher is only second to that of Buddha himself. He probably introduced not only the Buddhist scriptures, but also the art of writing among the Talein people.

The Burman alphabet is nearly the same as .the Mōn, or Talein. Some characters differ, however, in their phonetic values; and the Mōn possesses certain forms found in the *earlier* Pali, which are wanting in the Burmese.

Sir A. Phayre, in his 'History of the Burman Race,' says: 'The Burmese received religion and letters from India. Did they receive these through the Taleins, or from an independent source? It is certain, that they had no direct intercourse with the sea, probably until the second century of the Christian era. Their alphabet differs in some degree from that of the Taleins, though both are formed on the Nágari model. The circular form of the letters of both indicate the influence of the Tamulic letters. The Burmese appears the more perfect of the two, and has probably been formed at a later period than the other. It does not appear that the Burmese people received their religion and letters through the medium of their cousins, the Arracanese, for that people refer to the eastward as their own source of both. The passage of Indian Buddhist missionaries, therefore, from Gangetic India through Bengal and Munipore to Burma, is a probable event; but it took place later than has been represented. The only direct evidence we yet have on this subject is the discovery of a Buddhist image at the ancient capital of Tagoung, bearing an inscription in the Nágari character. This is not the only inscription of the same kind, that has been found at Tagoung, and the fact appears to indicate, that Tagoung received missionaries from Northern India.'

That the earliest Buddhist missionaries may have come into Burma through Assam and Munipore, can neither be affirmed nor denied. At the same time, the image found in Tagoung proves nothing. We learn from Fahian, that the Buddhist missionaries took with them images from the holy places in India; and we know that there were regular manufactories at Sarnath and Gaya, whence they were *exported* to Buddhist countries. The Tagoung inscription is of the same date as those, whence the Talein alphabet is derived (about the third century of the Christian era); and it is *at least* as likely, if not more so, that these images came in the usual course of trade through the seaports of Pegu, and that the Burmans received their first teachers through the same route, than by the far more difficult one across the wild mountain ranges lying between Assam and Upper Burma. As regards the Burmese alphabet, the 'Tamulic influence' to which Sir A. Phayre alludes could hardly have effected it through Bengal and Munipúr; but we can easily understand its effect through Talinga and Pegu, and is in itself almost decisive proof of the derivation of the Burmese literature from the Taleins. But why should we not unhesitatingly adopt the statement of their own national history, that letters were not introduced into Burma until long after they were used in Pegu, that is in A.D. 1057, when King 'Anaurahta brought Rahans and teachers versed in the sacred books from Thatone?' The Burmans were not likely without foundation to declare their indebtedness to a despised and conquered enemy, when they might have traced the origin of their literature to the sacred 'Middle Country' of India.

The peculiar circular form of the letters common to Burmese, Shan, Siamese, Singhalese, and the South Indian alphabets, has been with great probability ascribed 'to the habit of writing on the Talipot, or palm leaf, with an iron style.[1] It will be easily understood that horizontal lines on a palm leaf with a longitudinal fibre would be impossible, as the point of the style would split or tear the leaf. Another point which strikes a stranger to the language, is the apparent continuity of the writing, unbroken, as it seems, into words. But this is only apparent; all consonants which end a word have a sign called the 'Killing mark' thus C over them; a vowel not followed by a consonant must be the end of the word, besides which there are certain diacritical marks at the *end* of many words which also help the reader. The alphabet is a poor one,

[1] Beames's *Comparative Grammar.*

wanting the capacity to represent several sounds. If has no *f*, no hissing sibilant *s*, no *v*, and the Burmans find it almost impossible to pronounce final double consonants; such words as 'lands,' 'years,' 'strength,' are fearful stumbling blocks to them. My own name of 'Forbes' was always pronounced and written as 'paubee.'

The great bulk of the Talein-Burmese manuscripts consists of historical and religious works. Even the treatises on grammar and astronomy might be classed under the latter head, as the grammar only refers to the sacred Pali language; and their astronomy, borrowed from and mixed up with the extravagant cosmogony of the Hindus, forms a part of the religious system.

The historical works, or 'Radza-wins,' contain, as perhaps the histories of all ancient nations do, three periods, the pre-historic, the proto-historic, and the historic; and the latter with the Burmans may be considered to commence at much about the same era as the historic period in India, namely, the third century before Christ. When we quit the region of fable, these records reduce themselves to a very small compass, sometimes to a mere register of the dates and lengths of reigns; a compendium of history rather than history itself.

The religious literature is much more copious,

and comprises, besides the 'Bēda-gat' or 'Pittagat, that is, the collection of the Buddhist scriptures brought from Ceylon by Buddaghosa, various commentaries on these by later native teachers.

Buddhism has occupied the pens of the greatest Orientalists, and the European literature on the subject is nearly as extensive as that of the original itself, but comparatively little attention has been paid to the Burman, Shan, and other Indo-Chinese versions. Sanscrit and Pali were considered the sole trustworthy depositories of the religion, and its exegesis was to be sought in them. The Chinese Buddhist books have lately been more studied, and they are, many of them at least, of the same age and from the same source as the Talein, for Fahian was making his transcripts in Ceylon at about the same time as Buddaghosa. Yet if we seek for the purest remains of the Buddhist faith, we must turn to the Indo-Chinese countries, and above all to those of the Burman Peninsula. Since the reception of this faith by these races in the fourth century of the Christian era, they have remained almost uninfluenced by rival religions or by that restless spirit of inquiry, discussion, and philosophic refinement, that characterises to this day all Indian religious systems. They are orderly and law-abiding, ruled by custom and tradition, with obstinate tempers, and an intensely conservative spirit. Shut off from any close or frequent intercourse with foreign nations soon after the firm establishment of the faith of Buddha in the land, Burma has preserved that faith undisfigured by the gross esoteric doctrines of Tibetan Lamaism, and free from the Vishnuite influence, that has so largely leavened the Buddhism of Ceylon, the holy isle of Lankadwipa itself.

The 'Bēda-gat,' as said to have been copied by Buddaghosa from the sacred books in Ceylon, and brought to Thatone about A.D. 408, consists, according to the Talein-Burman canon, of seventy-one books or divisions. Of these thirty profess to contain the teachings and discourses of Gaudama himself: the first three form the 'Thootan,' or Moral lessons; the next five the 'Weenee,' or discipline of the Religious Order; the next seven the 'Abidamma,' or Philosophy of Buddhism; and the remainder the Miscellaneons discourses.

The other forty-one books contain the 'Attágáta,' or Commentaries of the disciples of Gaudama, illustrating and explaining his teachings. All these form the canon of the sacred books, the 'Bēda-gat,' in addition to which are the treatises of later writers on various points of Buddhist faith and philosophy.

The sacred literature of that country has all been borrowed from India, and is completely Indian in its form, its associations, and ideas. The scenes of all the narratives are laid in India; the manners are those of India, but not of Brahminical India. Of the 510 'Záts,' or 'Jatakas,' the stories of the various prior existences of Gaudama, many are well known in Europe, under the guise of 'Fables,' whether Æsop's or Pilpay's. All the moral teaching of Gaudama was conveyed in the common Eastern form of the apologue, or parable. In order to give some idea of the Talein and Burmese books, two extracts on different subjects are given.

I.

'A certain woman had a little son, whom she much loved, and when he died she took him in her arms, and went round to all the neighbours asking each one to cure him. They said to her, "Art thou mad, thus to carry about thy dead son?" But one wiser than the rest pondered within himself, It is because she knows not the law of death; I will help her. He said to her, "I cannot cure thy son, but I know one who can;" and when she asked who this was, he told her it was the Lord. Then she went to the Lord, and made obeisance, and asked, "Do you know the medicine to cure my son?" The Lord answered, "I know." Then she said, "What medicine do you want?" The Lord told her, "A handful of mustard-seed." She replied, "You shall have it, Lord." But the Lord said, "The mustard-seed must be from a house in which no son, no husband, no parent, no servant has died." She still answered, "Very well." Then she took the body of her son on her hips, and went to every house; and when they offered her the mustard-seed she begged for, she asked, "Has no son, no husband, no parent died in my friend's house?" Then the people said, "Oh! woman, what do you say? the living are very, very few, but the dead are many. Go to some other place.—I have lost a son.—I have lost a parent.—I have lost a servant." So she could not find one house without a death, and could not obtain the mustard-seed. Then she reflected, "I have greatly erred; my son is not the only one that dies; throughout the country, sons and parents die." Having laid the body of her son in the jungle, she returned to the Lord. (On being questioned, she relates what befel her as above.) Then the Lord said unto her, "Thy son alone is not dead; the law of death is, that there is no permanence in beings." And when he had finished preaching the law to her, she attained to one of the perfect states.'

II.

'Yes, the thickness of the earth is very great; compared with the love of a mother and father, it is but the thickness of a bamboo leaf. The universe is exceedingly broad; but compared with the kindness of a mother and father, it is but as the eye of a needle. The great Mount Meru is exceedingly high; but when measured by the kindness of a mother and father, it is like a small ant hill. The whole ocean, when compared with the kindness of a mother and father, is but as a small brook. The kindness of a mother and father cannot be measured.' Thus the excellent Lord spoke.

The abstruse and refined character of Buddhist philosophical treatises may be judged of from the following :—

'All sentient beings in the three worlds—heaven, earth, and hell—have in themselves only two attributes, viz. "Rupa" and "Náma" (form and name). "Rupa" is the materiality, the appearance of anything which can be acted on or destroyed. "Náma" is the faculty of knowing. In the five "khandas" or constituent elements of all sentient beings, *i.e.* materiality, the organs of sensation, of perception, of mutability, and of intellect, there is only "Rupa" and "Náma" (form and name.) Ideas are the result of the formation of the organs of the senses.

'The form and ideas, which thus constitute all beings, are liable to misery, to old age, and death, because there is production and decay; production exists because there are worlds; worlds exist because there is desire; desire exists, because there are organs of the senses; these organs exist, because there are form and name; form and name exist, because there are ideas; ideas exist, because there is merit and demerit; merit and demerit exist, because there is ignorance. Ignorance, therefore, is the real cause of all forms and ideas.'

One more extract—an old story from the Chronicles of Pegu.

'In the year 702 (A.D. 761) King Titha Radza succeeded to the throne of Pegu. Then King Titha Radza, falling into error, followed the teachings of heretical teachers in the way of Dewadat. He obeyed not the law which the Lord had preached, the Bēda-gat and Abidamma. He pulled down the pagodas, monasteries, and zédis. He threw the sacred images of the Lord into the rivers, and forbad the people, on pain of death, to reverence the three sacred objects, the Lord, the law, and the assembly, or to make offerings to the relics, images, or the phoongyees. All the people of Henthawaddee (Pegu) trembled before the orders of the king, and not one person was found, who dared to worship or make offerings.

'At this time there was in the city a young damsel, named Badya Daywee, the daughter a Thatay (rich man), who had been brought up by her mother, from the age of ten years, in the reverence of the three treasures of the law. When she was sixteen years old, the maiden went out with her companions one day to bathe in the river. While playing about in the water, she observed a golden image shining at the bottom. She asked, "Who has thus thrown the image of the Lord into the water?" Her nurse answered, "Lady, the king has ordered that any one reverencing the holy images and relics shall be punished." When Badya Daywee heard this, she said, "If so, I devote my life to the three treasures; do you all assist and wash the sacred image, and help me to place it in the zayat." Her attendants obeyed, and they washed the image and placed it in the zayat; and the place is known to this day in the Mōn tongue as "paun karow kyeik," the "washing place of the image," which is corrupted in the Burmese into "pan ta raw." While they were washing the image, some of the palace guards saw them, and quickly reported to the king. The royal anger broke forth like a raging fire, and he commanded the damsel to be called before him. When the guards went, they found Badya Daywee still washing the image, and she gave them a ring as a bribe, to allow her to finish. A second time the king sent messengers, who brought the maiden and her attendants into the palace yard, and reported to the king. The king, like a lion roaring at the sight of meaner animals, ordered that a "must" elephant should be made to trample the girl to death. The keeper of the elephants brought a savage elephant, and urged it to trample on her; but Badya Daywee, worshipping the three precious things, Buddha, the law, and the assembly, prayed: "Oh, ye five thousand Náts who guard the Faith; ye guardian Náts of the Universe, Náts of the Earth, of the Air, of the Forest; ye guardian Náts of the City, and of the Royal palace, I have offered my life to the three precious things. For the excellence of the three precious things, let the Thagyamin and the Náts assist, and deliver me from harm." Then she blessed the king, the elephant and his rider. The elephant, though urged on by the mahout, and driven forward again and again with lances, turned from Badya Daywee, and refused to touch her. When the officers reported this to the king, he ordered: "If the elephant will not trample her, heap a mountain of straw on her and burn her to death."

'The executioners heaped loads of straw around and above her; but, in spite of their efforts, they could no more set the heap on fire, than straw, that had been exposed to three months' incessant rain. Again and again they tried, but failed.

'This was also reported to the king, who ordered Badya Daywee to be brought into the presence, and addressed her: "Girl! thou hast taken thy teacher's image out of the river, and placed it in a zayat. If I see thy teacher's image fly through the air into my presence, I will spare thy life; if not, thou shalt be cut into seven pieces." Badya Daywee, making obeisance to the king, replied, "I will invite my teacher's image according to the royal order."

'Then, accompanied by the officers and guards, she went back to the zayat, and invoked the assistance of the three treasures and all the Náts. Then the golden image which she had washed, together with eight other images, were transported through the air, and, arriving at the king's palace, remained suspended over it.

'The damsel entered the palace, and begged the king to come and see what was happening. Titha Radza, his nobles, and all the people wondered and shouted with delight. Then Badya Daywee prostrated herself before the king, and said, "Oh, dread Lord! my most excellent teacher has long entered

Níbban, but yet his image has flown through the sky, and my Lord, the nobles, and the people have seen it. Now the teachers of my Lord the Ruler of the Sea and Land are here present; let them also fly through the air, so that all the people may behold."

'When she had said this in the presence of the nobles and all the people, King Titha Radza ordered the heretical teachers to fly through the air, but they could not. Then the king commanded, that all these heretical teachers according to the way of Dewadat should be driven out of the kingdom..

'Titha Radza wondered greatly, and admired at what had happened. He demanded Badya Daywee in marriage from her parents, and solemnly consecrated her Chief Queen. From that day King Titha Radza took refuge in "the precious things," and restored the pagodas, images, kyoungs, and zayats that had been destroyed, and built many new ones, and made proclamation that all the nobles and all the people should follow the law, and should reverence and make offerings to the sacred relics and to the Rahans.'

INDEX.